Project Advisory Committee:

Partners:
Paula Julian and Tang Cheam, National Indigenous Women's Resource Center and Christopher Foley, Indian Law Resource Center.

Alaska Native Women's Resource Center staff members:
Jacqueline Agtuca, Janelle Chapin, Michelle Demmert, Tami Truett Jerue, Candy Keown, Debra O'Gara, and Andrea Wuya.

Publication of this resource book was made possible by a grant from the Administration on Children, Youth and Families, Family and Youth Services Bureau, U.S. Department of Health and Human Services (Grant Number 90EV0454-01-00). Its contents are solely the responsibility of the authors and do not necessarily represent the official views of the U.S. Department of Health and Human Services.

Alaska Native Women's Resource Center
P.O. Box 80382
Fairbanks, AK 99708
AKNWRC.org

Alaska Native Women:

Ending the Violence, Reclaiming a Sacred Status

This book is dedicated to Shirley Moses, Inupiaq, a founding mother of the Alaska Native Women's Resource Center who passed away on June 13, 2021, and the generations of Alaska Native women who have suffered abuse, are missing, or have lost their lives due to domestic and sexual violence.

Contents

Acknowledgments

The Alaska Native Women's Resource Center (AKNWRC) extends our heartfelt appreciation to the following individuals for their support in making the publication of this crucial new Alaska Native resource book possible. These individuals have struggled for many years to establish safety and justice for Alaska Native women as discussed on the pages of this book:

> To the members of the board of directors of the AKNWRC who supported this project, Tia Holley, Inupiaq, King Island Native Community; Nugange (Lenora Hootch), Yup'ik, Native Village of Emmonak; Takurngailngq (Joann Horn), Yup'ik, Native Village of Bill Moore's Slough; Qunuruq (Priscilla Kameroff), Yup'ik/Inupiaq, Native Village of Emmonak; Naaqtauq (Shylena Lie), Inupiaq, Native Village of Kotzebue; Isabel Mills, Tlingit, Organized Village of Kake; and Nettie Warbelow, Athabascan, Native Village of Tetlin.
>
> To the AKNWRC federal partners at the Department of Health and Human Services, Family Violence Prevention Division, Family and Youth Services Bureau, Administration for Children and Families, particularly Shena Williams for her support of this project.
>
> To Paula Julian, National Indigenous Women's Resource Center, and Christopher Foley, Indian Law Resource Center, who have supported the AKNWRC and Alaska advocates over many years.
>
> To AKNWRC staff who assisted with the publication of this resource book, Jacqueline Agtuca, Janelle Chapin, Michelle Demmert, Candy Keown, Debra O'Gara, and Andrea Wuya.
>
> To AKNWRC consultant Tang Cheam for his design and publication efforts.

Our joint efforts are creating a safer world for Native women and their Nations.

Tami Truett Jerue, Executive Director
Alaska Native Women's Resource Center

Forward

First organized in 2015, the Alaska Native Women's Resource Center (AKNWRC) is a tribal nonprofit organization dedicated to ending violence against women in partnership with Alaska's 229 tribes and allied organizations.

AKNWRC board members are Alaska Native women raised in Alaska Native Villages and have 141 years of combined experience in tribal governments, nonprofit management, domestic violence, and sexual assault advocacy. This includes experience and individual advocacy to increase the safety of Native women at the local, statewide, regional, national, and international levels.

In 2017, AKNWRC was awarded a grant by the Family and Youth Services Bureau, Administration for Children and Families, U.S. Department of Health and Human Services, to serve as the first Alaska Native Tribal Resource Center on Domestic Violence. The award was historic and upheld the federal government's trust responsibility to assist Indian tribes in safeguarding the lives of Indian women. We were honored to receive the award, and like then, we continue to be excited at the potential the resource center provides for Alaska Native villages and women.

In the words of our beloved sister late Shirley Moses, a founding member of the center and chairperson of the board of directors, "With such support, we can address domestic violence working closely with Alaska Native tribal governments, and identify and remove barriers to victim safety and abuser accountability, especially in rural, remote Alaska Native villages across the state."

After decades of advocating for survivors, we understand domestic violence and recognize the authority, responsibility, and right of villages to protect women. We must address these issues at the village level because, in most villages, we are the only ones standing between a woman or girl and violence. We offer this resource book to support tribal leaders, advocates, and survivors in understanding the path forward to create the changes needed to end domestic and sexual violence.

Tami Truett Jerue, Executive Director
Alaska Native Women's Resource Center

Introduction

The AKNWRC resource book is a reference guide for advocates, tribal leaders, tribal courts, communities, and those addressing or concerned with domestic violence and the safety of Alaska Native women. It provides an overview of domestic violence and Alaska Native women from a distinctly Alaska Native perspective.

The book provides an Alaska Native view of domestic violence in the context of a spectrum of violence committed against Alaska Native women. It offers a path forward for support and healing from the violence by understanding how the current crisis of violence grew over time due to systemic barriers and a lack of protection of Native women from domestic and other forms of violence.

The first five chapters provide an understanding of the current dangerous reality of violence threatening the safety and well-being of Alaska Native women, how the violence was introduced to Alaska Native villages, and the development of the movement within villages to support, respond, and increase the safety of women from violence. This Indigenous perspective assumes violence against Native women was introduced by foreign governments to control and forcibly assimilate Alaska Native peoples for their labor and the taking of their lands and natural resources.

The following five chapters provide an understanding of the systemic legal and policy barriers embedded in the current political relationship between Indian tribes in Alaska and the United States. While violence is a reality in all communities, federal laws and policies deny Alaska Native women the same protections and resources from their respective tribal governments available to other populations of women. This in-depth view provides the context that such laws and policies were created by the United States and can also be corrected by Congress, as demonstrated by the 2022 reauthorization of the Violence Against Women Act.

The resource book identifies domestic violence as not traditional to Alaska Native peoples. The counterbalance to this belief is that Alaska Native culture offers the best protective and healing practice to support survivors and restore balance in their lives, families, and communities. By identifying the beginning point of domestic violence and disrespect of Native women, the resource book offers a path forward with a possible ending point from within the cultures of the Indigenous peoples of Alaska.

Chapter 1
The Crisis of Violence Against Alaska Native Women

When Congress and the Administration ask why the crime rate is so high in Indian country, they need look no further than the archaic system in place, in which Federal and State authority displaces Tribal authority and often makes Tribal law enforcement meaningless.[1]

To understand the current crisis facing Alaska Native women, one must recognize that the violence often takes place over a lifetime and not as a single incident against one Native woman.[2] The lifetime victimization rates for Alaska Native women are higher than those of Caucasian women on a national level.[3] 4 in 5 American Indian and Alaska Native women (84.3 percent) have suffered violence in their lifetime.[4] While domestic violence is a large part of the spectrum of violence committed against Native women, it also includes sexual assault, physical assaults, trafficking, and abductions by strangers and non-strangers. American Indian and Alaska Native women suffer a higher rate of violence than any other population group, including African American men. A United States Department of Justice (DOJ) report found the rate of violent crime victimization among American Indian females was "2½ times the rate for all females."[5] For these reasons, Native women's safety is of grave concern to Indian tribes in Alaska and should be to the nation.[6]

> The Indian Law and Order Commission is not the first advisory board to recognize the lack of access to safety and public safety services in Alaska Native communities. But it should be the last. The situation in

---

[1] Indian Law and Order Commission, *A Roadmap for Making Native America Safer: Report to the President and Congress of the United States*, Executive Summary, *x*, (2013). http://www.aisc.ucla.edu/iloc/report

[2] While Alaska Native men are also victims of domestic violence, this resource book is not a generalization about domestic violence but presents the actual lived experience of Alaska Native Women from the perspective of Alaska Native Peoples.

[3] André B. Rosay, U.S. Dep't of Justice, Nat'l Inst. of Justice, *Violence Against American Indian and Alaska Native Women and Men*, at 44, NCJ 249736 (2016). https://www.ncjrs.gov/pdffiles1/nij/249736.pdf

[4] *Id.* at 43.

[5] Steven W. Perry, U.S. Dep't of Justice, Bureau of Justice Statistics, *A BJS Statistical Profile, 1992-2002: American Indians and Crime*, 7, NCJ 203097 (2004). https://www.bjs.gov/content/pub/pdf/aic02.pdf

[6] Throughout this book, the terms "Indian tribes" and "Alaska Native Villages" are used interchangeably to refer to the 229 federally recognized Indian tribes located in the State of Alaska.

> Alaska is urgent and of national, and not just State or regional, importance. Only the combined efforts of Federal, State, and Tribal leaders will be sufficient to change course and put all Alaskans on a better path.[7]

Suffering this spectrum of violence over a lifetime and multiple generations in many, if not all, Native families have far greater consequences than single or multiple incidents of violence against individual women. It alters the very quality of life and causes immeasurable harm to the survivors, their families, communities, and tribes. The reality of experiencing violence over one's lifetime shapes how one understands the world and how the world understands Alaska Native women and violence. Living unprotected with this constant risk of violence is a reality that separates Alaska Native women from all other demographic groups. For mothers forced to raise their Native daughters to prepare for how to protect themselves from being abused, abducted, or murdered is an indictment of the laws, policies, and social norms that allow such violence from one generation to the next.

"[W]hen bodies are discovered, they have to sit there for sometimes days on end, in the wilderness, the inclement weather, snow and rain, the wildlife, bears, and ravens—what's left of a crime scene after so many days? This, however, is not the worst of it because while those bodies are waiting for someone to investigate, these women's mothers, fathers, grandfathers, uncles, aunts, children, nieces and nephews, and grandmothers must be forced to live with the

---

[7] Indian Law and Order Commission, *A Roadmap for Making Native America Safer*, at 56.

inhumane manner in which they died and walk past and around these bodies until law enforcement shows up."[8]

—Catherine Edwards, Vice President (one of six)
Central Council Tlingit and Haida Indian Tribes of Alaska

The life experience of generations of Alaska Native women and peoples is intertwined with federal law and policies that removed their individual decision-making and control over their lives. In 1867, without the consent of Alaska Natives, the United States signed a treaty with Russia and purchased what was then called Russian America.[9] The lives of Alaska Native peoples forever changed and became intertwined with federal Indian law and policies. This complicated legal relationship over decades diminished tribal sovereignty and, in this context, the safety of Alaska Native women.

The very concept of United States (U.S.) citizenship was bound to the cultural genocide of Alaska Native peoples. In 1915, the legislature of the Territory of Alaska passed a law defining the citizenship application process.

> Any native Indian of the Territory of Alaska who shall obtain a certificate … that a proper examination has been duly held and the applicant found to have abandoned all tribal customs and relationship, to have adopted the ways and habits of a civilized life and to be properly qualified to intelligently exercise the obligations of an elector in the Territory of Alaska, shall thereupon obtain an endorsement upon said certificate by at least five white citizens of the United States who have been permanent residents of Alaska for at least one year.[10]

The concept of abandonment of all tribal customs and relationships thought necessary to citizenship of the U.S. is found in the following declaration.

> We, the undersigned … declare that we have given up our old tribal relationships; that we recognize no chief of clan or tribal family; that we have given up all claim to or interest in tribal and communal houses; that we live in one family house in accordance with the customs of civilization; that we observe the marriage laws of the United States; that our children take the name of the father and belong equally to father and mother, and that the rights of the maternal uncle to direct the children are no longer recognized and that in the case of death of

---

[8] *Statement of the Central Council Tlingit and Haida Indian Tribes of Alaska, U.S. DOJ 2018 Violence Against Women Annual Government-to-Government Consultation*, Restoration Magazine, Vol. 15, Issue 3, at 42 (2018).

[9] Treaty of March 30, 1867, 15 St at 539.

[10] Legislature of the Territory of Alaska, SB 21, § 6, Ch. 119, 24 Stat. L., at 390 (1915). https://library.alaska.gov/hist/fulltext/ASL-KFA-1225.A3-1915.htm

either parent we recognize the laws of the United States relative to inheritance of property; that we have discarded the totem and recognize the Stars and Stripes as our only emblem; and that we are a self-supporting and law abiding people.[11]

The mandate of abandoning all "tribal customs and relationships" challenged and undermined the original cultural protections for women within their families, clans, and villages. As Indigenous women, we are bound to our tribal customs and relationships. The definition of indigenous is original, and to Alaska Native women, it includes our teachings, languages, voices, and our relationship to our homelands. The social foundations of what defines us as Native women were prohibited by the U.S. and held consequences, including physical punishment. The social foundations of what defined Native men similarly were prohibited and had dire consequences leaving men without their traditional role and unempowered. The history of our forced assimilation through federal laws and programs is a long and painful one for which the U.S. Congress apologized in 2009[12] and recognized in numerous reports.

> Unequal treatment of tribal governments and lack of full recognition of the sovereign status of tribal governments by state and federal governments, laws, and policies diminish tribal self-determination and negatively impact criminal justice, health, education, housing, and economic outcomes for Native Americans.[13]

> The foundation of our organizing to end violence against Alaska Native women is Indigenous. We understand, as peoples colonized by Russian and U.S. governments, the source and introduction of violence as a means of authority to control. The core principles of our efforts to end violence against Native women are the voices of our people, the teachings of our people, and the languages of our peoples, based within our villages and traditional homelands.[14]
>
> —Tami Truett Jerue, Executive Director
> Alaska Native Women's Resource Center

The removal of Native children from their parents and villages to the U.S. government residential schools is one of many historical examples of

---

[11] Gilbert McLeod, *Gilbert Said,* at 17 (Marian L. Swain, ed., 1992).

[12] Apology to Native Peoples, 2009, P.L. 111-118.
https://www.congress.gov/bill/111th-congress/senate-joint-resolution/14/text

[13] U.S. Commission on Civil Rights, *Broken Promises: Continuing Federal Funding Shortfall for Native Americans, Letter of Transmittal,* at 7 (2018). https://www.usccr.gov/pubs/2018/12-20-Broken-Promises.pdf

[14] Alaska Native Women's Resource Center, *Increasing Safety for Alaska Native Women, An Indigenous Grassroots Curriculum for Alaska Native Villages,* at 7 (2016).

colonization that continues to negatively impact Alaska Native peoples. These schools introduced violence and abuse as a legal means of control that destroyed lives, and severed belief systems passed from one generation to the next. Through the daily physical and emotional abuse of children, boarding schools normalized the use of violence to control and intimidate victims. The current social tolerance for violence against Alaska Native women we understand is connected to the physical and sexual violence girls experienced or witnessed during the boarding school era. Silence was learned as a means of self-protection.

Federal law and policies created settings where women and children were vulnerable to violence by persons authorized by the government for their care. For generations, such laws and policies have failed to hold perpetrators accountable for violence, including the military, law enforcement, extractive industries, and clergy. Understanding this political history allows Alaska Native women and Native peoples to see the current crisis of violence in a broader context, at its roots.

> As one Native advocate put it, sexual assault rates and violence against Native women did not just drop from the sky. Many of the current issues that American Indian and Alaska Native peoples face in the United States, particularly Native women, can be traced back to the legacy of abuse and systematic assault on Native culture, land, and people as a part of the colonization of the Americas. Gender-based violence against Native women was used by settlers as an integral part of conquest and colonization.[15]

The current failed response of the justice system is not new. Today's crisis of violence against Native women has its origins in the same laws and policies that colonized Alaska Natives since the U.S. purchased Alaska in 1867. Unfortunately, the harsh reality is that victims of domestic and sexual violence are not provided adequate protection and do not have available services following such victimization. A DOJ 2016 report found 38.2% of American Indian and Alaska Native women who needed services were unable to get the services.[16] This lack of access to services is a continuation of the disregard for the women the United States holds a responsibility to safeguard.

---

[15] *Native Women: Protecting, Shielding, and Safeguarding Our Sisters, Mothers, and Daughters: Hearing Before the S. Committee on Indian Affs.*, 112th Cong. 69 (2011) (Written testimony of Sarah Deer, Assistant Professor William Mitchel School of Law). https://www.indian.senate.gov/sites/default/files/upload/files/071411CHRG-112shrg71182.pdf

[16] André B. Rosay, *Violence Against American Indian and Alaska Native Women and Men*, at 50, Figure 6.3 Weighted Estimates of Inability to Get Needed Services.

The spectrum of violence against Native women includes many forms of physical abuse, with homicide being one end of the spectrum. According to the Centers for Disease Control and Prevention, in 2017, homicide was the fourth leading cause of death among American Indian and Alaska Native women between 0 and 19 years of age, and the sixth leading cause of death for women between 20 and 44 years of age.[17]

While the murder rate in Alaska leads the nation generally, the murder of Alaska Natives is disproportionately high. According to the Violence Policy Center in 2017, "Alaska ranked first as the state with the highest homicide rate among female victims killed by male offenders in single victim/single offender incidents."[18] According to the Alaska Violent Death Reporting System, between 2003 and 2008, Alaska Natives and American Indians were 33.1% of violent deaths[19] and 29.1% of homicides.[20] Native women were 39.8% of the violent deaths[21] and 38% of homicide victims in Alaska.[22]

In 2018, the Seattle Urban Indian Health Institute issued a report on missing and murdered Native women, referred to as MMIW, in 71 urban cities.[23] The report found that the State of Alaska was one of five states with the highest number of cases. An alarming 5,712 cases of missing and murdered Indigenous women were reported in the United States as of 2016.[24] For example, 116 of these cases were logged into the DOJ database, and at the end of 2017, Native American women accounted for only 0.7 percent of the active missing person cases—633.[25] The disparity between the number of known MMIW cases from the number reported in the federal crime database is an ongoing concern raised continuously by tribal leaders.

---

[17] *Leading Causes of Death, Non-Hispanic American Indian or Alaska Native, Females,* Centers for Disease Control and Prevention, United States (2017). https://www.cdc.gov/women/lcod/index.htm

[18] *When Men Murder Women, An Analysis of 2017 Homicide Data*, Violence Policy Center, at 14 (Sept. 2019). http://vpc.org/studies/wmmw2019.pdf

[19] *Alaska Violent Death Reporting System 2003-2008,* State of Alaska, Department of Health and Social Services, at 2 (Aug. 2011). http://dhss.alaska.gov/dph/Epi/injury/Documents/akvdrs/assets/AKVDRS.pdf

[20] *Id.* at 16, Table 3.1: Victim Count, Percent, and Rate of Homicide by Demographics.

[21] *Id.* at 4, Table 1.2: Victim Count, Percent, and Rate of Violent Death by Gender, Race and Ethnicity.

[22] *Id.* at 17, Table 3.2: Victim Count, Percent, and Rate of Homicide by Gender, Race and Ethnicity.

[23] Annita Lucchesi and Abigail Echo-Hawk, *Missing and Murdered Indigenous Women & Girls, A snapshot of data from 71 urban cities in the United States*, Urban Indian Health Institute, Seattle Indian Health Board (Nov. 2018). http://www.uihi.org/wp-content/uploads/2018/11/Missing-and-Murdered-Indigenous-Women-and-Girls-Report.pdf

[24] National Crime Information Center (2018). Federal Bureau of Investigation.

[25] *Missing and Murdered: Confronting the Silent Crisis in Indian Country: Hearing Before the Comm. on Indian Affs.*, 115th Cong. (2018) (statement of Robert Johnson, Assistant Director of the Criminal Investigative Division, FBI). https://www.fbi.gov/news/testimony/missing-and-murdered-confronting-the-silent-crisis-in-indian-country

The murders and disappearances of women and girls in Alaska are connected to the lack of protection from the state and the federal government and the failure of the federal government to provide resources to our tribes and other tribes to establish a comprehensive response.[26]

—Catherine Moses, Tribal Administrator,
Asa'carsarmiut Indian Tribe

[26] Catherine Moses, Tribal Administrator, *Statement of the Asa'carsarmiut Indian Tribe,* U.S. DOJ 2018 Annual Violence Against Women Annual Consultation, at 13 (2018). https://www.justice.gov/tribal/page/file/1161726

Did you know?

1. Researchers report that American Indian women suffer higher rates of violent victimization over a lifetime compared to other populations of women. This victimization is often referred to as a spectrum of violence.

2. The spectrum of violence suffered by Native women includes domestic violence, sexual assault, physical assaults, trafficking, and abductions by strangers and non-stranger. It takes place within their tribal communities and outside non-tribal communities.

3. The high rates of violence are linked to systemic barriers based on century-old federal law and colonization policies that separate and deny Native women access to legal protection from such violence.

4. The consequences of this violent victimization of American Indian women also negatively affect their families, communities, and nations.

Questions to consider:

1. How can we increase awareness that the high rates of domestic violence are connected to a larger crisis of violence Native women suffer because they are Native and women?

2. What changes are needed to reduce the lifetime victimization rates of domestic violence and violence often not considered domestic violence?

3. Do you agree that domestic violence against Alaska Native women is a crisis?

Chapter 2
Domestic Violence and Alaska Native Women

> *Since my journey began working and helping women in rural, remote Alaska villages, I have seen and listened to countless stories filled with so much pain and have heard the crying voices of our Native women, our sisters, our aunties, grandmothers, and children, often with nowhere to go for safety. In reality, there is no safe place to go in the villages ... women find shelter where they can. They hide in the local churches (if doors are left open), inside willows, in steam baths, or fish smokehouses. There are no readily available resources, and many women and children have no reliable police protection. We cannot simply get into a car and drive away—we run many times with five children with us as we hide under our homes in the dark, cold, winter months. Sometimes, if we're lucky, we might see a porch door open and we run inside the house, not knowing whom the house belongs to or whether someone is home . . . this we do to keep ourselves alive.* [27]
>
> —*Nugange (Lenora "Lynn" Hootch) Founding Mother*
> *Emmonak Women's Shelter and AKNWRC*

Domestic violence is often discussed as a single act, but it is commonly a pattern of abuse committed over weeks, months, years, or in many cases, decades by an intimate partner. This spectrum of abuse, known as domestic violence, includes a wide variety of acts, from non-criminal acts such as reproductive coercion to crimes of physical and sexual violence, stalking, kidnapping, abduction, and murder. Non-physical abuse, such as psychological aggression or mental abuse, economic abuse, and isolation from loved ones, is also common. Domestic violence victims have also shared being coerced by abusers to commit crimes, like prostitution, sex trafficking, theft, and the sale of drugs or alcohol. A study by the National Institute of Justice estimates that more than half (55.5 percent) of American Indian women have experienced violence by an intimate partner.[28]

The state of Alaska's justice system fails Alaska Native women; the lack of consequences for committing domestic violence against Alaska Native women sends a message to the public that such violence is acceptable. While acts of domestic violence, such as sexual assault, trafficking, abduction, and murder, include many crimes, the reality is that the state justice system's response, in many cases, is inadequate or non-existent to these crimes. Indian tribes throughout Alaska report that state troopers fail to respond or investigate, and prosecutors fail to charge domestic violence abusers, sexual assault predators, and sex traffickers. This lack of response leaves Alaska Native women

[27] As quoted in *Safety for Native Women: VAWA and American Indian Tribes*, at 19 (Dorma Sahneyah, ed., 2014).

[28] André B. Rosay, *Violence Against American Indian and Alaska Native Women and Men*, at 44, Table 6.1 Weighted Estimates of Violence Against Women.

unprotected, vulnerable, and targets for abusers and predators committing these crimes. It also sends the signal to abusers, predators, and traffickers that violence against Alaska Native women is acceptable, and they may feel emboldened to continue the abuse and violence as there are no meaningful consequences.

"As a Yup'ik woman who survived domestic violence, there were no services available for me. There were no services available to my children who witnessed domestic violence. We got little or no help from law enforcement."[29]—Gloria George, Councilwoman, Asa'carsarmiut Indian Tribe

The lack of accountability of perpetrators also supports common patterns of domestic violence abusers. Part of the pattern of domestic violence is the abuser's isolation of the victim from family and friends. The more isolated a victim is from her family, friends, and community, the less likely that she will have access to the support of those who will help her understand the abuse and support her in getting help to end the violence. Some victims may become more dependent upon the abuser and believe the perpetrator's excuses for the abuse, blame themselves, or may deny the violence. When a victim reports domestic violence and nothing is done, the victim receives the wrong signal, which may reinforce the abuser's excuses. She may think—It was my fault. No one cares.

Victims in villages often lack the means to leave their abuser. Housing in rural villages is very limited, and access to shelter services or a safe house is scarce. Harsh winters can create life-threatening conditions due to exposure. Matters may be even more complicated if a woman has relocated to her abuser's village. A woman may be dependent on the abuser for housing and literally have no other option. If a woman has children, shelter and food are very real concerns. And in many villages, due to the rural isolation, cost, or lack of transportation, leaving the village may take several weeks, depending on the weather and availability of planes. Faced with these challenges, when a woman reports her abuser and nothing is done, she may continue to live with the abuser. She may think—This is my only choice.

> In our village, safe housing is an urgent need because of our climate. The months of December, January, February, and March are the coldest times of the year. Temperatures reach -40°, and windchill can reach up to -60°. Imagine being out in the cold with your kids because you were getting away from domestic violence or being sexually abused. It is a terrible reality that women and children face because there is no other option, no other place to go, and no other house is

---

[29] Gloria George, Councilwoman, *Statement of the Asa'carsarmiut Indian Tribe,* U.S. DOJ Office on Violence Against Women, 2018 Consultation Report, at 12–13), https://www.justice.gov/tribal/page/file/1161726.

> available. Our women and children should not be out in the cold or have no place to go because they are being abused.[30]
>
> —Daphne Joe, Asa'carsarmiut Indian Tribe

Sexual violence is commonly used by abusers and is understood to be part of the spectrum of domestic violence. Alaska Native women are subjected to the highest rates of sexual assault, at least 7 times the non-Native rate. A 2016 study from the National Institute of Justice examined lifetime estimates for the prevalence of sexual violence against Native women. "More than 1 in 2 American Indian and Alaska Native women (56.1%) have experienced sexual violence in their lifetime."[31]

"Every woman you've met today has been raped. All of us. I know they won't believe that in the lower 48, and the State will deny it, but it's true. We all know each other, and we live here. We know what's happened."[32]

Sexual violence includes sexual abuse and assault but may also include other forms of sexual violence, such as prostitution and sex trafficking. Domestic violence victims have shared that they were coerced or forced into selling their bodies for sex because of abuse or the threats of violence. Sexual predators, by establishing intimate relationships with their victims, can use domestic violence to intimidate them into prostitution.

The Anchorage Police Department and the Federal Bureau of Investigation found that in 2009 and 2010, one-third of the women arrested for prostitution in Anchorage were Alaska Native women.[33] Yet Alaska Native people make up slightly less than 8% of the population in Anchorage.[34] The lack of response to sexual violence and trafficking is the same as the response to other crimes—inadequate to non-existent.[35]

---

[30] Daphne Joe, *Statement of the Asa'carsarmiut Indian Tribe Statement,* U.S. DOJ 2019 Violence Against Women Annual Consultation, Restoration Magazine, Vol. 16, Issue 3, at 21 (Oct. 2019).

[31] André B. Rosay, *Violence Against American Indian and Alaska Native Women and Men*, at 13.

[32] Indian Law and Order Commission, *A Roadmap for Making Native America Safer*, at 34. Tribal citizen (name withheld) statement provided during a Commission site visit to Galena, AK, Oct. 18, 2012.

[33] Alex DeMarban, *Alaska Natives Make Up One-Third of Anchorage Prostitution Arrest,* Anchorage Daily News, Dec. 3, 2010, https://www.adn.com/alaska-beat/article/alaska-natives-make-one-third-anchorage-prostitution-arrests/2010/12/03/.

[34] U.S. Census Bureau, 2010.

[35] As indicative of the federal government response to human trafficking for the years of 2013-2016, there were only 14 federal investigations and 2 prosecutions of human trafficking in Indian country. U.S. Gen. Accountability Office, *GAO-17-325, Human Trafficking Action Needed to Identify the Number of Native American Victims Receiving Federally-funded Services, at* 17 (2017). https://www.gao.gov/products/gao-17-325.

> My daughter was and still is a victim of sex trafficking. I reported it to the authorities and received no help. I told them the address, location, and names of her traffickers. The Anchorage Police Department would not listen to me until I got my two white friends to make a call for me. I contacted Priceless Alaska, but they would not help me unless a state trooper investigates and makes a referral to their organization. No one would help me. I also called the FBI, three times, and they did not respond. Through my two white friends, I reported her missing. My daughter was held, by traffickers, at Eagle River, Alaska, for four months. [36]
>
> —Martina Post, Native Village of Alakanuk

A part of the pattern of domestic violence by an abuser may include threats of death. Such threats or intimidation can prevent a woman from leaving an abuser. This is a concern for many victims of domestic violence, but for Native women in isolated off-road villages with no law enforcement or services, it is of increased significance to safety. The crisis referred to as Missing and Murdered Indigenous Women (MMIW) is a reality that Native women and Indian tribes in Alaska live with as part of their daily lives. Alaska Natives go missing at the highest rate in the nation. As of 2019, the National Crime Information Center (NCIC) Missing Person File contained 10,447 entries for American Indians.[37] Domestic violence can be lethal. Like the other forms of violence discussed above, cases of MMIW are often intertwined with domestic abuse. Domestic violence homicides, unsolved murders, and reports of missing Native women give credibility to death threats of abusers. She may think—He will kill me if I leave.

Over the last several decades, since VAWA became law in 1995, advocates and researchers have learned a lot about domestic violence abusers. Today a broader understanding of domestic abuse exists extending beyond single acts of violence by the abuser toward a victim. It is widely understood the threat or use of violence by an abuser to exercise power and control over an intimate partner takes on many forms. Domestic violence is recognized as a pattern of intimidation, through threats or acts of violence, including abuse of children or other loved ones, pet abuse[38], and spiritual abuse.

---

[36] Martina Post, *Statement of the Native Village of Alakanuk*, U.S. DOJ 2017 Violence Against Women Annual Consultation 2016, Restoration Magazine, Vol. 14, Issue 1, at 4 (Feb. 2017).

[37] FBI, Compilation of 2019 NCIC Missing Person and Unidentified Person Statistics, at 5 (2019), https://www.fbi.gov/file-repository/2019-ncic-missing-person-and-unidentified-person-statistics.pdf/view.

[38] "Often, abusers exploit the close, emotional bond shared by a victim and her companion animal to inflict harm upon the human victim. The abuser may harm or kill the animal in order to emotionally harm the human, use threats against the animal to gain compliance or control over the human, or use these methods to abuse the human or coerce her return after she leaves the household. These forms of abuse constitute one aspect of the broader pattern of control that

Domestic violence is harmful to children. Children are exposed to domestic violence in many ways, including seeing, hearing, or being told about it. In 1999, the U.S. Department of Justice (DOJ) launched the first National Survey of Children's Exposure to Violence (NatSCEV).[39] It found approximately 1 in 15 youth, had been exposed to some form of physical assault between their parents in the past year. Domestic violence is harmful to all children, and in the context of Alaska Native children, it is important to consider the history of colonization.

In 2014, the report of the U.S. Department of Justice Advisory Committee on American Indian and Alaska Native Children Exposed to Violence summarized: "Over the course of several months this Advisory Committee listened to hours of testimony about the trauma and suffering endured by our Native people—past and present. We heard story after story of abuse, loss, and tragedy. We heard about the legacy of historical trauma caused by loss of home, land, culture, and language and the subsequent abuse of generations of Native children in American boarding schools. We heard that, through a tragic history of broken promises and chronic underfunding, our country has failed to meet its trust obligations to Native Americans and their children. Yet at every hearing we also heard about the desire for healing and the importance of restoring traditional ceremonies and ancestral wisdom as ways of returning safety, dignity, respect, and well-being to our Indigenous people and their children."[40]

Addressing Domestic Violence

The current barriers to justice and the harmful effects of domestic violence upon Alaska Native women are further compounded by the years of confusing laws, policies, and inadequate allocation of resources by the federal and state governments. To address and enhance the national response to domestic violence and sexual assault, the United States enacted the Violence Against Women Act (VAWA) in 1994.[41]

---

characterizes an abusive relationship." Vivek Upadhya, *The Abuse of Animals as a Method of Domestic Violence: The Need for Criminalization,* 63 Emory L. J. at 1163 (2014). *See also* Sherry Ramsey, Mary Lou Randour, Nancy Blanney, and Mary Gupta, *Protecting Domestic Violence Victims by Protecting Their Pets,* Juvenile Justice Today, at 16-20, NCJFCJ (Spring 2010), https://pdfs.semanticscholar.org/c618/8d307c15d2e4e50f0b59bb777372327cccbe.pdf.

[39] Sherry Hamby, David Finkelhor, Heather Turner, and Richard Ormrod, *Children's Exposure to Intimate Partner Violence and Other Family Violence, U.S. DOJ, OJJDP, Bulletin National Survey of Children's Exposure to Violence* (Oct. 2011) https://www.ncjrs.gov/pdffiles1/ojjdp/232272.pdf

[40] U.S. Dep't of Justice, Office of Juvenile Justice and Delinquency Prevention, Office of Justice Programs, *Attorney General's Advisory Committee on American Indian and Alaska Native Children Exposed to Violence, Ending Violence so Children Can Thrive* (Nov. 2014), Letter from the Co-Chairs, https://www.justice.gov/sites/default/files/defendingchildhood/pages/attachments/2015/03/23/ending_violence_so_children_can_thrive.pdf.

[41] Violence Against Women Act, title IV of the Violent Crime Control and Law Enforcement Act of 1994, Pub. L. 103-322 (codified at 34 U.S.C. § 12291 *et seq.*), https://www.govinfo.gov/content/pkg/STATUTE-108/pdf/STATUTE-108-Pg1796.pdf.

Since that time, Congress has reauthorized VAWA to further strengthen the nation's response to domestic violence. Within each reauthorization, Congress has included historic reforms and increased resources consistent with its federal trust responsibility to assist Indian tribes and enhance tribal responses. Unfortunately, decades later, VAWA protections and resources have still only reached a small portion of Indian tribes in Alaska. Tribal leaders and advocates have expressed that the recognized authority and resources are needed to take action and effectuate change within their villages. The lack of federal and state response is not new. It is based on a history of the diminishment of tribal sovereignty and a failure to respond to violence against Alaska Native women.

While federal resources are needed and have a basis in the federal trust responsibility, the most effective response to domestic violence is a culturally meaningful and immediate local tribal response. Tribal leaders and advocates have stated that for change to be effective and meaningful, change must come from within the villages.[42]

Despite historical and current barriers, hope is found in the teachings, beliefs, and way of life of Alaska Native peoples. Hope rests in the cultural values of Alaska Native peoples as a source of change from within each village and tribal government. As governments, Indian tribes in Alaska are strengthening their responses to domestic violence to hold abusers accountable and support the safety of victims for the future generations of their communities.

> In one particular case back in the spring of 2013, a mother was beaten to death in front of her two children. The children thought their mother was sleeping and stayed by her side until the father sobered up and realized what he had done. Alcohol was a factor in this case! The father is now incarcerated, and the grandparents are left to finish raising the two children. Despite this horrible event, the children still love and miss both their father and their mother very much!
>
> Now the question is could this have been prevented? Has the father beat up the mother before this horrible event happened? Did the mother wish she had a safe place for her and her children to go before she passed away? Has the father seen his father beat his mother up when he was growing up? How damaged and broken are the children now for witnessing such an event and how broken are their hearts? Is there hope for the children's future to be living healthy lifestyles when they get older?

---

[42] Yup'ik Women's Coalition, Public Service Announcements (2017), http://www.yupikwomen.org/news-and-updates/ywc-psa/.

Not only do these questions pertain to this particular family but it pertains to all families everywhere!

Now we as leaders have to ask ourselves: Could we prevent such things from happening? Can we provide a safe place for our women and children? Can we help these families receive counseling to better themselves? Can we break the cycle of violence?

I believe we can! I believe we can provide a safe place for our women and children, and we can provide the necessary counseling for them. I believe the fathers can get better and treat their families better as well. I believe that we still have hope for tomorrow for our children's future!

If we provide them with temporary shelter, counseling, and treatment facilities, and educate the children at a young age about violence—that it is not appropriate and not our way of life.[43]

—Eric Olson, Sr., Chief, Native Village of Hooper Bay

---

[43] Eric Olson, Sr., Chief, *Statement of the Native Village of Hooper Bay,* U.S. DOJ 2019 Violence Against Women Annual Government-to-Government Consultation (2019) (on file with the AKNWRC).

Quick Facts
Domestic Violence and Alaska Native Women

More than half (55.5%) of American Indian and Alaska Native women have experienced physical violence by an intimate partner.[44]

More than 1 in 2 American Indian and Alaska Native women (56.1%) have experienced sexual violence in their lifetime.[45]

38.2% of American Indian and Alaska Native women victims of domestic violence who needed services were unable to get the services.[46]

Nationwide, homicide was the fourth leading cause of death among American Indian and Alaska Native women between 0 and 19 years of age, and the sixth leading cause of death for women between 20 and 44 years of age.[47]

In Alaska, American Indians and Alaskan Natives–both men and women–represented:

- 33.1% of all violent deaths include not only homicides, but suicides, unintentional firearm deaths, deaths of undetermined intent, and deaths due to legal intervention,[48] and
- 29.1% of all homicides.[49]

In Alaska, 127 Native women died a violent death in five years, 2003-2008, represented:

- 38% of all women homicide victims,[50] and
- 39.8% of the violent deaths of all women[51] occurred primarily as the result of firearms, poisoning, hanging, and strangulation/suffocation.

---

[44] André B. Rosay, *Violence Against American Indian and Alaska Native Women and Men*, at 43-44, Table 6.1 Weighted Estimates of Violence Against Women.

[45] *Id.* at 13.

[46] *Id.* at 50, Figure 6.3 Weighted Estimates of Inability to Get Needed Services.

[47] *Leading Causes of Death, Non-Hispanic American Indian or Alaska Native, Females,* Centers for Disease Control and Prevention, United States (2017). https://www.cdc.gov/women/lcod/index.htm

[48] *Alaska Violent Death Reporting System 2003-2008,* State of Alaska, Department of Health and Social Services, at 2 (Aug. 2011). http://dhss.alaska.gov/dph/Epi/injury/Documents/akvdrs/assets/AKVDRS.pdf

[49] *Id.* at 16, Table 3.1: Victim Count, Percent, and Rate of Homicide by Demographics, Alaska, 2003-2008.

[50] *Id.* at 17, Table 3.2: Victim Count, Percent, and Rate of Homicide by Gender, Race and Ethnicity, Alaska, 2003-2008.

[51] *Id.* at 4, Table 1.2: Victim Count, Percent, and Rate of Violent Death by Gender, Race and Ethnicity, Alaska, 2003-2008.

VAWA 2005
Title IX. Safety for Indian Women
§901. Findings

Congress finds that—
(1) 1 out of every 3 Indian (including Alaska Native) women are raped in their lifetimes;
(2) Indian women experience 7 sexual assaults per 1,000, compared with 4 per 1,000 among Black Americans, 3 per 1,000 among Caucasians, 2 per 1,000 among Hispanic women, and 1 per 1,000 among Asian women;
(3) Indian women experience the violent crime of battering at a rate of 23.2 per 1,000, compared with 8 per 1,000 among Caucasian women;
(4) during the period 1979 through 1992, homicide was the third leading cause of death of Indian females aged 15 to 34, and 75 percent were killed by family members or acquaintances;
(5) Indian tribes require additional criminal justice and victim services resources to respond to violent assaults against women; and
(6) the unique legal relationship of the United States to Indian tribes creates a federal trust responsibility to assist tribal governments in safeguarding the lives of Indian women.[52]

---

[52] Violence Against Women and Dep't of Justice Reauthorization Act of 2005, Pub. L. No. 109-162, § 901, 119 Stat. 3077 (2006). https://www.govinfo.gov/content/pkg/PLAW-109publ162/pdf/PLAW-109publ162.pdf

Did you know?

1. "American Indian/Alaska Natives are at a greater risk of violent victimization than are other Americans…"[53]

2. The term *domestic violence* has multiple definitions under federal, state, and tribal codes and ordinances. In general, it refers to an ongoing pattern of abuse, both physical and non-physical, intended to intimidate or control the victim of the abuser by an intimate partner.

3. The VAWA uses a more limited legal, criminal, and civil definition of domestic violence. The term domestic violence includes "felony or misdemeanor crimes of violence committed by a current or former spouse or intimate partner of the victim, by a person with whom the victim shares a child in common, by a person who is cohabitating with or has cohabitated with the victim as a spouse or intimate partner, by a person similarly situated to a spouse of the victim under the domestic or family violence laws of the jurisdiction receiving grant monies, or by any other person against an adult or youth victim who is protected from that person's acts under the domestic or family violence laws of the jurisdiction."[54]

Questions to consider:

1. How is domestic violence defined by your village?

2. Are the numbers of domestic violence cases in villages reported in law enforcement statistics accurate? If there is no law enforcement in your village, who responds to the domestic violence case?

3. How can an accurate reflection of domestic violence cases bring help to our communities in addressing domestic violence?

4. What changes are needed to gather an accurate understanding of the violence being committed against Alaska Native women?

5. In addressing domestic violence, should a village response include addressing other acts of violence against women? What about other crimes?

---

[53] Patricia Tjaden & Nancy Thoennes, Nat'l Institute of Justice, U.S. Dep't of Justice, NCJ 181867, *Extent, Nature, and Consequences of Intimate Partner Violence,* at 23 (2000). https://www.ncjrs.gov/pdffiles1/nij/183781.pdf

[54] VAWA 2005, Pub. L. No. 109-162, § 3, Universal Definitions and Grant Provisions, 119 Stat. 2965 (2006).

Chapter 3
Changes to Our Lives by the Outside World

Before the outside world came to our village our values were passed from generation to generation through training in the subsistence skills necessary for life in remote Alaska. We need to support those who have no voice. We need to speak out for those who are afraid and let them know that there is help and hope. You can reverse things. Nothing is ever impossible. Everything is possible.[55]

—Rose Borkowski, late Yup'ik elder, Advocate, Native Village of Emmonak

Why is the rate of violence against Alaska Native women so much higher than that against other women in the United States? There are many answers to this question, including the remote locations of many villages, the lack of immediate access to law enforcement, and the lack of services. While all these reasons contribute to the high rates of violence, they are just parts of a larger story, the broader history of violence against Native women. Unknown at the time to the original peoples of Alaska,[56] European Empires—Spain,[57] Portugal,[58] Great Britain,[59] and Russia[60]—claimed title to their lands through papal bulls[61] and international treaties. Later, the United States bought the territory of Alaska from Russia and consequently, claimed authority over the Indigenous Peoples occupying the lands. These international claims and the purchase by the United States occurred without the consent of those to be governed—the original, indigenous, peoples.

> When I read my grandpa's book. He was born in 1896. He talked about how their village used to run. It had harmony. Everyone tried to be at peace with each other. And when the whaling ship came, it brought

---

[55] Rose Borkowski, Video Statement, 2004 (on file with the AKNWRC).

[56] The word *Alaska* derives from the Aleut word *Alaxsxaq*, meaning "mainland."

[57] The 1493 Inter Caetera, a papal bull passed by Pope Alexander VI, purported to give Spain sovereignty over any territory west and south of a meridian line approximately 550 km west of the Azores and Canary Islands.

[58] In 1494, both the Spanish and Portuguese signed the Treaty of Tordesillas which created a new meridian line approximately 2000 km west of the Cape Verde Islands. This new meridian line granted Portugal all lands to the east and Spain all lands to the west of the line.

[59] In 1763, the Treaty of Paris settled land disputes between the United States and British North America and granted most of the land in Upper Canada to the British Crown. James Cook was the first British explorer to reach Alaska and execute territorial claims driven by the fur trade challenging Spain's claim.

[60] In 1741, Russian Captain Vitus Bering led a government-sponsored expedition that visited the shores of the Gulf of Alaska and later provided the bases for territorial claims. While searching for a passageway to Asia, the ships returned to Russia laden with furs providing an economic reason for exerting Russian sovereignty.

[61] A papal bull is an official letter or decree that the Catholic Pope issues.

> sexual abuse. It brought murder. It brought a lot of bad things that happened to our Native people. All my three aunties, even my grandmother, were on a whaling ship, and they hired them out. They would go out, and they would come back pregnant.[62]
>
> —Etta Tall, Traditional Advocate

Before foreign interference and colonization by Russia and the United States, a natural system of family and clan relationships existed based on a belief of respect for the spiritual nature of all things, including women and children. It is well known that violence against Alaska Native women was rare because such behavior was unacceptable within the cultural values of the original peoples. At the heart of this natural system were beliefs, traditions, and customs involving an extended family with clearly delineated roles and responsibilities.

When disrespectful conduct occurred, the village appropriately addressed the person's action. The wishes of the aggrieved woman were central to the response from the community. Accepting responsibility, correcting the wrongdoing, and apologizing for the disrespectful behavior was, and is, seen as essential to restoring balance in the community.

Abuse or violence against a woman or child was considered unacceptable behavior, and the well-being of the abused woman was the central concern of the community. The family, the clan, as well as spiritual and tribal leaders held essential roles in the process of holding abusers accountable for their actions. This high standard of accountability, while common to villages, was specific to each tribe in terms of consequences. Based on the beliefs and circumstances of the community, an abuser would be held accountable with direct and sometimes severe consequences.

The purpose of this accountability was to heal and restore the balance in the life of the woman and community, often including families and clans. The focus was on the woman, the victim, who suffered the abuse, wrongdoing, and disrespect. The goal was to correct the abuser's understanding that his disrespectful actions were unacceptable to the community. This focus and practice of community accountability is shared across Indian tribes and is the essential component of what are known as indigenous justice systems.[63]

---

[62] Etta Tall, Personal Video Statement, Yup'ik Women's Coalition Sexual Assault Planning Meeting (2017) (on file with the AKNWRC)

[63] Ada Pecos Melton, *Indigenous Justice Systems and Tribal Society,* In Wanda D. McCaslin, ed., Justice as Healing: Indigenous Ways, 2005. http://www.aidainc.net/Publications/ij_systems.htm

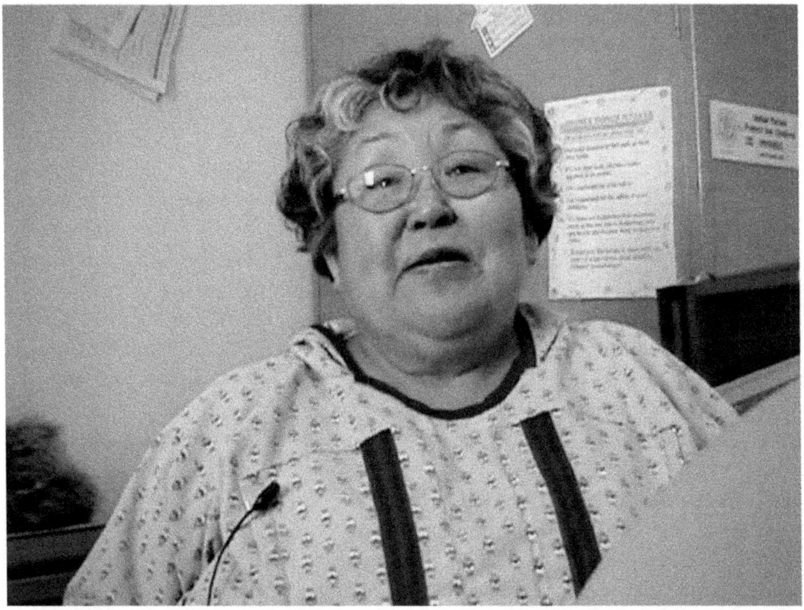

"The men talked to that person, and the object was to retrain the man on how to treat his wife, to show respect. If they were repeat abusers, if they didn't learn their lesson, then they'd be told to pack up, like, extra clothing, hunting gear, and food and told to go out into the wilderness, the tundra, and survive the experience of living alone. When the men checked him, he was allowed to come back into the village and to go back to his wife, instead of being punished like they are taken into jail today, fined, and all that. They were not actual council members, but everybody, all the men, were involved in this problem. If the man continued to be abusive, he was asked to go to another village not to have contact with his wife and children." [64]

—Rose Borkowski, late Yup'ik Elder, Advocate, Native Village of Emmonak

Destruction of Indigenous Justice Systems

Colonization severed the Haida people's ties with ourselves, each other, our nation, the land, and the sea, reflected in the disrespect for and rates of domestic and sexual violence against our women and children. Our potlatches are our ways of upholding our societal laws, and these were outlawed in Alaska in the early 1900s and in Canada the late 1800s.[65] Through Xaadas Kíl Kuyaas (Precious Haida Words) Foundation, we are focusing our time to re-connect these severed ties by bringing life back to our language and putting our Haida culture and

---

[64] Rose Borkowski, *Video Statement*, 2004 (on file with the AKNWRC).

[65] *See* Sara Davidson and Robert Davidson, *Potlatch as Pedagogy: Learning Through Ceremony*, (2018).

> worldview into action. This is key to healing from all the trauma our people have suffered for too long, and beyond the limitations of challenges with limited resource allocation.[66]
>
> —Lisa "Ka'illjuus" Lang, Xaadas Kíl Kuyaas Foundation

With the arrival of Europeans and other outsiders, the cultural standard of respect and safety was diminished as the original women suffered unimaginable violence ending or altering their lives, and that of their families' and tribes' forever. The attacks upon the original peoples by outside foreign governments destroyed entire villages and their ways of life, including their indigenous justice systems. Native women and children suffered physical violence, rape, murder, and became victims of what is today called sex trafficking. Unlike domestic violence today, this violence by foreign governments was viewed as legal. The indigenous justice systems could not protect Native women from these crimes of war as entire villages were destroyed, enslaved, or forced to assimilate.

When we think about why rates of domestic violence, rape, trafficking, and missing and murdered are so high–this story is the setting, the stage, and the historical context. Violence against Native women is tolerated today because for over two centuries, outsiders and foreign governments committed heinous acts of violence, and they were not considered crimes. This steady destruction and diminishment of the sovereignty of Indian tribes in Alaska, is the backdrop for the current crisis of violence confronting Native women. Today Alaska Native women continue to live unprotected by United States' laws and are vulnerable to violence. The legal barriers continue to prevent their tribal governments from protecting them.

This long history of foreign invasion, domination, and violence used against villages and women to gain control of their lands and resources is the history of genocide in Alaska, not unlike what happened in the lower 48 states. Under the Convention on the Prevention and Punishment of the Crime of Genocide, a treaty signed and ratified by the United States, genocide is defined as:

> "any of the following acts committed with intent to destroy, in whole or in part, a national, ethnical, racial, or religious group, as such:
> (a) Killing members of the group;
> (b) Causing serious bodily or mental harm to members of the group;
> (c) Deliberately inflicting on the group conditions of life, calculated to bring about its physical destruction in whole or in part;
> (d) Imposing measures intended to prevent births within the group;

---

[66] Lisa "Ka'illjuus" Lang, Xaadas Kíl Kuyaas Foundation, AKNWRC Webinar Presentation, *Part 2 of 2: Understanding Culture as a Protective Factor* (Aug. 13, 2020).

(e) Forcibly transferring children of the group to another group."[67]

Alaska Natives have experienced all of these acts.

Russia, 1784-1867, Eight Decades of Colonization

Russia dominated the indigenous lands and peoples of Alaska for more than eight decades, or just under three generations.[68] In search of sea otters, fur-trade centers were established. In many areas, the Native population was practically eliminated. Hostages were taken, individuals enslaved, families were split up, and others were forced to leave their villages and settle elsewhere. The frequent battles and the Russian massacre at Awa'uq of the Alutiiq people are told through Alutiiq stories and Russian accounts.[69] By 1800, little more than 50 years after the first Russian contact, the population had been reduced by some 80 percent, to about 2,500 people.[70]

The legal barriers and forced acceptance of violence perpetrated against Native women has its origins in this conquest of Native peoples by Russia. An outstanding characteristic of this conquest was the physical and cultural genocide of Alaska Native women. The violence used by Russia included using Alaska Native women for target practice to test the range of a bullet,[71] abduction of women and girls for sex trafficking on whaling and trading ships, and rape of women within their home villages. These and other crimes held no legal consequence for the Russian invaders.

> During the rule of the Russian-American Company the knut (stick) was used liberally, and the manner in which the Natives were forced to pursue the sea otter hunt in the services of their "white masters" was considered a form of slavery.
>
> Every morning a bell would ring, and all the men and women had to go to work. If a person did not come, he or she was sent for and soundly whipped. The wives of all the inhabitants of Kodiak, after their husbands leave with various hunting parties, are required to dig sarana according to the following quotas: wives and daughters of those who

---

[67] United Nations Convention on the Prevention and Punishment of the Crime of Genocide art. 2, Dec. 9, 1948. https://treaties.un.org/doc/publication/unts/volume%2078/volume-78-i-1021-english.pdf

[68] In 1741, a Russian expedition led by Danish navigator Vitus Bering sighted the Alaskan mainland. Russian fur-trade centers were established, exposing the Native Aleut populations to foreign diseases. The Three Saints Bay colony was founded on Kodiak Island in 1784.

[69] *Education Under Russian Colonization 1784-1867*, Alutiiq Education, alutiiqeducation.org.

[70] "*The Aleut Corporation Aleut History*," Our History - Aleut Corporation, https://aleutcorp.com.

[71] Kodiak Native Museum, Kodiak Island, presentation during U.S. DOJ OVW STOP training (July 2006) (on file with the AKNWRC).

travel as companions, not possessing their own baidarkas [sea kayaks], must collect four ishkats (native grass baskets) each; wives of men who own their own baidarkas must collect two, their daughters four ishkats each. When the berries ripen the company compels them to pick berries for winter reserve and each is obliged to provide one ishkat of cranberries, and a second one of crowberries. Other berries, such as raspberries, huckleberries, blueberries, cloudberries, and salmonberries, are collected, depending on the crop, as much as baidarshchik (company representative) orders. Those women who cannot fulfill this obligation because of poor health or because they have children at the breast, buy the berries from other women friends and deliver these to the company.

After the end of the berry-picking season, the women face another task: the bird hunters return then, and the company, having collected their catch, distributes it to the Alutiiq wives and daughters in all settlements to be processed and made into parkas. Following this they are assigned yet another obligatory labor: to sew kamleikas (parkas) from whale, sea lion, seal, and bear guts and to make out of sinew cordage for seal nets and to prepare sinew thread.[72]

The genocide that occurred during Russian colonization had near irreversible consequences for future generations as well because it severed the transmission of cultural knowledge traditionally conveyed from one generation to the next. This loss of family and culture is a historical trauma to which many attribute high rates of depression, suicide, alcoholism, and domestic violence. It represents a loss that cannot be calculated in numbers or lives.

[72] Sun'aq Tribe of Kodiak and Kodiak Native Women's Advisory Committee on Domestic Violence and Sexual Assault, *Violence Against Alutiiq Women Is Not Traditional Handbook*, (2006) (on file with the AKNWRC).

"We ask you … to understand how and why the history of violence against women in our village. Traditionally we are a culture based on respect and abuse was not tolerated. But today many of our challenges are legal challenges because of federal laws. Today, we do not have services and other programs due to the lack of resources. I have no choice that I was born Native, a Yup'ik Native from Alaska. My people survived and learned to live off the land and waters. They were knowledgeable with the harsh winters and understand what needs to be done for their families. We were civil in our way of life. We were never uneducated because we were educated to know our surroundings and to respect one another and love one another. My people felt pain and saw our own die from smallpox, influenza, and all the diseases. I see the pain my people went through. We are still in the process of learning who we are now. Please understand we have to learn two worlds now. Imagine if I invade your home and order you on how to live your life. Imagine if I made you speak only Yup'ik and punish you if you spoke any English, degrade you on how your way of life was wrong, and mine was correct. That is how my grandparents' generation lived. I watch my people literally die from alcoholism, not because they are alcoholics, but because they mourned over these changes."[73]

—Daphne Joe, Wellness Coordinator
Asa'carsarmiut Indian Tribe

[73] Daphne Joe, *Statement of the Asa'carsarmiut Indian Tribe Statement,* U.S. DOJ 2019 Violence Against Women Annual Consultation, Restoration Magazine, Vol. 16, Issue 3, at 21 (2019).

The United States, 1867-Present

In the 2009 Apology to Native Peoples, the U.S. recognized that there have been years of official depredations, ill-conceived policies, and the breaking of covenants by the federal government regarding Indian tribes.[74] The U.S. apologized for the many instances of violence, maltreatment, and neglect inflicted on Native Peoples. The release in 2018 of the U.S. Commission on Civil Rights Broken Promises Report also continues to affirm the need for the government to fulfill their trust responsibility.[75]

Within the United States, the body of law and policy that governs the legal relationship between Indian nations and the United States is known as federal Indian law. It is within this legal context that Alaska Native women continue to suffer from violence and injustice in their daily lives as a population. Federal Indian law has its origins in the outdated laws of colonization, laws that justified crimes of violence against Alaska Native women.[76] The living legacy of these laws are the legal loopholes that still permit such crimes of violence to go unpunished.

Historically, attacks on Indian tribes began with the taking of lands from the Indigenous peoples. The "legal fiction" for creating a basis for land title in North America was the "Doctrine of Discovery, pronounced on May 4, 1493, by Pope Alexander and later expanded. It granted European nations the right to claim the lands they discovered on behalf of Christendom. The legal foundation of the U.S. is bound to the Doctrine of Discovery, justifying the genocide, and forced assimilation of Indigenous peoples. For example, in 1823, Chief Justice John Marshall's opinion in the landmark case *Johnson v. M'Intosh* invoked the Doctrine, and as recent as the 2005 Supreme Court decision ruling against a land claim by the Oneida Indian Nation. On March 30, 2023, Pope Francis renounced the Doctrine of Discovery."[77]

"The Catholic Church therefore repudiates those concepts that fail to recognize the inherent human rights of Indigenous Peoples, including what has become known as the legal and political "Doctrine of Discovery."[78]

---

[74] P.L. 111-118, https://congress.gov/bill/111th-congress/senate-joint-resolution/14/text.

[75] https://usccr.gov/pubs/2018/12-20-Broken-Promises.pdf

[76] The reference to "colonization" is used in the context of European countries establishing control over Indigenous Nations of North America. Colonization is generally defined as an act of one nation controlling another for economic gain, https://un.org/en/sections/issues-depth/decolonization/index.html.

[77] Restoration of Native Sovereignty and Safety of Native Women, Restoration, Vol 20, Issue 2, (2023).

[78] Joint Statement of the Dicasteries for Culture and Education and for Promoting Integral Human Development on the "Doctrine of Discovery," 3.30.2023.

Unlike many Indian tribes in the lower 48, Alaska Native villages did not exchange their lands through treaties for peace and recognition of their sovereignty. On March 30, 1867, the agreement to sell 1.5 million hectares of Russian property in America for $7.2 million, about two cents per acre, was signed. These lands, by implication, included the Indigenous Peoples of the territory, even though they had not given their consent.[79]

Historically, U.S. federal policy toward Indian nations has eroded the protections and status of Native women within their respective villages, and more broadly, within the United States. American Indian laws and policies have had distinct goals and reasons for development. Generally, the ultimate reason was access to land and much desired resources. Certain policies during the American Indian Wars Era, the Boarding School Era, the Adoption Era, and Period of Forced Sterilization had a devastating impact upon the lives of Native women. While the purchase of Alaska from Russia came after the Indian Wars, the general policy of termination of Indian tribes remained and shaped U.S. relations with Alaska Native villages.

Alaska Native villages were impacted by the U.S. Boarding School Era, from the 1880s to the 1950s, followed by the Adoption Era, from the 1950s to the 1970s. During these two eras, children were removed from their mothers, families, and villages to be educated at federal or religious institutions. The 2009 Congressional resolution apologized for these and other actions. In 2021, Congress introduced a bill entitled "Truth and Healing Commission on Indian Boarding School Policies," which further acknowledges the harm this era has on our families and communities.[80]

> Whereas the federal government condemned the traditions, beliefs, and customs of Native Peoples and endeavored to assimilate them by such policies as the redistribution of land under the Act of February 8, 1887 (25 U.S.C. 331; 24 Stat. 388, chapter 119) (commonly known as the "General Allotment Act"), and the forcible removal of Native children from their families to faraway boarding schools where their Native practices and languages were degraded and forbidden…[81]

---

https://press.vatican.va/content/salastampa/en/bollettino/pubblico/2023/03/30/230330b.html

[79] 25 U.S.C. §71. During this time, it is notable that the Civil War had just ended, and the country was in the "Reconstruction Era," when the United States was reintegrating into the Union the states that had seceded, and determining the legal status of African Americans. Alaska Territory was a far-off world not part of this focus.

[80] S. 2907 and H.R. 5444 are identical companion bills.

[81] Apology to Native Peoples, 2009, P.L. 111-118. https://www.congress.gov/bill/111th-congress/senate-joint-resolution/14/text

Children were forcibly removed from their families and villages to further the federal policy of assimilation. The forcible removal of children was clearly a violation of many rights protected today under international law[82], as well as the concept of a "mother's right." It also negatively impacted the traditions and teachings of villages for the clan and the relatives to have the cultural responsibility for raising children.

> I did not want to go, but my mother said she had no choice. The BIA agent would come and take me. At the school, we were slapped, had our ears pulled, or hair pulled if we spoke Yup'ik. So, we cried with our tears, and I told myself I would never speak. I would not talk. I would keep quiet.[83]
>
> —Nugange (Lenora "Lynn" Hootch)

The intent of these two eras is reflected in the following statement of the 1886 Commissioner of Indian Affairs:

> It is admitted by most people that the adult savage is not susceptible to the influence of civilization, and we must therefore turn to his children, that they might be taught to abandon the pathway of barbarism and walk with a sure step along the pleasant highway of Christian civilization . . . They must be withdrawn, in tender years, entirely from the camp and taught to eat, to sleep, to dress, to play, to work, to think after the manner of the white man.[84]

The Impact of Colonization and Historical Trauma on Alaska Natives

The Administration for Children and Families describes "historical trauma" as something that can be traced back to first contact and the treatment of Native Americans throughout history.

> Historical trauma is multigenerational trauma experienced by a specific cultural, racial or ethnic group. It is related to major events that oppressed a particular group of people because of their status as oppressed, such as slavery, the Holocaust, forced migration, and the

---

[82] *See,* e.g., *U.N. Declaration on the Rights of Indigenous Peoples*, Art. 7(2), "Indigenous peoples have the collective right to live in freedom, peace and security as distinct peoples and shall not be subjected to any act of genocide or any other act of violence, including forcibly removing children of the group to another group. See also, American Declaration on the Rights of Indigenous Peoples, Article XVII.

[83] Video interview with Nugange (Lenora "Lynn" Hootch*)*, Board Member of AKNWRC, in Palm Springs, CA (Dec. 12, 2014) (on file with the AKNWRC).

[84] Monroe E. Price, *Law and the American Indian Contemporary Legal Education Series* (1973), quoted in Lila J. George, *"Why the Need for the Indian Child Welfare Act?"* Journal of Multicultural Social Work, Vol. 5, No. 166 (1997).

> violent colonization of Native Americans. While many in such a group will experience no effects of the historical trauma, others may experience poor overall physical and behavioral health, including low self-esteem, depression, self-destructive behavior, marked propensity for violent or aggressive behavior, substance misuse and addiction, and high rates of suicide and cardiovascular disease. Acute problems of domestic violence or alcohol misuse that are not directly linked to historical trauma may be exacerbated by living in a community with unaddressed grief and behavioral health needs. Parents' experience of trauma may disrupt typical parenting skills and contribute to behavior problems in children. Compounding this familial or intergenerational trauma, historical trauma often involves the additional challenge of a damaged cultural identity (Sotero, 2006).[85]

How historical trauma impacts individuals and communities is challenging to quantify and identify. However, nonetheless, we all know that it has an impact on where our communities are today with the disproportionate rate of violence, substance abuse, and suicide. Again, the ACF has acknowledged the impact on us over time.

> Considerable work has also been done with communities of Native Americans, who experienced repeated massacres and the forced removal of children to federal and mission boarding and day schools (Brave Heart, 2003). From her work with tribal communities, clinician and researcher Maria Yellow Horse Brave Heart describes historical trauma as the 'cumulative emotional and psychological wounding over the lifespan and across generations, emanating from massive group trauma experience.'
>
> ....
>
> Research is still emerging on the effectiveness of treatment methods for individuals experiencing historical trauma. Treatment approaches are grounded in traditional healing methods and ceremonial practices of communities. For example, Dr. Brave Heart has developed psychoeducational group interventions delivered at geographic locations that are sacred to members of tribal communities that involve ceremonies reinforcing cultural identity. Although even top researchers in this field acknowledge the literature about historical trauma is controversial, there is an important emphasis on the healing process, and overcoming the barriers to resolving grief.

---

[85] https://www.acf.hhs.gov/trauma-toolkit/trauma-concept

> [A key concept is] [h]istorical trauma is intergenerational trauma experienced by a specific cultural group that has a history of being systematically oppressed.[86]

Sadly, and arguably, American Indian and Alaska Native communities have experienced more oppression than any other group in the last few hundred years. We need to address this trauma so we can heal.

However, public acceptance of a system that offers one level of protection for Native women and another for all other women is an example of colonization. The violent and inhuman treatment of Alaska Natives continues the laws and policies of colonization. The fact that Native women are victimized at rates of more than double that of any other population of women in the United States is explained in this historical context.

Colonization has a destructive legacy for Alaska Native women. The destruction and diminishment of tradition, culture, and values in Alaska changed the foundation of how tribal peoples lived, leaving Native women and children unprotected and vulnerable to violence.

---

[86] *Id.*

"The changes to our lives as Native women by outsiders, Russia, and then the United States, cannot be undone. What can be done is recognizing and supporting the authority of villages to utilize their power of government to protect their well-being. Understanding the past can help us to make the changes needed today to protect Native women."

—Tami Truett Jerue
Executive Director, AKNWRC

VAWA 2005, Safety for Indian Women §902. Purposes

The purposes of this title are:
(1) to decrease the incidence of violent crimes against Indian women;
(2) to strengthen the capacity of Indian tribes to exercise their sovereign authority to respond to violent crimes committed against Indian women; and
(3) to ensure that perpetrators of violent crimes committed against Indian women are held accountable for their criminal behavior.

Did you know?

1. The United Nations defines *genocide* as: "any of the following acts committed with intent to destroy, in whole or in part, a national, ethnical, racial or religious group, as such: (a) Killing members of the group; (b) Causing serious bodily or mental harm to members of the group; (c) Deliberately inflicting on the group conditions of life, calculated to bring about its physical destruction in whole or in part; (d) Imposing measures intended to prevent births within the group; (e) Forcibly transferring children of the group to another group.[87]

2. The U.S. Boarding School Era impacted Alaska Native villages, and many Native children witnessed and experienced violence at these facilities. These facilities required children to speak only English and did not allow children to speak their Native languages. The impact of the Boarding School Era is not fully understood. The children were required to stay at the schools for holidays and other events. Lessons and family values were not considered, and children were forbidden from exercising their culture, religion, or any practice that conflicted with the teacher or priest. Children were also sexually abused at boarding schools.[88]

Questions to consider:

1. When did the disrespect of women begin in your community?

2. Did your village have outsiders come into your village to extract minerals, oil, animals, or timber? Did these outsiders treat your community as unworthy of respect, behave inappropriately, and disregard your women and their safety? Did violence against women become a problem after these outsiders came into your community?

3. How did families in your village explain to their children why they were being forced to leave and go to government schools during the U.S. Boarding School Era? What impact did boarding schools have on Native languages?

4. Is there a continuing impact of the physical and sexual violence committed against Native women by outsiders under Russia and the United States to establish control over the lands of the Native peoples of Alaska?

---

[87] *United Nations Convention on the Prevention and Punishment of the Crime of Genocide*, Article II, RES. 260 A, (III), 1948. https://www.un.org/en/genocideprevention/genocide.shtml

[88] https://www.adn.com/alaska-news/crime-courts/2018/12/26/the-list-these-are-the-priests-who-were-credibly-accused-of-sexual-abuse-across-alaska/.

Chapter 4
A Native Response to Domestic Violence

This subject is very sacred, because it addresses the heart of who we are, our religion. We have our way of living as Tlingit people. Being required to develop non-Tlingit responses is unrealistic because of the cost and because state and federal responses are not based on the worldview of the Tlingits.[89]

—Mike Jackson, Tlingit Elder and retired Alaska State Magistrate Judge

What are village-based responses from a cultural perspective to domestic violence? How can villages support women to regain what the abuse damaged in their lives? How is the traditional worldview of respect and harmony restored after such abuse or violence? How are relations within and between families and clans restored, so the woman is honored? How does the abuser fulfill his responsibilities for the damage caused by his abuse?

Each Alaska Native village, as a government, can determine the actions it takes to respond to domestic violence. However, the historical differences, treatment, and legislation by the federal government have created a lot of confusion about tribal structures and jurisdiction, which is typically defined by subject matter and territory. By understanding the history and current crisis of violence perpetrated against Native women, the important role of strong tribal governments becomes clear. Responding to domestic violence is at the heart of strengthening tribal governments to reestablish safety and cultural protections for women within the village.

Responding to domestic violence is commonly discussed as "providing victim services" and "offender accountability." These are terms used by the state and federal governments, the western criminal justice system, which have a different cultural foundation and organization. A village response to domestic violence can look differently and be more meaningful than a response from the state or federal system. Another major difference is that the offender, if from the village, has value and a place in the village and the community has an interest to see him healed and returned to the community.

---

[89] Paula Julian, *Indigenous Organizing Approaches, Addressing the Safety of Alaska Native Women,* Restoration Magazine, Vol. 14, Issue 3, at 38 (2017).

"We cannot let people blame the victim. We need to teach our traditional ways. Sometimes people do not want to report abuse, but if we as Alaska Natives stand up and speak up, victims may feel stronger."[90]

—the late Shirley Moses
Board Co-Chair and Founding Member, AKNWRC
[May 2, 1952 - June 13, 2021]

Alaska Native villages are tribal communities with family and clan relationships dating back over thousands of years.[91] These relationships have cultural and customary practices for resolving conflicts that are holistic. Respectful relationships in a village are important to maintain the stability of the entire village as a community, and as a nation. Each person in the village had an assigned role and purpose, which, if lost, could upset the harmony and well-being of the community. Domestic violence can destroy these relationships that weave the village together as a community. For this reason, and many others, the response of a village is and must be more than just arresting and prosecuting the abuser; rehabilitating the individual is in everyone's interest.

A village based on its way of life as indigenous people has the strength of being able to establish its response to domestic violence on the cultural values of its community. A strong, culturally based response of a village can serve as the

---

[90] AKNWRC, *Increasing Safety for Alaska Native Women*, at 27 (2016).

[91] The cave, "On Your Knees," located on Prince of Wales Island in Southeast Alaska, documents human remains from nearly 10,000 years ago, one of the earliest discovered on the west coast. https://en.wikipedia.org/wiki/On_Your_Knees_Cave

historical link connecting cultural teachings from past generations to the present and also to future generations. It recognizes the urgency of responding to single acts of domestic violence as it has greater meaning than a single act and is of central importance to the survival of the village as Native people. In this tribal context, victim services and abuser accountability have a greater meaning.

The village response, like an eagle or raven, requires two wings to be balanced. One wing being support services for Native women to heal from domestic violence. The other wing being accountability for abusers to end their violence. Creating services only for women cannot end the violence. Holding abusers accountable alone will not provide what Native women need to heal from the abuse. The abusers must also relearn the cultural value of respect to understand their own abusive behavior and, for many, acknowledge their own victimization.

Establishing these two wings and moving past the violence requires a strong, culturally supportive village as its body. The two wings must be connected to the tribal people, the body it serves. By planning and offering both wings based on the tribe's cultural values, a village can lift its community above the current violence to restore the respect and cultural protections within the tribe for present and future generations.

Indigenous Justice to Restore Wellness in the Community

Safety does not equal justice, and far too often, the criminal justice system does not create safety.

Colonization has a violent legacy that was justified by layering the colonizer's worldview and values upon the existing ways of life of the colonized. Safety and justice have deeper meanings among Alaska Native peoples. The logic of why or how the systems imposed were better or superior was only rational from the colonizer's point of view. The years and history have demonstrated just how destructive colonization was to Indigenous people.

The first intrusion of the federal government into what was the sole authority of Indian tribes is an example of this western view of justice. Federal jurisdiction over Indians was imposed upon Indian Nations because the United States disagreed with a customary tribal response to a murder case.[92] The tribe's response was based on concern for the continued support of the victim's family. It required the person who committed the killing, to pay the victim's family restitution. The U.S. penalty for the murder was death by hanging. At the time, the federal government did not have jurisdiction over crimes occurring between two Indians on a reservation. The U.S. government found this tribal justice

[92] *Ex Parte Crow Dog*, 109 U.S. 556 (1883).

approach unacceptable, and as a result, Congress enacted the Major Crimes Act.[93] The Act provided for the first time in U.S. history concurrent federal authority with Indian tribes over the crime of murder, and other crimes, when it was between two Indians. The hanging of Crow Dog, the murder in the case, would have achieved American justice but left the family of the victim with no customary justice, thus no restitution.

Indigenous justice systems. The definition of indigenous is "original," and indigenous justice systems are the original ways in which Native peoples lived. Indigenous justice is based on the beliefs and teachings of a defined people. It is often referred to as customary law. The goal of indigenous justice is often restoring the person who was injured to their former place. Indian tribes throughout the United States continue to live by their specific indigenous justice system. These culturally based systems were created in many cases over thousands of years. Indigenous justice reaches far beyond a court imposing a prison sentence. It is a way of living, providing for accountability and restoration.

"The laws we live under day-to-day are our village law, and a large part of village law is unwritten."[94]—Nettie Warbelow, Native Village of Tetlin

> Our unwritten law we have abided by as traditional aboriginal people within the U.S. It is not the intention of this written code to undermine or eliminate our unwritten law. We will continue to value and implement the knowledge of those customs and beliefs which cannot be written. In order to strengthen this written law, parents must teach their children the unwritten law of our Tetlin Athabascan heritage. Parents need to teach their children who they are.[95]
>
> —Donald Adams, Chief of Tetlin, 1998

Foundation of customary law. Across Indian tribes, the foundation for resolving conflict is customary law based on a cultural view of the world as Native peoples. Whether a village has created a western tribal court or maintained a traditional response to handling domestic violence cases, the foundation continues to be concerned with restoring balance and maintaining harmony in the community. Tribal leaders have consistently stated the importance of maintaining their integrity as Native people in responding to domestic violence. The goal of immediate protection of the victim rests on the foundation of restoring balance within the close community and healing. Accountability of the abuser is viewed as a long-term change involving

---

[93] Major Crimes Act, 18 U.S.C.A. 1153 (1885).

[94] *Indigenous Curriculum Pilot Trainings: Alaska Native Villages of Emmonak, Anvik, and Kake*, Restoration Magazine, Vol. 12, Issue 1, at 22 (2015).

[95] *Id.*

relearning the cultural value of respect for all living things, particularly women and children. In many communities, the society is matrilineal; thus, women have a prominent place in society, including as life-givers.

Choice of response. The authority of tribal governments arises from their status as indigenous nations—the recognition that our governments were here before Europeans or Russians. Traditional and effective customary practices have been central for Indigenous peoples for hundreds of generations. The suppression of our traditional laws by western colonial laws have only been in place for 8 or 9 generations. While it may seem colonization has become fully entrenched, our ancestors still guide us, and we still hear them. As Indigenous peoples, we can resurrect our indigenous justice system to address violence against Native women and restore protections for our well-being.

While national discussions acknowledge tribal authority "to choose" its response to domestic violence, it is often only acknowledged in the context of western justice as a beginning point. From a Native perspective, a more accurate statement is, "do we add" western justice responses to our village response to domestic violence?

For Alaska tribal governments, the western response is not the beginning point or only response. In fact, many tribal governments perceive the western response as a failure and one that has endangered our women in disproportionate ways. How to support victims, children, families, and others impacted by domestic violence is a village decision. How to hold abusers accountable to correct the wrongs they have committed is a village decision. The solutions are derived from determining how the village chooses to live as a people, community, and tribe. It is a choice of how to ensure the tribe's survival for future generations.

"Understanding the only way to change things is to do it ourselves. We have to make the change. It's not going to come from anyone else."[96]—Joel Jackson, Vice President, Organized Village of Kake

Villages, as governments, continue to rely on their customary responses to support the victims of domestic violence and to hold abusers accountable for their abuse. Villages using federal funds have strengthened their governmental response, and some have developed western-based tribal courts, adopting domestic violence codes and ordinances. These additions to their indigenous justice systems are viewed as necessary to access much-needed resources and a response that western court ideologues understand.

---

[96] Paula Julian, *Indigenous Organizing Approaches*, Restoration Magazine, Vol. 14, Issue 3, at 40 (2017). Joel Jackson has served as President of the Village of Kake since 2018.

Indigenous justice systems are not based on the government having to prove the abuser committed the violence. Speaking the truth is a standard of conduct. From this Native perspective, the abuser would admit to their wrongdoing. Acknowledging committing the abuse is not based on being proven guilty in court. Accountability is more about finding the solution for moving beyond the abuse to solutions that exterminate the abuse, but not the abuser from the community. Pleading guilty or not guilty are not the beginning point for an indigenous justice system.

The purpose of the indigenous justice response is how to resolve the wrongdoing to restore balance. The adversarial prosecutor and defense counsel that are so central in western criminal courts are not essential to indigenous justice systems. The concept of the judge as an unbiased uninvolved trier of the facts is also not a focus of indigenous justice systems. Indigenous justice involves all parties and typically includes families and involved members of the community. The concept of justice is not time served in prison as a form of retribution. Justice is a broader concept involving an examination of the action of the wrongdoer, why he did it, and trying to find a way to help the victim feel safe.

In state and federal meetings, indigenous justice systems are generally not seen as the foundation for village-based responses to domestic violence. Instead, they are often talked about in the context of western-based justice. Sometimes indigenous justice systems are narrowly seen merely as an "alternative" to a western court. This limited view fails to understand indigenous justice as an extension of how Native people choose to live.

"The American paradigm has its roots in the worldview of Europeans and is based on a retributive philosophy that is hierarchical, adversarial, punitive, and guided by codified laws and written rules, procedures, and guidelines." [97]—Ada Pecos Melton, Executive Director, American Indian Development Associates

What Do We Want? A Victim Centered Response

The beginning of creating a village-based response is listening to the voices of the women who have suffered or are suffering from domestic violence. What do women want to restore? What was taken from them? How did the violence destroy their lives?

These questions were discussed in community engagement meetings on domestic violence across Alaska tribal communities. In these discussions, Native

---

[97] Ada Pecos Melton, *Indigenous Justice Systems and Tribal Society,* In Wanda D. McCaslin, ed., Justice as Healing: Indigenous Ways (2005). http://www.aidainc.net/Publications/ij_systems.htm

women, many of whom were victims of domestic violence, stated clearly what they wanted in their lives to address domestic violence.

Native women have said—
I want the violence to stop.
I want to be safe in my home.
I want our children to be safe.
I want to live in my village.
I want him to be good again.

Strengthening a village-based response to domestic violence begins with listening to the voice of the victim of the abuse. It begins by understanding what is important to the victim. Simply stated, what does the victim want the abuser "to do" or "to stop doing"?

The agreement of the abuser to the wishes of the victim, such as stopping the violence, not contacting her, not coming to their home, or places she goes to regularly is essential. Moving out of the family home and continuing to support the family may be one of the most significant changes to help a domestic violence victim. The wishes of the victim concerning children in common with the abuser are also very important. Ensuring that the abuser respects the victim's wishes is central to creating safety for a victim. Personal responsibility for one's action is a quality and value among Native cultures.

Respect and speaking the truth are foundational values of Alaska Native people. These two beliefs can serve as strong village protections for victims of domestic violence. Village accountability of the abuser is not new, and traditionally disrespect and abusive behavior were not accepted. The customary responses of shunning, limiting the abuser's behavior, retribution to the victim, and in extreme measures the elders or chiefs used banishment to send a strong message to the abuser that the violent behavior was not acceptable. These examples reflect a customary non-adversarial approach to correcting the abusive behavior through community accountability.

Just as the sovereignty of Indian tribes in Alaska was undermined, so were these values and beliefs. Communities have struggled against the federal government's efforts to destroy our Indigenous languages, clans, maternal familial rights, and other cultural practices to uphold these values. Some say leadership has embraced the colonizers' actions of oppression—disrespect, abuse, and violence. These behaviors were shocking for the community to address, and often it led to silence in the communities—women suffered in silence.

"Our women carry the clan, and it is important that we restore our cultural values so that our mothers, daughters, granddaughters, and sisters are protected from violence."[98]—the late Joyce Skaflestad, Hoonah Indian Association advocate and Alaska State Magistrate

With the VAWA movement and the important legal changes, women are regaining their voices and will not be silenced. Alaska Native women and tribal organizations are taking action to increase awareness and pass laws to protect Native women.

> Central Council is taking steps to address and end violence against women and children. We have passed Judy's Law, where if you murder your wife and endanger your children then your parental rights will be terminated. Judy Lee was murdered by her husband; he claimed to not know what happened to her; they searched for her and when they found her body, they came to arrest her husband for murdering her. He then held their children hostage during an armed encounter with law enforcement, so we passed this important law in her name. Her crime two years later is still not prosecuted. We also started a DV task force and we called on the States of Washington and Alaska to recognize the National Day of Awareness for MMIW. We held a rally and march in Juneau in April to bring awareness to this important work.[99]
>
> —Catherine Kashkaani Edwards, Vice President (one of six)
> Central Council of Tlingit and Haida Indian Tribes of Alaska

Village-Based Solutions from Within Each Tribe

> Anvik is a small tribe and has many cultural and traditional practices that uphold respect for our women. These practices may seem strange in the context outside of our village, but we believe these traditional practices and activities will strengthen respect and safety for women.[100]
>
> —Carl Jerue, First Chief, Native Village of Anvik

Since the passage of VAWA in 1995, tribal leaders and advocates have worked to strengthen their response to DV with the support of increased resources to exercise their tribal authority. Through these efforts, Alaska tribes or "villages" have steadily increased their response to hold abusers accountable and support domestic violence victims. While increased federal resources are essential, it is also recognized that the strongest response is the one that holds the greatest significance to those involved—victim, abuser, and community.

---

[98] Paula Julian, *Indigenous Organizing Approaches*, Restoration Magazine, Vol. 14, Issue 3, at 38 (2017).

[99] *Statement Central Council Tlingit and Haida Indian Tribes of Alaska,* U.S. DOJ Violence Against Women Annual Consultation 2018, Restoration Magazine, Vol. 15, Issue 3, at 43 (2018).

[100] *New Civil Diversion Agreement Recognizes Village Authority, Native Village of Anvik Signs Landmark Agreement with the State of Alaska*, Restoration Magazine, Vol. 14, Issue 1, at 38-39 (2017).

Villages are distinct governments, and it varies how each village chooses to address the abuse and how the abuser will be held accountable. Abuser accountability mechanisms such as oral or written apologies to victims, parents, or to the whole village are extremely significant. Helping to repair or pay for damages caused by the abuse is a way to make amends and relieve the hardship caused by the abuser.

Domestic violence is a learned behavior. Unlearning the use of abuse to control another person happens over time. The commitment to regularly meet with an elder, participate in a cultural activity, subsistence gathering, or an elder's group to discuss cultural practices and beliefs that teach the foundational understanding of respect is an important way to unlearn abusive behavior. Abusers cannot be coerced to change their belief system. While unlearning the use of violence requires a personal commitment to change, the village also commits to address the change and reform the abuser. These forms of accountability by an abuser are significant to the victim, family, and the community. The role the abuser can play in the community recognizes that abuse is not a traditional value and can be unlearned.

> A lot of times the men are abusive because of the trauma they had. We want to help them so they can get healthy. We're always going to have this revolving door of domestic violence and sexual assaults unless we start teaching, young to old, why abuse is happening. And when we can identify things that have happened historically that have affected them negatively, they say that's why my grandma quit talking. She won't talk about the trauma that happened in the village. They need to start talking about their own trauma as individuals and understand why they are abusive.[101]
>
> —Shirley Moses, Founding Board Member, AKNWRC

The victim may find greater healing in acknowledgment of the wrongdoing by her abuser or support from family and elders then testifying in a case against her abuser in a western-style court. The abuser may learn new forms of respectful behavior more effectively by meeting consistently with village elders to discuss cultural beliefs than by serving time in prison. Each village faces the challenges of finding meaningful pathways for recovery and change.

Many abusers, because of their belief that violence is acceptable learned behavior will not change. And many fail to understand the conflict between respect as a way of life and their personal justifications for the use of violence. These abusers, while members of their village, are dangerous to the victim, their

[101] Video interview with the late Shirley Moses, former Board Member of AKNWRC, in Palm Springs, CA (Dec. 12, 2014) (on file with the AKNWRC).

families, and the community. Village governments are challenged to develop a response to these abusers who refuse to accept responsibility.

In addition, many non-Natives have married or live within villages and do not have a cultural foundation or Native worldview. Customary practices hold meaning only to the extent they are believed to be part of a person's being. Responding to these cases requires careful resolve to maintain the injured at the center of the village response.

Achieving Safety by Coming Together as Native Villages

Villages are actively working from within their respective tribes and also coming together as Indian tribes to increase safety for Native women. In 2013, the Alaska Federation of Natives (AFN), the largest organization of Indian tribes in Alaska, passed a resolution to address violence against Native women.[102] Six years later, in 2019, AFN passed three resolutions addressing violence against Alaska Native women. The first called for increased coordination at the federal, state, and tribal levels of government to address violence against Native women, including missing and murdered Native women.[103] The second resolution called upon Congress to recognize the jurisdiction of Alaska Indian tribes to prosecute non-Indians in domestic and sexual violence, child abuse, and related crimes in Alaska Native villages.[104] The third resolution supported a federal, tribal set-aside under the Victims of Crime Act to assist victims, particularly "Native women victimized by domestic and/or sexual violence."[105]

Another example of tribal government action from within is the 2018 vote by the Tribal Assembly of the Central Council of Tlingit and Haida Indian Tribes, to establish a task force to begin to address the disproportionate level of violence in its communities.[106]

---

[102] AFN Convention Resolutions 13-14, *Protect Alaska Native Women* (2013). https://www.nativefederation.org/wp-content/uploads/2018/07/2013-AFN-Convention-Resolutions.pdf

[103] AFN Convention, Resolution 19-8, *Calling Upon the Inherent Responsibility of the State, Federal, and Local Government to Acknowledge the Disproportionately High Rates of Violence Against Women of Indigenous Communities and Missing and Murdered Indigenous Women* (2019). https://secureservercdn.net/198.71.233.161/ekq.405.myftpupload.com/wp-content/uploads/2019/10/2019-AFN-Convention-Resolutions-final-4.pdf

[104] *Id.,* Resolution 19-9, *Calling Upon Congress to Promptly Enact "The Alaska Tribal Public Safety Empowerment Act" Legislation Recognizing the Jurisdiction of All Tribal Nations in Alaska to Prosecute Domestic Violence, Sexual Violence, Child Abuse, and Related Crimes in Alaska Native Villages.*

[105] *Id.,* Resolution 19-7, *Support for a Dedicated Tribal Set-Aside in the Victims of Crime Act (VOCA) Fund,* (2019).

[106] Pamela Dalton Sterns, *Violence Against Women Task Force Established,* Restoration Magazine, Vol. 15, Issue 2, at 49 (2018).

Alaska tribes as members of the National Congress of American Indians have also led in the passage of resolutions to address violence against Alaska Native women and to educate non-Alaskans about the disproportionate violence in rural Alaska and the lack of law enforcement in nearly 40% of our communities. These efforts at the tribal, regional, and national levels are steps forward in strengthening and developing tribal responses to increase safety for Native women.

The cultural worldview of Native people are strengths villages can draw upon in facing the difficult challenges of responding to the current crisis of violence. Villages also have the dedication of those in the community that are committed to ending the violence. Our families did not know violence as a means of control until it was introduced to colonize and enforce foreign government authority of Russia, and then the United States. Our ancestors lived in a balanced world, free of domestic and sexual violence, for hundreds of generations. With commitment and perseverance, we can find that wisdom and balance again for our communities. These resources are invaluable because they are local tribal resources, many of whom are already involved in responding to domestic violence.

We cannot change the past, but we can change the present, and create a safer world for our future. Indian tribes across the United States have led in replacing old federal laws and policies with new ones more supportive of tribal sovereignty, which reflects cultural values and teachings. What is critical is that every village recognizes and uses its government authority to support and honor victims of domestic violence by holding abusers accountable to end violence against Native women.

"As sovereign nations, since time immemorial we reassume tribal authority to protect Native women from harm because they're our backbone, feeding and caring for us."[107]
— *Ivan Ivan, Chief, Akiak Native Community*

[107] *Id.*

Did you know?

1. The Family Violence Prevention and Services Act is the only federal funding stream dedicated to domestic violence shelter and supportive services and provides 10% of the annual appropriation to Indian tribes.[108]

2. The Violence Against Women Act of 2005 created a specific title for American Indian tribes called Safety for Indian Women and has the following statutory purposes:
   a. to decrease the incidence of violent crimes against Indian women;
   b. to strengthen the capacity of Indian tribes to exercise their sovereign authority to respond to violent crimes committed against Indian women; and
   c. to ensure that perpetrators of violent crimes committed against Indian women are held accountable for their criminal behavior.[109]

3. The practices of the village-based responses to domestic violence may have a greater impact on abusers than a western-based approach of prosecution and/or incarceration. Village-based solutions that teach respect and accountability seek to correct the foundational beliefs abusers use to justify their violence of disrespect and right to use violence over their spouse or partner.

4. Prior to contact with the United States and Russia, domestic violence was not part of village life.[110]

Questions to consider:

1. How are village-based solutions to domestic violence different from state-based solutions?

2. How do traditional and cultural activities provide a strong foundation to support respect for victims of domestic violence? Some villages organize cultural activities such as skin sewing, beading, dance, food gathering, and group gatherings to support women to heal from domestic violence. Are these examples your village might use to support victims? Are there other cultural examples of honoring women and upholding respect for their important roles?

3. Some villages use subsistence activities to teach or help abusers to understand or relearn the belief of respect. Some villages work with elders to organize the time for abusers to unlearn abusive behavior and violence

---

[108] 42 U.S.C. 110 § 10409, (2010).

[109] VAWA 2005, Pub. L. No. 109-162, § 902, 119 Stat. 3078, (2006).

[110] Alaska Native Women's Resource Center Board member, Nettie Warbelow, has stated this during numerous consultations and training sessions.

to control their victim. Is it possible that understanding their Native language, teachings, stories, and history will help an abuser learn to respect all things, including their victim? Are these examples your village might use to reteach respect to abusers?

4. What are village responses for women who do not want the state involved in their lives, families, or homes? What are village solutions to allow a woman to stay in her village and be safe? What other village-based solutions are used in your village?

Chapter 5
Our Movement: Survivors, Advocates, Tribal Leaders, and Elders

> *I am a survivor of domestic violence. I was in and out of the shelter program for many years with my kids, and I didn't want them to see me being abused. So, I said I am not going to take it anymore. Our movement is like a seed that has grown. I know if we organize ourselves as Alaska Natives, we can end the violence in our villages.*[111]
>
> —*Joann Horn, Director, Emmonak Women's Shelter*

Respect is the foundation of the way we see and live in our world, and because of this view, disrespectful behavior has no place in our communities. We have no words in our language for behavior such as domestic violence. It is not part of our tradition, and when abuse happened, the elders and tribal leaders took action. Women were honored.

The invasions of outsiders into our world changed our lives, and one of the most devastating changes was the violent attacks upon Native women. Native women, their families, clans, and villages resisted the rape, beatings, abuse, abductions, trafficking, and murders and stood against the violence from the beginning. However, few heard our voices and acted to assist until recently.

The aftermath of the violence perpetrated by outsiders is the erosion of respect for Native women as reflected in the current crisis of violence we endure on a daily basis. It is also reflected in the diminishment of the authority of villages as tribal governments to protect Native women, and confusion of tribal status brought on by the Alaska Native Claims Settlement Act.

Birth of a Movement

In the 1970s, women in their villages began to organize to support other women suffering from abuse. The grandmothers, mothers, aunties, sisters, and daughters of women being abused opened their homes to those needing a safe place from the violence. This support was offered as a responsibility to assist family and community members. In some villages women organized to create community shelter services.

The first village-based shelter, the Emmonak Women's Shelter, was created in 1977 in the Yup'ik Village of Emmonak. The help offered was not "funded" by the state or federal government but supported by donations from community members in the village—smoked fish, clothing, and blankets. The Emmonak

---

[111] AKNWRC, *Safety for Alaska Native Women,* at 41 (2016).

Village Council donated the use of the building space for the shelter. This support was not provided by paid "advocates" but by community members committed to preventing abuse. In the 1970s funding for such support for Native women was not available as it is today under the Family Violence Prevention and Services Act (FVPSA).[112]

Native women who organized to support other women from domestic violence are the heart of our movement in Alaska to end violence against Native women. They are the grandmothers of our movement for safety and justice. Nationally, Native women also organized within their tribal nations to respond to domestic and sexual violence.

'In the early years, women opened their homes to other women in need and the children that came with their mothers. In the 1970s, we did this as women helping other women, sisters helping sisters. Since that time, our movement has grown to open the eyes of this country and the world to better understand violence against women."[113]

—Tillie Black Bear, Sicangu Lakota, Rosebud Sioux Tribe

---

[112] Family Violence Prevention and Services Act, 42 U.S.C., Ch. 110 (2010).

[113] Jacqueline Agtuca, *Safety for Native Women: VAWA and American Indian Tribes*, at 11 (Dorma Sahneyah, ed., 2014).

Growth of the Movement

In 1993, the U.S. Department of Interior (DOI) reaffirmed that Alaska Native villages are Federally Recognized Indian Tribes. This clarification and the names of Alaska villages included on the list of federally recognized Indian tribes were published in the Federal Registry.[114] Ada Deer, then-Secretary of Indian Affairs, stated:

> This list is published to clarify that the villages and regional tribes listed below are not simply eligible for services, or recognized as tribes for certain narrow purposes. Rather, they have the same governmental status as other federally acknowledged Indian tribes by virtue of their status as Indian tribes with a government-to-government relationship with the United States; are entitled to the same protection, immunities, privileges as other acknowledged tribes; *have the right, subject to general principles of Federal Indian law, to exercise the same inherent and delegated authorities available to other tribes*; and are subject to the same limitations imposed by law on other tribes.[115] (emphasis added).

This acknowledgment supported both recognition of tribal government authority to respond and federal trust resources to implement that authority. The change in federal recognition status opened the doors for villages to hold abusers accountable as sovereigns and made available funding for services to women and children.

> Back in the early to mid 70s the national domestic violence movement started. And there were pockets of us around the state that were getting together here in Alaska, planning to create safe places. Just like the women in Emmonak. I was in Valdez, and we were part of an underground group helping women who were abused or raped. Horrific cases. There were about five of us. We would borrow cars to take women over the mountain to Anchorage to try to get them safe or on a plane. There was a lot of underground work going on back then. We didn't even think of calling the police.
>
> Before 1995, our movement, primarily made up of volunteers, worked across villages and the state to help our sisters seeking safety and developed an informal network of advocates. Informally we also worked with our tribal sisters in the lower 48 to support Alaska Native women being abused to return to their villages or to leave Alaska.

---

[114] Indian Entities Recognized and Eligible to Receive Services From the United States Bureau of Indian Affairs, 58 Fed. Reg. 54364 (Oct. 21, 1993). https://www.govinfo.gov/content/pkg/FR-1993-10-21/pdf/FR-1993-10-21.pdf

[115] *Id.* at 54366.

> Through this advocacy, we met and developed relations with other advocates for battered women on a national level and joined them to advocate for changes to the system at the federal and state levels.[116]
>
> — Tami Truett Jerue, Executive Director, AKNWRC

The passage of the Family Violence Prevention and Services Act in 1984 (FVPSA)[117] and the Violence Against Women Act in 1995 (VAWA)[118] set the United States as a country on a new course by creating a strong response to domestic violence and sexual assault. FVPSA provided dedicated funding for domestic violence shelter and supportive services. VAWA established domestic violence and sexual assaults as national issues for the United States. Advocates such as Tillie Black Bear worked to include support for Indian tribes under FVPSA and VAWA. These two landmark federal statutes, as a result, were passed recognizing tribal authority and providing the needed resources for tribally based services.

The clarification of the status of federally recognized Indian tribes supported Alaska Native villages' choice to access resources for domestic violence shelters and services under FVPSA. It also provided access to new federal legal reforms under VAWA.

FVPSA and VAWA provided villages in Alaska with direct access to federal resources needed to support the development of village-based responses to domestic violence and sexual assault. Nearly three decades ago, in 1984, FVPSA provided "demonstration grants to Indian tribes and tribal organizations for projects designed to prevent family violence and to provide immediate shelter and related assistance to victims of domestic violence and their dependents."[119] The FVPSA reauthorization in 2000 required not less than 10% of the annual appropriation to be used to support Indian tribes.[120] "The purpose of these grants is to assist Tribes in efforts to increase public awareness about, and primary and secondary prevention of, family violence, domestic violence, and dating violence, and to provide immediate shelter and supportive services for victims of family violence, domestic violence, or dating violence, and their

---

[116] Video interview with Tami Truett Jerue, Executive Director, AKNWRC, in Palm Springs, CA (Dec. 12, 2014) (on file with the AKNWRC).

[117] Child Abuse Amendments of 1984 (PL 98–457). https://www.govinfo.gov/content/pkg/STATUTE-98/pdf/STATUTE-98-Pg1749.pdf#page=1

[118] VAWA 1994, title IV of the Violent Crime Control and Law Enforcement Act of 1994, Pub. L. 103-322 (codified at 34 U.S.C. § 12291 et seq.). https://www.govinfo.gov/content/pkg/STATUTE-108/pdf/STATUTE-108-Pg1796.pdf

[119] Family Violence Prevention and Services Act, Title III, 98 Stat. 1758 (1984). https://www.govinfo.gov/content/pkg/STATUTE-98/pdf/STATUTE-98-Pg1749.pdf#page=1

[120] 42 U.S.C. 110 § 10409, (2010).

dependents."[121] VAWA required 4% of specific funding to be dedicated to Indian tribes. In 1995, the Sitka Tribe of Alaska was one of the first Indian tribes in the U.S. funded under VAWA. The Tanana Chiefs Conference and other villages also applied and were funded in the early years under VAWA. Funding under FVPSA and VAWA since the 1990s has increased, providing essential resources to more Alaska Native villages.

Maturation of the Movement

The movement for safety and sovereignty has steadily grown in Alaska. In 2000, Alaska Native advocates joined together with the national movement to increase the tribal funding stream under the VAWA from 4% to 5% to provide critically needed resources. VAWA 2000 also included a program to fund tribal coalitions to provide local and regional tribal training and assistance. Today two tribal coalitions exist in Alaska: the Yup'ik Women's Coalition[122] in the Yukon delta region and the Healing Native Hearts Coalitions[123] for the Athabascan region.

In 2005, the national movement successfully educated and partnered with members of Congress to include a title specifically for Indian tribes within VAWA called Safety for Indian Women. The tribal title recognized the unique legal relationship of the United States to Indian tribes and women. Congress explicitly provided that the title was "to strengthen the capacity of Indian tribes to exercise their sovereign authority to respond to violent crimes committed against women."[124]

The tribal title has many important sections, but one of the most important for Alaska Indian tribes is the mandated tribal-federal annual consultation on violence against women with the Departments of Justice, Health and Human Services, and Interior. Alaska tribes have participated in every consultation since the first one in 2006. Many of the national reforms specifically for Alaska villages are a result of this active participation. Village tribal leaders and advocates have attended to present the concerns and recommendations of villages to enhance the response to violence against Native women. There continues to be a need to educate about the unique challenges within Alaska.

In 2010, Alaska Native advocates worked to educate Congress and national public policy leaders on the urgent need for safe shelter. Tribal advocates played

---

[121] https://www.acf.hhs.gov/fysb/programs/family-violence-prevention-services/programs/tribes.

[122] http://yupikwomen.org

[123] http://hnhcoalition.org

[124] VAWA of 2005, Title IX. Safety for Indian Women, §902, Purposes.

an important role in the 2010 reauthorization of FVPSA[125] to include a national Indian resource center.[126] Resources under FVPSA are essential for Indian tribes to provide shelter and services for victims of domestic violence.[127] In 2013, VAWA included a historic amendment affirming inherent tribal authority over non-Indians committing specific acts of domestic violence, or dating violence, or violation of certain protection orders in the Indian country of the tribe. This return of partial tribal jurisdiction, recognizing the inherent authority over non-Indians failed to include 228 of Alaska Native villages due to the requirement that the offense was committed within a tribe's Indian country. Only one tribe of the 229 in Alaska has a defined Indian country.[128] This exclusion of 228 Indian tribes in Alaska, or 40% of Indian tribes nationally, was a terrible injustice. It is one example of why the movement must understand the complex history of violence against Alaska Native women and legal barriers to their safety.

The VAWA 2022, includes "Subtitle B: Alaska Tribal Public Safety Empowerment." These provisions reaffirm the inherent authority of and empower Alaska tribal governments to work in partnership with state and federal authorities to address public safety in Alaska Native Villages. The law clarifies tribal authority to address civil and criminal matters, including protection orders, involving Alaska Natives in the Village or within their authority. The law also creates a limited criminal jurisdiction pilot project modeled after the successful pilot project implemented by tribes outside Alaska that was included in VAWA 2013. These provisions were called for repeatedly by advocates since VAWA 2013 and demonstrate the continued role of the grassroots movement in educating about the needs within our communities.

The combination of national reforms over more than a decade increased awareness of the urgency to address violence against Alaska Native women. In

---

[125] Child Abuse Prevention and Treatment Act of 2010, P.L. 111-320. https://www.congress.gov/111/plaws/publ320/PLAW-111publ320.pdf

[126] The National Indigenous Women's Resource Center serves as the U.S. Department of Health and Human Services, National Indian Resource Center Addressing Domestic Violence and Safety for Indian Women.

[127] The FVPSA Grants to Native American Tribes and tribal organizations are formula grants funded through a 10% set-aside within the FVPSA appropriation. The purpose of these grants is to assist Indian tribes in efforts to increase public awareness about, and primary and secondary prevention of, family violence, domestic violence, and dating violence, and to provide immediate shelter and supportive services for victims of family violence, domestic violence, or dating violence, and their dependents. https://www.acf.hhs.gov/sites/default/files/fysb/fvpsa_tribaldvservices_071818_508.pdf

[128] 48 U.S.C. §358 (1891). The Annette Islands, south of Ketchikan at the extreme lower end of the Alaskan archipelago, were 'set apart as a reservation' by Congress for the Metlakatlans and other Indians, 'to be held and used by them in common, under such rules and regulations, and subject to such restrictions, as may be prescribed from time to time by the Secretary of the Interior."

2013, advocates from across Alaska came together with the National Indigenous Women's Resource Center to form the Alaska Native Women's Resource Center. In 2017, as a result of the years of organizing to increase the safety of Alaska Native women, Congress appropriated funds under FVPSA to support a dedicated Alaska Native Tribal Resource Center on Domestic Violence.

> I want to take a moment to thank you for your dedication, patience, and leadership in advocating for the safety of Alaska Native women and villages. Because you've never given up and persisted in reaching out and speaking your truths and realities in your villages, OVW funded our collaboration. This is a first, which has either never happened since OVW began in 1995 or has only happened a handful of times. Most, if not all of the technical assistance that OVW has funded has been national in scope, so this says a lot for your perseverance. You changed the way OVW and the Federal government does its business. Congratulations! We look forward to supporting you in continuing to make life-saving changes for your women, families, and villages, and are excited about how you will inspire your sister Tribes in the lower 48 as well as internationally. Thank you for letting NIWRC be your ally from here on forward.[129]
>
> —Lucy Simpson, Executive Director,
> National Indigenous Women's Resource Center

> With such support, we can address domestic violence by working closely with Alaska Native tribal governments, and identify and remove barriers to victim safety and abuser accountability, especially in rural, remote Alaska Native villages across the state.[130]
>
> —Shirley Moses, AKNWRC Board Co-Chair, and
> Executive Director, Healing Native Hearts Coalition

> This funding will give us the opportunity to break the deafening silence surrounding victims and bring healing to our people with laws, policies, and local response rooted in Alaska Native voices, languages, and teachings. AKNWRC's philosophy is that violence against Native women is rooted in the colonization of Indigenous nations. The solutions to ending the violence will come from our villages and people.[131]
>
> —Joann Horn, AKNWRC Board Co-Chair, and
> Executive Director, Emmonak Women's Shelter

---

[129] Memorandum from Lucy Simpson, Executive Director, National Indigenous Women's Resource Center, to Tami Truett Jerue, (2017) (on file with the AKNWRC).

[130] *A New Alaska Native Tribal Resource Center,* Restoration Magazine, Vol. 14, Issue 3, at 41 (2017).

[131] *Id.*

In 2018, after more than a decade of the movement educating Congress about the need to include a dedicated tribal funding stream under the Victim of Crime Act (VOCA), Congress appropriated tribal funds under the Act.[132] This combination of increased resources for Indian tribes to develop tribal responses and victim services at the village level has provided new hope for women in many villages by providing the needed services and protection to live free of violence.

Today our movement continues to grow across Alaska Native villages and the state working to strengthen village-based responses and services and create changes needed to increase safety for Native women. Our efforts since the 1970s to support the immediate safety of women in our villages has grown into a social justice movement engaging both the federal and state governments.

March 26, 2017, Fairbanks, Alaska, the first meeting of the newly created AKNWRC board of directors and staff. Standing from left to right, Tami Truett Jerue, Candy Keown, Tia Holley, and Joann Horn. Sitting left to right, Marie Taylor, Lenora (Lynn) Hootch, Priscilla Kameroff, and Shirley Moses.

[132] Commerce, Justice, Science, and Related Agencies Appropriations Act of 2018, (Pub. L. No. 115-141) for the U.S. DOJ created a 3% tribal set-aside in the Crime Victims Fund (CVF) receipts allocated to OVC.

Creating Working Partnerships Among Villages

The Alaska Native Women's Resource Center is organizing to create working relationships among villages on priority issues to increase safety for Native women. Many of these issues at the village level are directly connected to the authority of villages as governments to respond and hold abusers accountable. Issues such as recognition of village-based responses, the lack of village police, recognition and enforcement of village protection orders, and funding of village-based shelter services are not only state issues but are now national issues.

Advocates and tribal leaders have joined together during the Alaska Federation of Natives (AFN) to share, inform, and develop a joint response to address violence against women. The annual convention of AFN is a meeting point for the largest number of Indian tribes in Alaska. In 2013, violence against women received focused attention from AFN with the passage of the Protect Native Women resolution.[133] Additional resolutions addressing specific concerns and actions have passed since 2013.

Creating Partnerships with Indian Tribes Nationally

Native women across the country have advocated for the safety of women for decades. Alaska Native women and Indian tribes have developed close working relationships nationally to address violence against Native women. Tillie Black Bear from the Sicangu Lakota Indian Tribe located in South Dakota was one of the first Native women to advocate at the national level. She is considered a grandmother of the movement for the safety of Indian women.

> [O]ur movement has grown to open the eyes of this country and the world to better understand violence against women.... Our role has and will continue to be to connect the violence beyond individual acts to the oppression that gives rise to the violence. As Native women this violence is linked to the colonization by the United States of our nations, lands, and peoples. As women of the movement, we play many roles. One is to understand and reform those laws, policies, lack of resources, and so much more that continues to separate us as Native women. Another is to restore the sovereignty and protections that are original to our Indian tribes.[134]
>
> —Tillie Black Bear, Sicangu Lakota (1946-2014), Founding Mother of the White Buffalo Calf Woman Society Shelter (1977) and National Indigenous Women's Resource Center (2010)

---

133 Alaska Federation of Natives, 2013 Annual Convention, Resolution 12-14, submitted by the Village of Tetlin, Kenaitze Indian Tribe, Village of Dot Lake, and the Village of Anvik.

134 Tillie Black Bear, *Safety for Native Women: VAWA and American Indian Tribes Foreword*, NIWRC (2013).

Alaska Indian tribes and the Alaska Native Women's Resource Center continue to organize to build these relationships nationally. The focus of these efforts is on priority issues to address violence against Native women. The National Congress of American Indians (NCAI) is the oldest and largest membership organization of Indian tribes in the United States. NCAI created a Task Force on Violence Against Women in 2001 that has met annually three times a year since 2003. Alaska tribes, advocates, and tribal coalitions play an active role and provide leadership to the NCAI Task Force and the NCAI. While villages share many of the barriers preventing Indian tribes in the lower 48 from holding abusers accountable, other barriers are specific to Alaska.

"In closing, we thank our Indian brothers and sisters from the lower 48 who have organized and stood with us to elevate the injustices Alaska tribes have faced as national issues for immediate resolution."[135]—Michael Williams Sr., Secretary-Treasurer, Native Village of Akiak

Creating Partnerships at the International Level

Violence against Indigenous women happens around the world. Tribal leaders, advocates, and the Alaska Native Women's Resource Center are part of an international effort to address violence against Indigenous women. These international relations have provided insight and support to the efforts to increase safety for Native women in Alaska.

In 2003, a delegation of tribal domestic violence and sexual assault coalitions funded under the Office on Violence Against Women met with the Māori advocates in Aotearoa, the Māori name for New Zealand. This international exchange provided a new view of the struggle to increase the safety of Indigenous women from domestic violence. It marked the beginning of an increased understanding of the shared experience of Indigenous women and colonization. The delegation included representation from the Alaska tribal coalition. Lessons learned from the exchange provided part of the inspiration and logic for the separate tribal title, Safety for Indian Women of VAWA 2005.[136]

In 2010, the United Nations Special Rapporteur on Violence Against Women visited the Eastern Band of Cherokee Indians' tribal lands called Qualla Boundary. The official report to the United Nations expressed concern about

---

[135] Michael Williams Sr., Secretary-Treasurer, *Statement of the Native Village of Akiak,* U.S. DOJ 2019 Annual Violence Against Women Government-to-Government Consultation (2019) (on file with the AKNWRC).

[136] Terri Henry, *Summary Report to the Office on Violence Against Women, International Indigenous Women's Seminar: National Collective of Independent Women's Refuges and Māori Justice System,* Aotearoa (2003) (on file with the AKNWRC).

the rates of violence against Native women. It recommended specific changes to address the concerns, including the return of jurisdiction over non-Indians committing violence against Native women.

Alaska Native tribal leaders and advocates have continued to engage internationally at the United Nations and other global spaces. This work has included organizing special side and parallel events during the annual sessions of the U.N. Commission on the Status of Women, participating in the World Conference on Indigenous Peoples in 2014, and in a 2018 Thematic Hearing before the Inter-American Commission on Human Rights. AKNWRC has also participated in meetings of the North American Trilateral Working Group on Violence Against Women. The Working Group, created during the Obama administration, is made up of the governments of Canada, Mexico, and the United States. It meets annually to engage in dialogue and share knowledge about best practices and lessons learned addressing the high rates of violence against Indigenous women and girls across the North American continent and advancing initiatives to increase self-sufficiency.

'The Tri-lateral meeting created the opportunity for Native advocates in the United States to directly connect with Indigenous advocates from Mexico and Canada, as well as to provide expert testimony to government representatives from all three countries concerning barriers to and promising practices for effectively working with Tribal communities on criminal justice

responses to violence against Indigenous women and girls."[137]*—Michelle Demmert, Law and Policy Director, AKNWRC*

Organizing Efforts Rooted Within Alaska Native Villages

Over the decades, the movement has learned that the center of the efforts to increase the safety of women is themselves–Alaska Native peoples. "The changes required must come from within our villages. Nonetheless, as citizens of the United States, we deserve to have access to resources."—Frances Andrews, Operations Manager, AKNWRC

Today, while abusers can be Native or non-Native, the introduction and origins of violence against women came from outsiders seeking to profit from the taking of local natural resources. Our teachings, voices, languages, and the customary laws of our peoples are the foundation for the changes needed. We can and must restore the respect of women to prevent the destruction of our Native way of life.

In organizing at the village, state, national, and international levels, our efforts are shaped by, and support, our Native worldview, and ways of life. Ending violence against women within our villages should affirm and strengthen who we are as a people.

Voices of Our Movement

The story of our village-based movement for the safety of women is reflected in the experiences of Alaska Native women. Our journey in Alaska is shared with thousands of tribal women across the United States who are part of this movement for social justice. These women have spent much of their lives advocating for the safety of their Native sisters decade after decade. In Alaska, many of these advocates helped to found and are members of the board of directors of the AKNWRC. Their stories are shared on the pages of this book to support the changes needed to create safety for their sisters and protect future generations of women. In 2022, advocates celebrated the reauthorization of VAWA with a specific subtitle within the Tribal title to address the unique issues in Alaska.

---

[137] *Third Meeting of the Trilateral Working Group on Violence Against Indigenous Women*, Restoration Magazine, Vol. 15, Issue 3, at 50 (2018).

I am a mother of five children and seventeen grandchildren. I have lived in the Native Village of Emmonak my entire life. Over the last 37 years, I have dedicated my life to working within Emmonak, the surrounding villages, and with the state and allies in the lower 48 to uphold Yup'ik values, customs, and traditions in advocating for an end to violence against Alaska Native women.

I joined the movement for safety when I was just a teenager and helped to found and served as Director of the Emmonak Women's Shelter, a Native village–based shelter in Alaska that has been operating since 1979. Concerned village members and volunteers like me established the shelter—the second oldest known Native women's shelter in the United States—because we saw a critical need to provide safety for women and their children victimized by domestic violence, sexual assault, and other forms of abuse. We opened the shelter to provide emergency shelter and assistance to victims. Since our beginning we have helped women from all over the state, more often than not, on a volunteer basis and without funding.

As the founder and Director of the Yup'ik Women's Coalition and Member of the Board for the Alaska Native Women's Resource Center, I know VAWA and the Alaska Tribal Public Safety Empowerment section within the Tribal Title are our hope for the future. I realize I have spent much of my life focusing on violence-related issues. Over the last 37 years, we have worked hard to create the changes needed so women will be safe. Like so many other women now involved in this movement and our mothers before us, we really have no choice. Domestic violence, rape, suicide, and sex trafficking threaten the future of our people and villages. Our people are living daily in peril.

VAWA finally includes the 229 villages of Alaska. We must stand together and build our national movement to end this violence.

Quayana Cak'naq!
Nugange (Lenora "Lynn" Hootch),
Executive Director, Yup'ik Women's Coalition,
Board and Founding Member, AKNWRC

September 21, 2022, Anchorage, AK, "Qaspeq Ceremony," a traditional opening to the 17th Annual Government-to-Government Violence Against Women Tribal Consultation. Standing from left to right, Joann Horn, Travis Bird, Tasha Pauken, Priscilla Kameroff, Candance Fratis, Janelle Chapin, and Tiana Teter. Photo courtesy of Kelsey Foote.

Did you know?

1. In 2005, based on tribal organizing efforts to increase awareness of violence against Indian women, Congress reauthorized the VAWA to include a specific title for Indian tribes called Safety for Indian Women. This new title was based on the unique legal relationship of the United States to Indian tribes."

2. The Safety for Indian Women title of VAWA provided for government-to-government consultation on addressing violence against Indian women. Tribal leaders and advocates understood addressing the legal barriers and lack of resources required federal accountability to create the changes needed to protect and support Native women. Alaska Native villages have attended every annual government-to-government consultation since the first, following the passage of the Violence Against Women Act of 2005.

3. The safety for Indian women movement consistently reaches out to Indigenous peoples on an international level through the United Nations. The initial idea for the Safety for Indian Women tribal title of VAWA 2005 came from an international exchange of advocates for Indigenous women. The representatives of tribal coalitions in the United States traveled to Aotearoa (New Zealand) and met with Māori advocates and their shelter movement. The Māori advocates shared many lessons learned since the 1980s in building their movement for the safety of Māori women.[138] The delegation of American Indian women included a representative from Alaska.

Questions to consider:

1. Tillie Black Bear is considered the grandmother of the battered women's movement and also the safety for Native women's movement. Tillie often said, "We are a resistance movement." What do you think she meant by this statement?

2. American Indian women and Māori women live in separate countries and parts of the world but have similar social justice movements to increase the safety of women. How can we continue to share lessons on an international level? Why is this international involvement important?

3. Following the passage of the Safety for Indian Women title of VAWA in 2005, tribal governments and tribal advocates stressed the importance of building the movement for safety and sovereignty. The Alaska Subtitle of

[138] Toni McCallum first published in Women Together: A History of Women's Organizations in New Zealand (1993), Kate Burry 2018 update, *National Collective of Independent Women's Refuges 1981*. https://nzhistory.govt.nz/women-together/national-collective-independent-womens-refuges

VAWA 2022 and other legislative reforms are the beginning of change, not the end. How do you think the movement will continue to grow?

October 3, 2017, We-Ko-Pa Conference Center on the reservation of the Fort McDowell Yavapai Nation in Fountain Hills, Arizona, Mike Jackson speaking for the Organized Village of Kake during the 12th Annual Government-to-Government Violence Against Women Tribal Consultation.

Chapter 6
Tribal Courts: Strengthening Community Protections

Many villages, while lacking the resources to fully develop western justice systems do have village traditional justice approaches that can be strengthened or be reestablished to create protections for women in the village.[139]

—Mike Jackson, Keeper of the Circle, Organized Village of Kake
Retired State Justice Magistrate

Tribal communities have a choice of how to respond to domestic violence. How to hold abusers accountable to correct the wrongs committed by the abuse. How to support victims of domestic violence, the children, families, and others impacted within the village. This response is a choice of how the village chooses to live as a people, community, and tribe.

In the broadest sense, tribal justice systems are the fundamental expression of the tribe as a sovereign. In exercising this authority, many tribes have created tribal courts with the power to direct or restrict the actions of an abuser in their homes and the community. This powerful authority is possessed by governments—federally recognized Indian tribes, states, and the federal governments.

In this way, tribal courts can serve as an essential component in the immediate and long-term process of holding domestic violence abusers accountable and ending their violence. A tribal court and justice system can increase and strengthen a tribe's response to domestic violence and other crimes of violence against women. A tribal court can provide a local, culturally-based, holistic response to restore respect for women, address the victim's concerns, and provide a path to community healing.

Tribal courts are organized based on the needs expressed by the village or villages served. Indian tribes in Alaska decide how to organize their government's response to domestic violence. Villages, like the Native Village of Anvik, are using the tribal council to decide how to hold an abuser accountable. Tribes, like Central Council Tlingit and Haida Indian Tribes of Alaska are using a tribal court to hear and decide how to hold an abuser accountable for domestic violence. And, villages, such as the Organized Village of Kake, are using traditional peacemaking courts.

---

[139] Mike Jackson, *AKNWRC MMIW Awareness Card* (2019) (on file with AKNWRC).

How a village or villages organizes its tribal court varies and is shaped by the decisions of the village governments. Tribes have established various types or styles of justice systems—the single court, a regional court or justice forum, an intertribal court, peacemaking or talking circles, and traditional councils which could be made up of elders, an elected council, or a community panel forum. This is not an exhaustive list as each tribe has the sovereign authority to decide how best to resolve disputes.

The various styles of justice can also be mixed and matched. For example, a tribe may choose to implement a western style court process for criminal offenses committed by adults, an elder's panel or a talking circle for youth offenders, and a family wellness court for child welfare and guardianship cases. It is important and highly encouraged for tribes to thoroughly explore the possibilities, hold community discussions, establish desired values needed for the justice system that will serve the community needs, and carefully plan with input from the community, elders, and elected officials. Tribal courts are also using a range of western-based responses such as protection orders, arrest, and prosecution.

> Keex' Kwaan's Core Tribal Values, passed on today orally (unwritten) are the "Laws of the Land" that have held our association of Clans together for thousands of years to form Keex' Kwaan. Yesterday our ancestors formed the process of Peacemaking. No moiety, of the Eagle or Raven, claims this animal as their Clan Symbol, because no one can own the process of Peacemaking. Today we begin to write down a living document that will grow with us and be amended by Keex' Kwaan to meet the needs of the Tribe.[140]
>
> —Establishment and Purpose of the Keex' Kwaan Peacemaking Court.

The Benefits of a Tribal Court

A court or forum for resolving disputes is an essential component of tribal sovereignty. Tribal justice systems protect and preserve sovereignty by providing a forum for the interpretation of tribal laws, rules, and policies to resolve disputes in a manner that is consistent with the values, customs, and traditions of the tribe. A justice forum that is based in the culture and values of the specific tribe and region is often less intimidating, more accessible and results in broader holistic resolutions for all those who participate in the process.

Establishing tribal justice systems prevents or reduces the need for tribal citizens to be involved in the federal or state courts to resolve some or all disputes. As the Alaska tribal justice systems develop, expand and gain visibility to

[140] Organized Village of Kake, Keex' Kwaan Peacemaking Court. Chapter 1, Section 1.

successfully bridge the gaps created over the last 200 years of colonization and forced imposition of western courts, greater respect and appreciation for traditional justice will emerge. Tribal courts and justice systems can also provide a forum for enforcing orders from outside jurisdictions, such as civil protection, child custody, or child support orders.

The underlying authority for a tribal government to create or establish a court or justice system is often found in the tribe's constitution or a similar governing document. The tribal governmental body, whether elected or appointed, is the designated lawmaker, and the law can be written or oral, depending on the tribe's traditions and values.

Types of Courts and Justice Systems

The individual tribal court is a court that is organized and run by only one tribal government with laws, rules and policies developed by the one tribe.

A regional court is a centrally located justice system that provides various justice services for a specific region, i.e., Southeast Alaska. The regional court can provide judicial services for tribal citizens and their families from a number of tribes located in a particular region. This sharing of resources can be based on historical cooperation among the tribes or through modern day cooperative agreements. The benefits are one court, shared personnel, and common application of laws, practices, and outcomes to disputes.

An intertribal court involves two or more tribes sharing resources and professional services usually by way of intertribal agreements. This consortium of tribes can be located in a small distinct area or spread out over a larger region. The tribes agree to pool resources, including funds and grant funded projects, equipment, and personnel, but each member tribe retains its own laws, rules, values and decides which types of justice services it wants to exercise, i.e., criminal, civil, family, children.

The member tribes that are a part of the intertribal agreement share personnel such as trial judges, appellate judges or panels, circle facilitators or peacemakers, presenting officers, code writers, administrators, or clerks. There are a few examples of successful intertribal court systems with the Northwest Intertribal Court System (NICS) being the closest in Washington State.[141] The shared court personnel have a home office just north of Seattle and they travel by car to the individual member reservations on a regular designated schedule to conduct court hearings where each member tribe is located. With 229 tribes and distinct state-wide regions and sub-regions, there are many opportunities for creating

[141] https://www.nics.ws

inter- tribal courts or justice systems among the Alaska Native tribes.

Peacemaking courts, talking circles and wellness courts have been re-emerging among the Alaska tribal communities in the last several years. These forums are much different than the western style courts where there is a judge or decision maker that determines the final resolution and issues a written order. Peacemaking and talking circles are based on helping the victim to heal after a harm has been done and to address the offender[142] regarding why or how the harm was done. This process is focused on repairing and healing rather than simply finding blame or fault and punishment. This is a horizontal system of justice where people coming into the peacemaking process are on an equal basis and equally participate in the presentation and discussion of the dispute, and finally in determining the resolution. The peacemaking process is non-adversarial and the resolution is based on agreement of all who participate.

The peacemaking and/or wellness courts or forums can also be set up to be done jointly with a State court and can be designated to address only certain types of disputes, such as youth criminal offenses or adult drug offenses or family disputes such as custody or child abuse/neglect.

Village Law is Essential to the Court's Response to Domestic Violence

Today tribal courts are using a range of actions to hold abusers accountable, including customary and western-based law. The law governing how a village responds to domestic violence is important to the abuser, victim, and entire village in understanding that abusive behavior, violence, and the threats of violence as a means of control are not acceptable. The tribal courts in Alaska offer meaningful pathways to safety and justice in many forms.

Many tribal leaders at annual consultations on violence against women and in Congressional hearings have stated that the state-based system does not provide an acceptable response to domestic violence in villages. Tribal leaders have clearly stated responding to domestic violence requires a local response and holding abusers accountable is a village responsibility. Each tribe decides what laws it uses or adopts.

> I was in the state courts for 11 years. The thing that keeps coming into my head is we have written law that is written by people that probably have not stepped foot in a court. They make up these laws that sound good to them, and it doesn't work. And, you know, we had judges that weren't a part of the community. They didn't grow up in the community. I actually grew up in Angoon, so I knew the people. They

---

[142] In Peacemaking courts, the offender can be called the wrongdoer, defendant, or abuser.

don't know the culture. They don't know how everything works. And coming from the state court to the tribal court to do some pro tem work has been truly a breath of fresh air because the tribal courts have something that works for our communities. That's a really great thing to see because I know that some of those laws don't work. Throwing somebody in jail because that's what the law says doesn't always work. They're going to come out. They might be worse. They might be resentful. The healing courts that we have now, the peace circles, all those things work.[143]—Elaine Jack, Pro Tem Tribal Judge, Central Council Tlingit and Haida Indian Tribes of Alaska Tribal Court.

As Sovereigns, Tribal Courts Use Unwritten and Written Law

The response of the federal and state governments to domestic violence is governed by a code enacted or passed by the citizens of the specific government. Alaska tribes as sovereigns have this same authority to pass a domestic violence code or rely on customary law that is meaningful to the village in responding to domestic violence. The choice of developing a written code is decided by the village and should be based on the beliefs of the village members.

"Years ago, our elders were the tribal councils of our communities. They made sure that the laws of the village were taken care of. They were in control of the community to make sure that

[143] Tribal Court Roundtable, Fairbanks, Alaska (Nov. 2019) (transcript on file with the AKNWRC).

people abide by the law of the village; and written and unwritten laws are two different things. For me as a young person growing up in the village, I was only aware of the unwritten laws that I carry in my heart as a Native person. These are the things that were never written down. This is what we were taught, and we carry it in our hearts, and we practice it in our community. It's from one generation to another. So, in 1993, they asked us to work on an ordinance. This is for Tetlin, and it was very difficult to put it in writing, because I know my law in my heart because that's where I carry it. And it's a knowledge that I have within myself as a Native person for my community. So, when we started writing it, it was very difficult, but we did. And it's in black and white. It's there. You can read the law of the village. But unwritten laws are what we carry in our heart as Native people."[144]

—Nettie Warbelow, Tribal Court Judge, Native Village of Tetlin
Board and Founding Member, AKNWRC

Clarity on the Response of the Village and Court

In the most practical sense, domestic violence requires an immediate response to stop the violence and protect the victim. How a village implements its immediate response to a domestic violence case is important. While a tribal court may not be involved in stopping the actual violence it is critical the tribe decide who will respond and how they will respond to a domestic violence case, a repeat case, or on-going abuse. In many small off-road villages, elected tribal leaders serve many roles. A tribal leader has intervened to stop the actual violence and protect the victim, and also later as a member of the tribal council acting as the tribal court to hear the domestic violence case.

Domestic violence often is not a single act of violence. It happens more often as a pattern of abuse and in many cases, daily. The size and close proximity of homes in some off-road villages increase the ability to monitor and hold an abuser accountable. Small villages can allow the tribal council or court to know whether a victim of domestic violence is safe or continuing to be abused.

> If you look around the world, there are all sorts of justice models and then of course we have our Indigenous models. We didn't really identify them as justice systems, but they were how we maintained law and order within our communities. So I think that tribal courts in Alaska have a real opportunity to define what sovereignty is. You define what is appropriate for your community and what that looks like. There are some basic tenants you need to follow, which are essentially a due process model. And that means, you know, in any proceeding you need to give notice, provide an opportunity to be heard, and a decision from a fair and impartial decision maker. That is pretty straightforward and how your justice looks is really up to you.

[144] *Id.*

> I've done some work with Kake on their codes and they have a three-panel court system or a peacemaking court system and that's what they defined as being appropriate for them. And at Tlingit and Haida right now we have a hybrid system that leans towards the Western system. And I think we're trying to figure out how to incorporate more of our traditional ways of approaching problem solving into our court system. Our laws reference our clan systems and our family structures. We need to try to really look at what your values are, what's important to your community, and what's going to provide the most meaning. And we really need to acknowledge the fact that the Western judicial systems are in crisis and they are not working. I think in all the years that I've been a judge, there's probably five, maybe 10% of the individuals that I've had before me, where they needed to be incarcerated. Most need services and healing.[145]
>
> —Michelle Demmert, Law and Policy Director, AKNWRC

Restorative Approach

Tribal courts as restorative justice systems are focused on the victim of domestic violence and their children but also safeguard the Native worldview and lifeways of the entire village for future generations. Western-based justice, state and federal prosecution, is focused on the punishment of the abuser. This retribution or penalty is in the form of loss of the person's freedom—arrest, jail, prison. It is not restorative in terms of addressing the needs of the victim, family, or village. It is not restorative or concerned with maintaining balance within the village. Accountability must be meaningful to the abuser. It must hold significance in the life of the abuser to provide a means to unlearn the violence and relearn a Native view of the world based on respect. A village court as a reflection of the people it serves has the knowledge and, in many cases, the relationship to fulfill this role in holding abusers accountable.

> When we have our hearings and proceedings, at the beginning we pray and at the end we pray. We pray for the abuser, we pray for the victim, and we pray for every one that is involved. When domestic violence occurs, village families are involved and the elders are involved, the husbands and wives and children are involved. I think when we deal with some of these cases that are given to us by the law officers, we as sovereign people can help our people, by using our methods, and our ways that we've been practicing and what we learned from our elders.[146]
>
> —Herman Hootch, Chief Judge, Native Village of Emmonak

---

[145] *Id.*
[146] *Id.*

Voice of the Victim

In holding an abuser accountable, one of the most important roles a tribal court can play is listening to the voice of the victim of the abuse. Listening to and understanding what is important to the victim. Simply stated, what does the victim want the abuser "to do" or "to stop doing." The agreement of the abuser to the wishes of the victim, such as stopping the violence, not contacting her, not coming to their home, or places she goes to regularly. Moving out of the family home and continuing to support the family may provide important changes to support a domestic violence victim. The wishes of the victim concerning children in common with the abuser are also very important. The tribal court or council should include the victim's requests as a priority for creating safety for a victim and restoring balance in her life, and that of the family and village.

Tribal Court Usage of Customary Laws

The customary responses of a village have a meaning because of the belief and lifeways of a village. These same responses without such a belief system may have no meaning in holding abusers accountable. Shunning, limiting the abuser's behavior, restitution to the victim, and in the most severe cases, banishment, sends a strong message to the abuser that disrespectful behavior is unacceptable. Customary responses also include having the abuser make amends to the community for the disrespectful, violent behavior. Making amends is specific to the victim, abuser, and village. It is based on the abuser taking meaningful actions for the victim, and often the village. Villages have used a range of actions by the tribal courts to respond to the needs of the victim, families, and community.

Apology. Abuser accountability, such as oral or written apologies to victims, parents, or the whole village, is extremely significant. It is an acknowledgment by the abuser of his wrongdoing and commitment to unlearning his abusive behavior. It can provide an important statement that abuse and violence are not the victim's fault.

Making amends. This response is based on the concept of the abuser showing accountability for the abuse or violence through his actions. Making amends to the victim when requested may include providing items needed even though the abuser is not living in the home. Helping to repair the damages caused by the abuse is also a way to make amends and relieve the hardship caused by the abuser. Each victim is unique and providing other items the victim and or her family might need can be very helpful in showing accountability for the abuse. Making amends to the community may include work services such as cleaning or repairing a village building or community hall, or chopping wood needed for heating a building. These examples reflect a non-adversarial approach to correcting abusive behavior through community accountability.

Unlearning the violence and relearning Native beliefs of respect. Unlearning abusive behavior begins with one's individual belief system. Meeting regularly with an elder or an elder's group to discuss beliefs such as respect and other traditional practices is a strength available in villages for abusers to change their thought processes.

> Tribal courts are a healing center for the people, not punishment. Not sending them out to jail but providing a resource like the Emmonak Women's Shelter does. They provide shelter for women and counseling. Putting people away only destroys our people. I like what Emmonak is doing. They're working with all the resources they have there in order to empower their tribal court, not be influenced by the state or federal government.[147]—Moses Owens, Vice Chief, Native Village of Akiak

Recognition of Village-Based Responses

The Alaska Supreme Court confirmed in 1999 that "...tribes have the 'power to make their own substantive law in internal matters and to enforce that law in their own forums.' Similarly, the Supreme Court has stressed that tribal sovereignty is valuable precisely because it enables Native Americans 'to control their own internal relations, and to preserve their own unique customs and social order.' "[148]

Each tribal government has the authority to determine its specific response to holding abusers accountable and supporting the victim of the violence and, in many cases, the victim's family. Once this decision is made, how the village government makes the consequences for those committing domestic violence known to its members and those living in the village is very important. By informing the entire village of the consequences of committing domestic abuse, it becomes widely known that such behavior will not be accepted. It also alerts other jurisdictions (tribal, state, and federal) of the consequences the village will place on an abuser. Coordination with these other jurisdictions is important because victims and abusers do not remain in their villages and may leave for various reasons.

Tribal courts bring not only local knowledge, cultural sensitivity, and

---

[147] *Id.*

[148] *John v. Baker*, 982 P.2d 738 (Alaska 1999). The court found that a tribe had inherent sovereignty to hear a custody case between tribal members in its courts, recognizing tribal court jurisdiction over civil matters.

expertise to the table, but also are a valuable resource, experience, and have a high level of local trust. They exist in at least half the villages of our State and stand ready, willing, and able to take part in local justice delivery. Just as the three branches of State government must work together closely to ensure delivery of justice throughout the State court system, State and Tribal courts must work together closely to ensure a system of rural justice delivery that responds to the needs of every village in a manner that is timely, effective, and fair.[149]

[149] Indian Law and Order Commission, *A Roadmap for Making Native America Safer*, at 49.

Did you know?

1. "Indian tribes possess the inherent authority to establish their own form of government, including tribal justice systems."[150]

2. According to the Violence Against Women Act of 2005 "[t]he term 'courts' means any civil or criminal, tribal, and Alaskan Village, Federal, State, local or territorial court having jurisdiction to address domestic violence, dating violence, sexual assault or stalking, including immigration, family, juvenile, and dependency courts, and the judicial officers serving in those courts, including judges, magistrate judges, commissioners, justices of the peace, or any other person with decision making authority."[151]

3. As of January 2022, 149 Alaska tribal courts have completed a court assessment in preparation to develop and improve their justice systems.[152]

4. The Full Faith and Credit provision of VAWA provides that a civil or criminal domestic violence order issued by a court in one state, tribe, or territory shall be accorded full faith and credit by the court of another state, tribe, or territory.[153] It is to be enforced as if it were a court order of the issuing court's jurisdiction. This law applies to the various types of protection orders including permanent, temporary, and ex parte protection orders. It does not require registration of protection orders in the enforcing jurisdiction. The order to be enforced must comply with the VAWA statute by providing the person to be restrained with reasonable notice and an opportunity to be heard in court, in a manner consistent with due process.

Questions to Consider:

1. Do you have elders or respected leaders available that can assist in facilitating peacemaking circles or filling the role of a judge in court proceedings?

2. Does your community have safe houses? If not, what options do you have or can create that will provide safe places for women and children?

3. Who in your community is available to help with establishing accountability for those who are being violent?

---

[150] Indian Tribal Justice Act, 25 U.S.C.A. Sec. 3601(4).

[151] 42 U.S.C. Sec. 13925 (a)(2).

[152] January 2022 BIA TJS PowerPoint presentation from Tricia Tingle, Alaska Native Justice Center training presentation. See also, Indian Law and Order Commission, *A s for Making Native America Safer: Report to the President and Congress of the United States*, at 39, (2013). http://www.aisc.ucla.edu/iloc/report. The Alaska Legal Services Corporations 2022 Court Directory for a list of tribal court in Alaska, https://courts.alaska.gov/courtdir/docs/tribal-court-directory.pdf

[153] VAWA 2005, 18 U.S.C. § 2265.

4. Who is responsible in your community for enforcing protection orders?

"Every single Alaskan, and I'll just add, every single Indigenous person in this state has the right to be safe in their home and free from violence. And that is not the case."[154]

—Debra Dzijúksuk O'Gara, Attorney, Professor, and Tribal Judge

[154] Yereth Rosen, *Alaska budget items and policy changes recommended to help protect Indigenous women and girls*, Anchorage Dispatch News (March 24, 2023).

Chapter 7
Legal and Policy Barriers to the Safety of Alaska Native Women

What do I tell a niece or a nephew when their mother disappears, or her lifeless body is laying in the village—what do I say to them about why it's still there? What do I say when the man that killed her still hasn't been arrested? What do I tell my tribal citizens when they ask me, what can I do about it? Is it really an acceptable answer to say that it's out of our jurisdiction? Leaving that body there, or not arresting perpetrators, sends a strong signal to the community that women and children don't matter, we don't care if you die, there is nothing anyone can do for you. This doesn't help when you want victims to come forward. They won't report. The powers that be have already delivered the message that she doesn't matter. The last girl laid dead for days. The man that killed her hasn't been arrested. It just further drives home the message: there is no use in coming forward, no one can protect you.[155]

—*Catherine Edwards, Vice-President (one of six)*
Central Council Tlingit and Haida Indian Tribes of Alaska

Survivors of domestic violence and their families in villages across Alaska have voiced frustration and anger at the lack of response to the abuse they endure. They also express great fear of future violence by the abuser because nothing is done to stop the abuse. Victims of domestic violence are vulnerable and need immediate support to help prevent future abuse.

As a movement of survivors, tribal leaders, and advocates, we struggle to understand the legal and policy barriers preventing Indian tribes in Alaska from holding abusers accountable and protecting victims. When there is little or no law enforcement response to domestic violence, this sends a signal to the abuser, the victim, and the community that domestic violence is acceptable and not a crime. Recognition of the importance of government accountability of abusers was the foundation of the Violence Against Women Act of 1995. This Act changed federal laws and public policy to support victims of domestic violence and hold abusers accountable.

Recognizing the urgent need to respond to violence against Native women, Congress passed a specific tribal title as part of VAWA 2005 named Safety for Indian Women. This title recognizes and supports tribal governments' authority

---

[155] Catherine Kashkaani Edwards, *Statement Central Council Tlingit and Haida Indian Tribes of Alaska, U.S. DOJ 2018 Violence Against Women Annual Consultation*, Restoration Magazine, Vol. 15, Issue 3, at 44 (2018).

to respond to domestic violence and related crimes. The first section of the VAWA Tribal title lists three specific purposes that provide guidance on the implementation of the title.

> VAWA 2005 Sec. 902. Purposes
> The purposes of this title are—
> (1) to decrease the incidence of violent crimes against Indian women;
> (2) to strengthen the capacity of Indian tribes to exercise their sovereign authority to respond to violent crimes committed against Indian women;
> (3) to ensure that perpetrators of violent crimes committed against Indian women are held accountable for their criminal behavior.[156]

Strengthen the Village Response in Holding Individuals Accountable

Nationally it is agreed that domestic violence is the result of learned behavior supported by social norms, laws, and policies, not substance use or other causes that often are given as excuses for the abuse. It is a learned behavior of someone who has reached a point in their life where they believe violence is acceptable. The difficult questions villages must answer are—How will abusers unlearn their use and acceptance of violence? What actions can village governments take to send strong and immediate signals to stop the abuse? What legal reforms are needed to strengthen the village response to hold those who use violence accountable?

Domestic violence requires a local response. Tribal leaders have testified during annual consultations, government meetings, and national conferences that public safety in Alaska villages is a local matter. They ask for support and resources to respond to the violence, not ineffective assistance from the state or federal governments. Addressing domestic and family violence is a great way to increase the health, safety, and welfare of tribal villages. How to achieve placing this responsibility under the authority of the local village government is challenging because of federal laws limiting village authority. These federal laws, often called barriers, include acts of Congress and Supreme Court cases that diminished the authority and capacity of villages to protect their citizens, particularly women, from domestic violence and related crimes such as sexual assault.

---

[156] VAWA 2005, § 902, 119 Stat. 3078.

> Our villages can and have for centuries taken responsibility and now is the time to let us do so again. The federal and state governments need to recognize their old laws of the past need to be changed so villages can do so again.[157]
>
> —Michael Williams Sr., Secretary/Treasurer
> Akiak Native Community

Recognize the Full Authority of Alaska Native Villages to Respond to Domestic Violence

Sovereignty is the authority to determine, as Indigenous people your laws, practices, rules, and other forms of self-governance. Alaska Native villages have lived according to their traditions and beliefs for thousands of years. While the sovereignty of villages has been challenged by outside governments, since Western contact, villages continue to exist and govern themselves as unique and distinct peoples.

The U.S. recognizes the sovereign authority of tribal villages to self-government as clearly indicated by the inclusion of the 229 tribes in Alaska on the Department of Interior Federally Recognized Indian Tribe List.[158] "The 1993 list named the Alaska villages recognized under ANCSA as tribes. It specifically stated that they have all the immunities and privileges available to other federally acknowledged Indian tribes by their government-to-government relationship with the United States as well as the responsibilities, powers, limitations, and obligations of such tribes."[159]

The sovereignty of tribes is inherent and has never been given up. The U.S. Congress has the plenary power to pass legislation regarding relations with Indian tribes. However, the U.S. has diminished and, in specific instances, refused to recognize or respect the existence of the sovereignty of Alaska Native villages. Since the 1970s, the movement has chipped away at some of the U.S. dominance, reawakening the traditional ways that kept balance and order. This village government authority is essential to responding to domestic violence in

---

[157] Michael Williams Sr., Secretary Treasurer, *Statement of the Native Village of Akiak*, U.S. DOJ 2019 Violence Against Women Annual Government-to-Government Consultation (on file with the AKNWRC).

[158] Federally Recognized Indian Tribe List Act of 1994, 25 U.S.C. 5130. https://www.federalregister.gov/documents/2015/01/14/2015-00509/indian-entities-recognized-and-eligible-to-receive-services-from-the-united-states-bureau-of-indian

[159] On October 21, 1993, during the term of Assistant Secretary of Indian Affairs Ada Deer, the Department of the Interior issued a list of tribes in the United States eligible for services from the Department. See Federal Recognition of Alaska Tribes and Relations with the State of Alaska https://www.uaf.edu/tribal/112/unit_4/federalrecognitionofalaskatribesandrelationswiththestateofalaska.php

villages and protecting women. The authority to order an individual to not go to a victim's home or job, to leave the village, or attend a village program to end abuse are examples of the importance of village government actions. These examples are often included in orders of protection issued by village tribal courts or tribal councils.

> Tetlin Village has a written code of tribal ordinances and is the product of many minds and many hours of work. Through the knowledge gained from listening to our grandparents and elders, these individuals were able to construct this code, which reflects the traditional values of the Tetlin people. Moreover, as a result of our combined and thoughtful efforts to address issues within Tetlin, our tribal court is a competent and strong court system, which is better structured than distant state courts to handle local prosecutions. The Tetlin tribal court currently handles domestic violence and sexual assault cases. As such, the tribal court hears cases and can provide an order of protection and oversee protection order violations. Our tribal court orders are stamped with a Tetlin Tribal Court stamp.[160]
>
> —Nettie Warbelow, Tribal Court Judge, Native Village of Tetlin

Eliminate the Legal Barriers Preventing Tribes from Responding to Domestic Violence

Many victims of domestic violence have never left their village or ever met a federal employee, but the response to their abuse is determined by federal and state law, not their village government. Tribal governments have the authority to decide how it will respond to domestic violence, but this response is impacted by what is called federal Indian law. The response of the state and federal governments is also determined, or controlled, by federal Indian law. This complex body of law is commonly called a jurisdictional "maze of injustice."[161]

Federal Indian law consists of three general categories of law including Congressional Acts, rulings of the Supreme Court, and Presidential Executive Orders of the United States. Understanding the current legal maze that controls the response of tribes in Alaska to domestic violence is essential to answer many of the questions of victims. Questions like – Why do I need to call the state trooper? Why do I have to leave my village to testify in state court? Why is my rape handled by an outsider? – are heard across Alaska.

---

[160] AKNWRC, *Increasing Safety for Alaska Native Women,* at 51 (2016).

[161] The phrase 'maze of injustice' became a common reference following the 2007 report by Amnesty International, *Maze of Injustice: The failure to protect Indigenous women from sexual violence in the USA.* https://www.amnestyusa.org/pdfs/mazeofinjustice.pdf

Answering these questions and improving the response to domestic violence in villages requires more than training and education. The improved response to domestic violence at the village level requires changes to specific federal laws regarding Alaska tribal governments. These are changes to remove legal barriers, clarify the authority of villages, and provide increased resources to villages to exercise their authority to hold abusers accountable.

In the body of federal Indian law, two Congressional acts and two U.S. Supreme Court cases resulted in confusion regarding the authority of villages. Over time each of these federal acts and cases created more confusion, not clarity, regarding tribal authority resulting in the current state of inconsistency and disagreement at the state, village, and federal levels. This confusion is highlighted by the disagreement of state and federal departments on their interpretations of existing law leaving victims in physical danger unprotected. Given the current jurisdictional challenges, it is difficult for victims to understand how the law can prevent future abuse.

Understanding how tribal government authority was changed by Supreme Court decisions in the *Oliphant* case (1978) and the *Venetie* case (1998), the Alaska Native Claims Settlement Act (1976), as well as Public Law 83-280 (1953)[162], is essential to addressing domestic violence in villages. It is also essential to understand what these Supreme Court rulings and Congressional Acts did not change.

Understanding these federal and case laws help to navigate within the broader context of unanswered questions regarding domestic violence. Why are Alaska Native women vulnerable to abusers, rapists, traffickers, and predators? Why do Alaska Native women have the highest rates of domestic violence victimization of any population of women?

"We have all these questions. Why? Why? Why? Unresolved questions."[163]

"My mom told me she was molested by a man, and I thought, is this genetic? Passed on from my mom to me? And is it going to be passed on to my children? And then to my children's children?"[164]

---

[162] P.L. 280 was applied to Alaska in 1958.

[163] Video Public Service Announcement, Yup'ik Women's Coalition (2017). https://www.youtube.com/watch?v=uh5fIUoBKTA&feature=youtu.be

[164] Survivor statement, Yup'ik Women's Coalition, First Sexual Assault Conference (2017). https://www.youtube.com/watch?v=ECUyRR96XQw&feature=youtu.be

The Connection between Federal Indian Law, Tribal Jurisdiction, and Village Accountability of Abusers

Alaska Native villages, as federally recognized Indian tribes, have the authority to act as sovereign governments. This sovereignty was not given or delegated by Congress but is inherent and existed before the United States was created. Tribes existed as self-governing peoples long before the U.S. Constitution was adopted. Originally Indian tribes exercised full tribal authority over all people, Indians, and non-Indians, within their territory.

Over time the United States has restricted the government authority of Indian tribes, and some have been applied to Alaska tribes.[165] Some of these old federal laws and practices are today recognized as harmful to Indian tribes and have been amended or abolished as federal law or policy.

In the 2013 reauthorization of VAWA, Congress recognized the impact some of these restrictions had on holding domestic violence offenders accountable. VAWA 2013 reaffirmed the jurisdictional authority of Indian tribes over non-Indians in certain cases of domestic violence. Unfortunately, VAWA 2013 failed Indian tribes in Alaska and Maine without the needed authority to protect victims and hold abusers accountable. VAWA 2022, enacted on March 15, 2022, recognized the limitations of VAWA 2013 and has the potential to change the landscape for tribes in Alaska.[166] The Alaska Public Safety Empowerment Subtitle creates a process for Alaska tribes to take advantage of expanded jurisdiction over non-Indian offenders and the ability to take advantage of reimbursement programs for their tribal justice systems. This new law provides such groundbreaking and historic provisions that we are devoting Chapter 9 to the discussion of this new section.

Indigenous justice systems existed before the United States and continue to resolve conflicts today. Unfortunately, these tribal justice systems often lack financial support and may not be recognized by state governments. This lack of recognition and support of Alaska tribes denied the validity of actions taken by tribal justice systems and also denied access to federal resources to support the development of traditional justice systems.

"There is no coordination (with the state) that I am aware of … We are here because there is none, almost as if the state is absolved from all responsibility

[165] For additional description of the history and current law regarding Alaska Native villages see David S. Case & David A. Voluck, *Alaska Natives and American Laws* (2012).

[166] Violence Against Women Act 2022, Title VIII, Division W, Safety for Indian Women, 847-862, Tribal jurisdictional provisions of H.R. 2471, codified into 25 U.S.C. 25 U.S.C.§§ 1304.

because they do not have the resources."[167]—Patricia Alexander, Co-Chair, Tlingit and Haida Task Force on Violence Against Women

The state and federal justice systems are dual systems, addressing criminal and civil matters, and their authority requires jurisdiction over persons and territory. In Alaska, village justice approaches that have been used for centuries are known as customary law. While many villages have adopted domestic violence codes, others have not and use unwritten customary law to hold offenders accountable. Customary law is recognized to be valid under VAWA and many other federal statutes.

Jurisdiction Overview

Jurisdiction is described in three categories: Personal jurisdiction which describes how a tribe will have jurisdiction over an individual; territorial jurisdiction, which describes the area in which a tribe can exercise the jurisdiction, and subject matter jurisdiction through inherent tribal authority that may be defined in a constitution or other law.

Jurisdiction over persons

The power of an Indian tribe to exercise control over an abuser exists in the context of Western justice in two forms called civil jurisdiction and criminal jurisdiction. Many Indian tribes in Alaska issue orders of protection to protect victims of domestic violence, which could restrict the behavior or exclude the wrongdoer. The most common examples of criminal authority over an abuser are arrest, prosecution, and incarceration. One village, the Native Village of St. Paul's Island, exercises such criminal jurisdiction through a cross-deputization agreement with the City of St. Paul to enforce village laws.[168]

Oliphant v. Suquamish

In the area of criminal jurisdiction, Indian tribes exercised jurisdiction over all persons in their territory until a U.S. Supreme Court ruling in 1978 in the case of *Oliphant v. Suquamish*. In *Oliphant,* the Supreme Court ruled that Indian nations lacked authority to prosecute crimes committed by non-Indians.[169] This landmark restriction of tribal criminal jurisdiction by the Court altered the ability

---

[167] Response of Patricia Alexander, Co-Chair, Violence Against Women Task Force of the Central Council of Tlingit and Haida Indian Tribes of Alaska, to questions during the *Senate Committee on Indian Affairs, Oversight Hearing on Missing and Murdered, Confronting the Silent Crisis*, held December 12, 2018. https://www.indian.senate.gov/hearing/oversight-hearing-missing-and-murdered-confronting-silent-crisis-indian-country

[168] St. Paul Island Village and City agreement. https://www.theguardian.com/us-news/2018/feb/08/alaska-domestic-abuse-st-paul-island-alcoholism-shelters

[169] *Oliphant v. Suquamish Indian Tribe*, 435 U.S. 191 (1978).

of all federally recognized Indian tribes to hold accountable non-Indian offenders committing domestic violence, sexual assault, and other related crimes. Indian tribes, while continuing to exercise civil jurisdiction over non-Indian abusers, could no longer impose criminal sanctions on these abusers. The abuser and the public understood that non-Indians could commit such crimes without any significant consequences.

The *Oliphant* decision created a jurisdictional loophole for non-Indian perpetrators of violence against Native women living on tribal lands. This loophole created by the Court allowed non-Indians to commit heinous acts of physical and sexual abuse without fear of any legal consequence from tribal governments. In 2013, due to a national groundswell, Congress addressed this jurisdictional race-based loophole by amending federal Indian law and reaffirming partial criminal jurisdiction to Indian tribes over non-Indians in three specific cases—domestic violence, dating violence, and violation of an order of protection.[170] This historic step forward, however, only applied to cases within Indian country. All Indian tribes in Alaska, except one, were excluded from this life-saving reform as not fitting the federal definition of Indian country.

Jurisdiction over territory

The authority of an Indian tribe to hold an abuser accountable is also limited by federal Indian law in the realm of territorial jurisdiction. Congress by statute links tribal territorial jurisdiction to the definition of Indian country.[171] In 1998, the U.S. Supreme Court restricted the territorial jurisdiction of Alaska Indian tribes in the case of *Alaska v. Native Village of Venetie Tribal Government.*[172] The Court in its ruling regarding the Alaska Native Claims Settlement Act held that except for the Annette Island Reservation, the Village of Metlakatla in Southeast Alaska, there is virtually no Indian country in Alaska.[173]

In the context of addressing domestic violence, the authority of the tribal governments in Alaska is limited by the *Venetie* ruling and the current legal definition of Indian country. The Special Domestic Violence Criminal Jurisdiction (SDVCJ) provision of VAWA 2013 is not available to 228 villages to arrest and prosecute non-Indian abusers because the statute is limited to

---

[170] Violence Against Women Reauthorization Act of 2013, Tribal Jurisdiction Over Crimes of Domestic Violence, Pub. L. No. 113-4, § 904, 127 Stat. 120 (2013) (codified at 25 U.S.C. § 1304).

[171] 18 U.S.C. § 1151.

[172] *Alaska v. Native Village of Venetie Tribal Government*, 522 U.S. 520 (1998).

[173] 18 U.S.C. § 1162 (Except as otherwise provided in sections 1154 and 1156 of this title, 28 U.S.C. § 1360.)

specific offenses committed within the Indian country of an Indian tribe.[174] Only the Village of Metlakatla, one of 229 villages, is eligible to exercise certain laws under VAWA 2013.

Indian country is defined as a confined area of territorial jurisdiction tied to a tribe[175] and the term Indian country as:

> (a) all land within the limits of any Indian reservation under the jurisdiction of the United States government, notwithstanding the issuance of any patent, and including rights-of-way running through the reservation,
> (b) all dependent Indian communities within the borders of the United States whether within the original or subsequently acquired territory thereof, and whether within or without the limits of a state, and
> (c) all Indian allotments, the Indian titles to which have not been extinguished, including rights-of-way running through the same.[176]

With the growing increase in public awareness and congressional concern regarding violence against Alaska Native women, the importance of providing the same authority to villages is now recognized. As witnessed during past reauthorization of VAWA, it is clear that Congress has the authority to enact legislation to address this non-Native race-based loophole in Alaska. VAWA 2022 included Alaska Native Villages, but instead of applying the term Indian country to the territorial jurisdiction, it uses the term "village," to mean the "Alaska Native Village Statistical Area" from the Tribal Statistical Area Program Verification map of the Bureau of the Census."[177]

The impact of the Alaska Native Claims Settlement Act (1971) on territorial jurisdiction

The Alaska Native Claims Settlement Act (ANCSA)[178] came at the tail end of the Termination Era of federal Indian policy, the mid-1940s to mid-1960s, and came to fruition after being in the works for several years. The Termination Era was designed to abolish tribes and assimilate individual Indians.[179] After natural resources were found in Alaska on tribal lands, the United States saw a pressing need to resolve disputes regarding land claims.

---

[174] VAWA 2013, 127 Stat. 121.
[175] 18 U.S.C. § 1151.
[176] *Id.*
[177] https://tigerweb.geo.census.gov/tigerweb/
[178] 43 U.S.C. 1601 et seq. (1971).
[179] The federal "Termination Policy" focused on legally ending the historic government-to-government relationship with Indian tribes.

The ANCSA created a new approach to tribal land tenure. Rather than recognize sovereign tribal lands, ANCSA created for-profit corporations and transferred tribal lands in fee to these entities to manage more than 40 million acres of land. ANCSA divided the State into 12 regional corporations and over 200 village corporations that would identify with their regional corporation. Many of these villages had corresponding tribal village governments, but with the passage of ANCSA, any meaningful land base that had existed evaporated. As a result, unlike most court systems that have defined territorial jurisdiction and personal jurisdiction, Alaska tribal courts generally exercise authority through tribal citizenship and not through a geographic space defined as Indian country.

A difference of opinion exists on the impact of ANCSA on Indian tribes in Alaska. This difference was addressed by the Indian Law and Order Commission's (ILOC) report to Congress noting the opinion of the Department of the Interior Solicitor in 1993 that ANCSA had not terminated the status of villages as tribes. It also referenced the Alaska Supreme Court's 1999 decision in *John v. Baker* that Alaska Native tribal courts can regulate internal domestic affairs even if tribes do not have federally recognized Indian country.[180] Based on an extensive review of the issue, the ILOC made the following recommendations:

> 2.1 Congress should overturn the U.S. Supreme Court's decision in Alaska v. Native Village of Venetie Tribal Government by amending ANCSA to provide that former reservation lands acquired in fee by Alaska Native villages and other lands transferred in fee to Native villages pursuant to ANCSA are Indian country.
>
> 2.2 Congress and the President should amend the definitions of Indian country to clarify (or affirm) that Native allotments and Native-owned town sites in Alaska are Indian country.[181]

The Current Applicability of Public Law 83-280 (1953) to Alaska

Public Law 83-280 (P.L. 280) is frequently referred to as the reason why Alaska tribes lack authority to respond to cases of violence against Native women. In reality, P.L. 280 did not change tribal authority.[182] Indian tribes in Alaska retain their inherent authority over their members and certain lands. For many decades the misinterpretation of P.L. 280 created confusion, but today the concurrent authority of Indian tribes with state governments is commonly accepted.

[180] *John v. Baker,* 982 P.2d 738 (Alaska 1999).
[181] Indian Law and Order Commission, *A Roadmap for Making Native America Safer*, at 51-52.
[182] U.S. DOJ, Office of Tribal Justice, Position Paper (Nov. 9, 2000).

> The State of Alaska rests its argument for exclusive criminal law jurisdiction on P.L. 83-280. Yet, courts within and outside Alaska have unanimously affirmed that P.L. 83-280 left concurrent State and inherent Tribal jurisdiction intact within Indian country. The State cannot simultaneously assert that, outside the Metlakatla Reservation, there is no Indian country in Alaska and that P.L. 83-280 prevails.[183]

Congress passed P.L. 280 to transfer specific jurisdiction away from the federal government and confer it initially on five states, adding Alaska in 1958 after statehood. [184] Congress by transferring or withdrawing federal criminal jurisdiction on reservations in these six states authorized those states to assume its authority on Indian lands.[185] Before P.L. 280, these states did not have legal authority as governments to act on these reservations. Thus P.L. 280, created for the first time in these states government authority to prosecute serious crimes, such as sexual assault, under the Major Crimes Act. In 1953, at the time Congress enacted P.L. 280, it was the end of what is known as the Termination Era, a time where it was the policy of the U.S. to terminate Indian tribes.

> For many years it was erroneously assumed that P.L. 280 was a broad grant of exclusive state criminal and civil jurisdiction over Indians for all purposes, but it is now agreed that it does not deprive tribes of concurrent jurisdiction.[186]

Jurisdictional Uncertainty After *Alaska v. Venetie*

The 1999 U.S. Supreme Court decision in *Alaska v. Venetie* further reduced the applicability of P.L. 280 for the Alaska state government. The federal authority transferred under P.L. 280 was the authority the federal government held or possessed—its federal Indian country criminal authority. The Court's ruling in *Venetie* found limited Indian country in Alaska. Since P.L. 280 as a statute is specifically limited to Indian country, the state authority that continued following *Venetie* is also restricted to these very specific Indian country lands—restricted allotments and townsite lands—and other tribal trust or restricted lands.

---

[183] Indian Law and Order Commission, *A Roadmap for Making Native America Safer*, at 45.

[184] The six named states, known as the "mandatory states," are California, Minnesota (except Red Lake Reservation), Nebraska, Oregon (except the Warm Springs Reservation), Wisconsin, and, as added in 1958, Alaska (except the Annette Islands with regard to the Metlakatla Indians).

[185] Public Law 280 provided that the General Crimes Act (18 U.S.C. 1152) and the Major Crimes Act (18 U.S.C. 1153) no longer applied to areas covered by P.L. 280 in the mandatory states. 18 U.S.C.A. 1162.

[186] David S. Case, David A. Voluck, *Alaska Natives and American Laws*, University of Alaska Press Fairbanks, p. 407 (2012).

The clarifying question to ask whenever P.L. 280 is raised as justification for state authority should be: "Is the state action on land that is a restricted allotment or townsite? Or another restricted trust land?" If the answer is no then simply stated P.L. 280 does not, cannot, legally apply. Under P.L. 280, the federal government transferred to the state of Alaska specific federal jurisdiction, which is limited and only applicable to Indian country. Tribes have always maintained their inherent sovereignty to govern over time.

P.L. 280 Applies to Indian Country in Alaska

The 1999 *Venetie* decision held that only the Metlakatla Indian Community on the Annette Island and "restricted allotments and townsite lands" were Indian country. It is also important to note regarding Metlakatla that an amendment by Congress in 1970 permitted Metlakatla and the state to exercise concurrent criminal jurisdiction.[187]

Congress, recognizing this pattern of failed responses to cases of domestic and sexual violence under P.L. 280, created a legal path under the Tribal Law and Order Act of 2010[188] for Indian tribes to petition the federal government to reassume—take back—the federal jurisdiction it transferred to the state governments. On March 15, 2013, the Department of Justice announced that it had granted the first resumption request and would accept concurrent jurisdiction with the White Earth Indian Nation over its reservation in Minnesota. Other Indian tribes have successfully petitioned for the resumption of concurrent federal jurisdiction. Given the minimal application of P.L. 280 since the *Venetie* decision this option while available to Alaska Native villages may not be practical.

Federal Policy Barriers: Funding Exclusion of Tribes Located in P.L. 280 Jurisdictions

In many discussions, it is said that the reason for the lack of tribal justice systems in Alaska is because tribes lack the legal authority to operate a justice system. This conclusion is inaccurate. The reality is that many tribes in Alaska do not have government infrastructures, such as law enforcement or courts, due to lack of funds to support such systems. In the past, federal policies based on faulty or poorly reasoned interpretations by the Bureau of Indian Affairs (BIA) denied Alaska tribes access to federal resources essential to holding abusers accountable.

Following the Act's passage, the BIA instituted a federal policy not to fund Indian tribes located in P.L. 280 states like Alaska. Many tribes in Alaska, like

---

[187] Act of November 25, 1970, Pub. L. No. 91-523, 84 Stat. 1358.18 U.S.C. § 1162, as amended.
[188] Tribal Law and Order Act, §234(a)(3).

those found in other P.L. 280 states, do not have an emergency or other law enforcement services because they were, and continue to be, denied funding from the federal government to develop such services.[189]

Today, while Alaska tribes generally have the same access to federal resources as other Indian tribes, the BIA continues to deny access to law enforcement funding. Tribal governments located in P.L. 280 states were denied federal funds to support the development of tribal justice systems until just recently.[190] For this reason, the Tribes in Alaska are decades behind in developing funded justice and public safety systems. Lack of access to BIA law enforcement funding is an essential barrier Indian tribes in Alaska face in developing and maintaining a law enforcement response to domestic violence. While a complicated issue until Alaska tribes have access to adequate law enforcement funding, they cannot develop a full response to domestic violence.

Barriers Preventing Tribes Access to the National Crime Information Center

Tribes across the nation were denied equal access to the National Crime Information Center (NCIC), despite there being provisions in VAWA 2005 specifically designed to provide tribal access. In the Tribal Law and Order Act of 2010 (TLOA), Congress again required the Attorney General to ensure that tribal agencies that met applicable requirements be permitted access to national crime information databases and the ability of tribes to fully participate in national criminal justice information. Tribes were dependent upon the states in which they were located, for accessing the databases via state networks has been determined by various regulations, statutes, and policies of the states. Tribal access to the national databases was made permanent with the passage of VAWA 2022.

Under the Tribal Access Program (TAP), Alaska tribes were still denied access to these databases until August 2018.[191] This denial of access to NCIC based on the eligibility criterion for the TAP was based on a policy interpretation and not a legal barrier.[192] The Congressional statutes clearly gave the directive to allow Indian tribes to have access to enter and obtain information from NCIC. This

---

[189] *See generally* Carole Goldberg-Ambrose, *Planting Tail Feathers: Tribal Survival and Public Law 280* (American Indian Studies Center, 1997).

[190] *See generally* C. Goldberg-Ambrose and D. Champagne, *A Second Century of Dishonor: Federal Inequities and California Tribes*, Report to the Advisory Council on California Indian Policy, 47–59 (1996).

[191] https://www.justice.gov/opa/pr/department-justice-announces-expansion-program-enhance-tribal-access-national-crime-1

[192] https://www.justice.gov/tribal/tribal-access-program-tap

Department of Justice policy position stood in stark contrast to the acknowledgment of the importance of tribal access to NCIC as stated below.

> "Federal criminal databases hold critical information that can solve crimes, and keep police officers and communities safe," said Deputy Attorney General Sally Quillian Yates. The Tribal Access Program is a step forward to providing tribes the access they need to protect their communities, keep guns from falling into the wrong hands, assist victims and prevent domestic and sexual violence. Empowering tribal law enforcement with information strengthens public safety and is a key element in our ongoing strategy to build safe and healthy communities in Indian country.[193]

The eligibility to apply under TAP was expanded in 2018 to include civil courts issuing orders of protection, restraining orders, or keep away orders, sex offender registration programs, and matters related to child welfare. Initially, the Metlakatla Indian Community was the only village with TAP access. The TAP eligibility criterion is now broader, but the test will be whether the expansion of the TAP will result in the inclusion of more than just a few tribes in Alaska.[194]

VAWA 2022 has expanded the tribal permitted uses of the NCIC database. Tribes can now legislate to use the database for emergency placement of children, background checks for those working with our elders, and other governmental usage. How the U.S. DOJ will interpret section 802 and regulate tribal use is yet to be seen. Furthermore, how these new provisions will be applied to Alaska tribes, most without law enforcement, is yet undetermined and Alaska tribes may continue to have access challenges.

Exclusion From the Full Protections of the VAWA 2013

"Because of the 1998 Supreme Court ruling that excluded Alaska Native tribes (except the Metlakatla Indian Community) from "Indian country," Alaska Native women are excluded from the protections afforded other women in Alaska and the rest of the country."[195]—Chief Carl Jerue, Native Village of Anvik

---

[193] U.S. Dep't of Justice, Press Release, *Department of Justice Announces Program to Enhance Tribal Access to National Crime Information Databases* (Aug. 19, 2015). https://www.justice.gov/opa/pr/department-justice-announces-program-enhance-tribal-access-national-crime-information

[194] https://www.justice.gov/tribal/tap-faq

[195] Carl Jerue, Chief, *Statement of the Native Village of Anvik*, U.S. DOJ 2014 Violence Against Women Annual Government-to-Government Consultation (on file with AKNWRC).

Congress enacted historic tribal reforms for Indian tribes to increase their response to violence against women under VAWA 2013.[196] It recognized and affirmed the inherent sovereign authority of Indian tribal governments to exercise criminal jurisdiction over non-Indians who violate protection orders, or commit domestic, or dating violence, against Indian victims on tribal lands.[197]

> VAWA 2013's limited reaffirmation of inherent tribal criminal jurisdiction over non-Indians, known as Special Domestic Violence Criminal Jurisdiction (SDVCJ), has fundamentally changed the landscape of tribal criminal jurisdiction in the modern era. By exercising SDVCJ, many communities have increased safety and justice for victims who had previously seen little of either. SDVCJ has allowed tribes to "respond to long-time abusers who previously had evaded justice"[198] and has given a ray of hope to victims and communities that safety can be restored.[199]

As of 2018, Indian tribes implementing SDVCJ reported "143 arrests of 128 non-Indian abusers. These arrests ultimately led to 74 convictions, 5 acquittals, and 24 cases"[200] were pending. Unfortunately, the provision limits the exercise of the SDVCJ restored to Indian tribes to crimes committed in Indian country.

SDVCJ is essential to abuser accountability and protection of Native women. The National Institute of Justice (NIJ) examined inter-racial violence against women in Indian country and documented a high rate of domestic violence by non-Indians. The NIJ reported that more than half of American Indians and Alaska Native women have experienced physical violence in their lifetime. Of these victims, 90 percent report being victimized by a non-Indian intimate partner.[201]

Until the VAWA 2022 Alaska tribal amendments, because of the Indian country restriction, 228 of the Indian tribes in Alaska could not implement this provision of the VAWA 2013. Alaska Native women, like other Native women are abused by non-Indian abusers. Alaska Native women should not be denied this essential

---

[196] VAWA 2013, § 902, 119 Stat. 3078.

[197] 25 U.S.C. § 1304.

[198] *Draft Legislation to Protect Native Children and Promote Public Safety in Indian Country: Hearing Before S. Comm. on Indian Affs.,* 114th Cong. 11–13 (2016) (statement of Tracy Toulou, Director of the Office of Tribal Justice, U.S. DOJ). https://www.govinfo.gov/content/pkg/CHRG-114shrg21390/pdf/CHRG-114shrg21390.pdf

[199] *VAWA 2013's Special Domestic Violence Criminal Jurisdiction Five-Year Report*, NCAI, at 1 (2018). https://www.ncai.org/resources/ncai-publications/SDVCJ_5_Year_Report.pdf

[200] *Id.*

[201] André B. Rosay, *Violence Against American Indian and Alaska Native Women and Men*, at 46, Figure 6.1 Interracial Violence: Weighted Estimates for Lifetime Victims.

legal reform. Indian tribes across the United States have called for Congress to amend the SDVCJ section of VAWA 2005.[202]

The 228 Indian tribes in Alaska without federally recognized Indian country were also excluded from the OVW Tribal Jurisdiction Grant Program. While this program was created to assist Indian tribes in preparing and implementing SDVCJ, it provides important resources to strengthen tribal justice systems and address domestic violence.

Untying the Current Legal Knot Preventing Safety for Alaska Native Women

The current barriers to the safety of Alaska Native women are like a Fisherman's Knot. They can only be untied by the way they were created. The legal foundation for the protection of women in their villages rests on an archaic system of governance, the very system that created the vulnerabilities to abuse and violence in their everyday lives.

The broad legal parameters created by federal Indian law limit the response of Indian tribes in Alaska to domestic violence. While many of these legal barriers are from past decades, the United States continues to restrict the authority of Alaska Indian tribes to hold abusers accountable and protect Native women. VAWA 2013 is one such example.[203]

These legal barriers also produce an inoperable state and federal response to domestic violence at the village level. Simply stated, the legal barriers created a false expectation of a state law enforcement response and removed the expectation of a federal law enforcement response. The vulnerabilities created by federal Indian law regarding tribal jurisdiction in Alaska are ongoing, are well known, and were addressed explicitly by the Indian Law and Order Commission.

> The strongly centralized law enforcement and justice systems of the State of Alaska are of critical concern to the Indian Law and Order Commission. They do not serve local and Native communities adequately, if at all. The Commission believes that devolving authority to Alaska Native communities is essential for addressing local crime. Their governments are best positioned to effectively arrest, prosecute, and punish, and they should have the authority to do so—or to work

---

[202] National Congress of American Indians, *Calling Upon Congress Promptly to Enact Legislation Recognizing the Jurisdiction of Tribal Nations in Alaska to Prosecute Domestic Violence, Sexual Assault, Child Abuse, and Related Crimes in Alaska Villages,* Resolution #REN-19-011, 2019.

[203] VAWA 2013 excluded 228 tribes from implementing SDVCJ due to the requirement that the offense occur in Indian country.

> out voluntary agreements with each other, and with local governments and the State on mutually beneficial terms.[204]

This failed government response has been referred to as an archaic system of governance. Understanding the impact of federal Indian law and policies on the response of tribes in Alaska to abusers—and also rapists, sex traffickers, and the crisis of MMIW—is the foundation for addressing these crimes. While there has been progress toward securing safety and justice for Alaska Native women, the current pace of change is unconscionably slow given the scale of suffering and the loss of human life caused by current laws and policies.

> Section 205 of the Tribal Law and Order Act of 2010 (TLOA) states, "Nothing in this Act limits, alters, expands, or diminishes the civil or criminal jurisdiction of the State of Alaska, any subdivision of the State of Alaska, or any Indian tribe in that State." Yet, the Indian Law and Order Commission's opinion is that problems in Alaska are so severe and the number of Alaska Native communities affected so large, that continuing to exempt the State from national policy change is wrong. It sets Alaska apart from the progress that has become possible in the rest of Indian country. The public safety issues in Alaska–and the law and policy at the root of those problems–beg to be addressed. These are no longer just Alaska's issues. They are national issues.[205]

"There is no coordination (with the state) that I am aware of … We are here because there is none, almost as if the state is absolved from all responsibility because they do not have the resources."[206]—Patricia Alexander, Co-Chair, Tlingit and Haida Task Force on Violence Against Women

---

[204] Indian Law and Order Commission, *A Roadmap for Making Native America Safer*, at 35.

[205] *Id.* at 33.

[206] Response of Patricia Alexander, Co-Chair, Violence Against Women Task Force of the Central Council of Tlingit and Haida Indian Tribes of Alaska, to questions during the *Senate Committee on Indian Affairs, Oversight Hearing on Missing and Murdered, Confronting the Silent Crisis*, held December 12, 2018. https://www.indian.senate.gov/hearing/oversight-hearing-missing-and-murdered-confronting-silent-crisis-indian-country

Did you know?

1. One of the purposes of the VAWA, Safety for Indian Women Title is "to strengthen the capacity of Indian tribes to exercise their sovereign authority to respond to violent crimes committed against Indian women." Numerous federal grant programs are available to support Alaska tribes in developing a tribal government response to hold offenders accountable and services to support victims and survivors.

2. Villages with civil courts that issue orders of protection, restraining orders, or keep away orders are now eligible to apply to the Tribal Access Program (TAP) and to have direct access to enter and obtain information from the federal databases.

3. P.L. 280 did not impact the authority of Alaska Indian tribes—tribal authority is not referenced under this federal statute. P.L. 280 only created a change to federal and state authority by transferring specific federal jurisdiction to the state. The Act was very limited at the time and today because of the U.S. Supreme Court decision in the *Venetie* case it has even less impact.

4. "Tribes 'have power to make their own substantive law in internal matters, and to enforce that law in their own forums.' "[207] And tribal courts may also have jurisdiction to 'resolve civil disputes involving nonmembers, including non-Indians'[208] when the civil actions involve essential self-governance matters such as membership or other areas where 'the exercise of tribal authority is vital to the maintenance of tribal integrity and self-determination.'[209] *John v. Baker,* 98 P.2d 738 (Alaska 1999).

Questions to consider:

1. How are legal barriers different from other challenges such as the lack of resources to create programs?

2. Why do tribal villages under federal law have "specific" government authority and not "full" authority to respond to domestic violence?

---

[207] *Santa Clara Pueblo v. Martinez,* 436 U.S. 49, 55-56, 98 S.Ct. 1670, 56 L.Ed.2d 106 (1978) (citations omitted).

[208] *Duro v. Reina,* 495 U.S. 676, 687, 110 S.Ct. 2053, 109 L.Ed.2d 693 (1990) (citing *Santa Clara,*436 U.S. at 65-66, 98 S.Ct. 1670; *Williams v. Lee,* 358 U.S. 217, 223, 79 S.Ct. 269, 3 L.Ed.2d 251 (1959)).

[209] *Id.* at 688, 110 S.Ct. 2053 (citing *Brendale v. Confederated Tribes & Bands of the Yakima Indian Nation,* 492 U.S. 408, 109 S.Ct. 2994, 106 L.Ed.2d 343 (1989)).

Chapter 8
The Crisis of Missing and Murdered Native Women

> *We want to make a clear statement to every federal employee at consultation this year. The murders and disappearances of women and girls in Alaska are connected to the lack of protection from the state and federal government. They are connected to the government disputing the authority of our tribal government to respond to the violence our women and girls face every day. And the murders and disappearances are connected to the failure of the federal government to provide resources to our tribes and other tribes to establish a comprehensive response.* [210]
>
> *—Catherine Moses, Tribal Administrator, Asa'carsarmiut Indian Tribe*

In 1994, with the passage of the VAWA, Congress funded research to further understand domestic violence. Over the last two decades, the lethality and connection between domestic violence and homicide has increased. The National Violent Death Reporting System reports 1 in 2 female murder victims and 1 in 13 male murder victims are killed by intimate partners.[211] It is now well documented that domestic violence homicides impact more than the victim of abuse, taking the lives of the victim's family members, people who intervened in the attempt to prevent the abuse, law enforcement, and others.

The current crisis of missing and murdered Indigenous women, referred to as MMIW, is connected to this harsh reality of domestic violence. It is also related to the larger issues of denying Native women access to basic resources and justice services needed to live in safe and stable communities. The crisis of MMIW happens as a result of a spectrum of violent crimes committed against Alaska Native women because they are women and as significant because they are Native.

While not all MMIW cases are the result of domestic violence, a large number of murders are related to domestic violence. Similarly, in many cases of missing Native women, the suspects in the disappearances are not strangers, and include intimate or former intimate partners. Cases of MMIW clearly fall within the continuum of domestic violence. In developing a village response to domestic violence this potential lethality should be considered.

---

[210] Catherine Moses, Tribal Administrator, *Statement of the Asa'carsarmiut Indian Tribe*, U.S. DOJ 2018 Violence Against Women Annual Government-to-Government Consultation (on file with the AKNWRC).

[211] Ertl A, Sheats KJ, Petrosky E, Betz CJ, Yuan K, Fowler KA. *Surveillance for Violent Deaths - National Violent Death Reporting System, 32 States,* 2016. https://www.ncbi.nlm.nih.gov/pmc/articles/PMC6818131/

Homicide and Native Women

The federal and state governments gather information concerning violent deaths. The National Violent Death Reporting System (NVDRS) provides a census of violent deaths that occur within the United States to both residents and nonresidents. The NVDRS defines a death due to violence as "a death resulting from the intentional use of physical force or power against oneself, another person or against a group or community." Suicide is included in this definition because far too often homicide/suicide cases do occur where the abuser kills the victim and commits suicide.

Homicide is one of the leading causes of death for women in the United States.[212] Over half of these homicides nationally, 55.3%, were intimate partner violence (IPV) related; for example, the victim was the current, former, or unspecified spouse or girlfriend of the suspect. IPV related deaths also included victims who were not the intimate partner; family, friends, or others who intervened in the IPV. Nearly half of female victims are killed by a current or former male intimate partner.[213]

The Centers for Disease Control and Prevention operates the NVDRS and gathers information from three separate sources: death certificates, coroner/medical examiner reports, and law enforcement reports. The NVDRS creates a depiction of who dies from violence, where and when victims die, and factors perceived to contribute to the victim's death. NVDRS provides a census of violent deaths that occur within the United States to both residents and nonresidents.

Unfortunately, not all states with high populations of American Indians report to the NVDRS. The State of Alaska has participated in NVDRS since 2004. These reports provide information helpful to understanding violent deaths of Alaska Native women in cases where the circumstances are known. Unfortunately, less information about violent deaths of Alaska Native women occurring outside the state is available because not all states participate in the national reporting system.

Based on the NVDRS American Indian/Alaska Native women experienced the second-highest rate of homicide, 4.3 per 100,000 population, in the country.[214] Based on the State of Alaska violent death reporting system, Alaska Native

---

[212] Petrosky E, Blair JM, Betz CJ, Fowler KA, Jack SP, Lyons BH. *Racial and Ethnic Differences in Homicides of Adult Women and the Role of Intimate Partner Violence—United States, 2003–2014.* MMWR Morb Mortal Wkly Rep 2017;66:741–746. DOI: http://dx.doi.org/10.15585/mmwr.mm6628a1.

[213] *Id.*

[214] *Id.*

women also experienced the second-highest homicide rate, 38%, 8.6 per 1,000 population,[215] and 39.8% of violent deaths.[216] These rates, nationally and in Alaska, are shocking and illustrate the injustice faced by Native women. The violent death rate of Native women is far higher than their portion of the population.[217]

General Vulnerabilities

There are many stories of Alaska Native women and girls who have faced victimization because they are Indigenous. Many Native women have suffered abuse and death because of a government system that fails in its "federal trust responsibility to assist tribal governments in safeguarding the lives of Indian women."[218] Simply stated, for Alaska Native women, there is little, if any, help available. At least 75 communities in Alaska lack any law enforcement presence at all."[219]

> We have no closure with many of our women who die unexpectedly and unnaturally. The manner of death, while often considered "suspicious" and often with visible injuries, is classified as accidental, suicidal, or undetermined. In the village of Klawock, police suspected "foul play" in the unnatural death of 37-year-old Francile Ella Turpin on January 14, 2018, as of printing, there is no resolution.[220] Why is it that our women and their families do not receive the closure regarding the cause of death that the general population takes for granted?[221]
>
> —Tami Truett Jerue, Executive Director, AKNWRC

Alaska has the highest number of MMIW of any state. As of May 2022, out of the 755 missing Alaska Native and American Indian people in the National

---

[215] *Alaska Violent Death Reporting System 2003–2008,* State of Alaska, Department of Health and Social Services, at 17 (Aug. 2011). http://dhss.alaska.gov/dph/Epi/injury/Documents/akvdrs/assets/AKVDRS.pdf

[216] *Id.* at 4, Table 1.2: Victim Count, Percent, and Rate of Violent Death by Gender Race and Ethnicity, Alaska, 2003-2008.

[217] *See* Ronet Bachman, *et. al*, U.S. Dep't of Justice, *Violence Against American Indian and Alaska Native Women and the Criminal Justice Response: What is Known,* at 18 (2008). https://www.ncjrs.gov/pdffiles1/nij/grants/223691.pdf

[218] VAWA 2005, Pub. L. No. 109-162, § 901, 119 Stat. 3078 (2006).

[219] Indian Law and Order Commission, *A Roadmap for Making Native America Safer*, at 39.

[220] https://www.ktva.com/story/37289178/klawock-police-say-foul-play-suspected-in-womans-death

[221] *Unmasking the Hidden Crisis of Murdered and Missing Indigenous Women (MMIW): Exploring Solutions to End the Cycle of Violence*, *Hearing Before the H. Comm. on Natural Resources Subcommittee for Indigenous Peoples of the United States, 116 Cong.* (2019) (statement of Tami Truett Jerue, Executive Director AKNWRC). https://naturalresources.house.gov/imo/media/doc/Written%20Testimony_Tami%20Jerue.pdf

Missing and Unidentified Persons System (NamUs) 292 of those were from Alaska—the most of any state.[222] The Violence Policy Center reports that Alaska is ranked first among the states with the highest homicide rates of women killed by men and is the most violent state.[223] Anchorage is ranked among the most violent cities in the country. The Seattle Urban Indian Health Institute reports that Alaska is among the top ten states with the highest number of missing and murdered Native Americans and Alaska Natives.[224]

Increased Awareness of Missing and Murdered Alaska Native Women

Through the voices of survivors, their families, tribal leaders, and advocates calling for justice, there is increased awareness of the crisis of MMIW. In lifting the voices of MMIW, this social justice movement focuses on foundational changes needed to prevent future disappearances and murders. In addition, it is educating national leaders and policymakers to understand the relationship of the MMIW crisis to the importance of village-based responses, and tribal authority to protect women. Until movement efforts put the MMIW crisis on the national agenda, it was a silent crisis. Today the MMIW crisis in Alaska and other parts of the country is recognized by Congress and the United Nations.

---

[222] https://namus.nij.ojp.gov/sites/g/files/xyckuh336/files/media/document/namus-stats-ai-an-may-2022.pdf

[223] https://vpc.org/studies/wmmw2019.pdf

[224] https://www.uihi.org/wp-content/uploads/2018/11/Missing-and-Murdered-Indigenous-Women-and-Girls-Report.pdf

September 19, 2018, Fairbanks Alaska, AKNWRC staff and board from left to right Marie Taylor, Shirley Moses, Janelle Chapin, Michelle Demmert, intern, and Healing Native Hearts staff member Elizabeth Jeru.

Violence Against Women Annual Consultations and Federal Accountability

Indian tribes in Alaska have a government-to-government relationship with the United States. Based on this legal and political relationship, Congress created a specific consultation mandate under the VAWA 2005, Safety for Indian Women Title.[225] It requires the U.S. Departments of Justice, Health and Human Services, and Interior to consult with Indian tribes on "Enhancing the safety of Indian women from domestic violence, dating violence, sexual assault, and stalking."[226] Indian tribes in Alaska have attended every consultation since the first in 2006. One of the priority issues raised by tribal leaders at each consultation is the crisis of MMIW. Over the last two decades, awareness concerning the MMIW crisis has increased because tribal leaders persistently testified during government consultations.

Tribal leaders consistently raise their concerns regarding the inadequate response to cases of MMIW Alaska Native women. The U.S. DOJ summarized tribal leader testimony on this issue in its report to Congress in 2016.

---

[225] VAWA 2005, Pub. L. No. 109-162, § 903, Consultation, 119 Stat. 3078 (2006).
[226] *Id.* § 903(b)(2).

> At the 2016 consultation, many tribal leaders testified that the disappearance and deaths of American Indian and Alaska Native (AI/AN) women are not taken seriously enough and that increased awareness and a stronger law enforcement response are critical to saving Native women's lives. They noted that missing AI/AN women may have been trafficked, and they also provided examples of abusers who murdered their partners after engaging in a pattern of escalating violence for which they were not held accountable. Tribal leaders also raised concerns that cases involving Native victims are often mislabeled as runaways or suicides and that cold cases are not given sufficient priority. Recommendations included creating a national working group to address these issues, an alert system to help locate victims soon after they disappear, and the development of an Indian country-wide protocol for missing Native women, children, and men.[227]

The U.S. Congress has the authority to restore tribal protections for women and authorize the resources to support tribal justice systems and services needed to implement and support victims in becoming safe. In response to the ongoing testimony of tribal leaders during the annual consultations, the voices of families calling for justice, and the actions across tribal communities, Congress recognized the need for federal legislation to address the crisis of MMIW. In 2017, 2018, and 2019, the Senate Committee on Indian Affairs held hearings and proposed legislation to address the concerns of tribal leaders and family members. In 2020, the House also held a hearing on proposed legislation addressing MMIW. Unfortunately, it was not until 2020 that Congress passed the Savanna's Act and the Not Invisible Act.

The Savanna's Act[228] was first introduced in October 2017.[229] The Act was in response to the murder of Savanna LaFontaine-Greywind, who was murdered while pregnant and her infant taken by her murderers. The Act aims to improve tribal access to federal crime information databases, such as the NCIC and requires data collection on missing and murdered Native people. The Act also calls on the U.S. DOJ to develop law enforcement and justice protocols to address missing persons. Finally, it requires an annual report to Congress.

---

[227] U.S. Department of Justice, Office on Violence Against Women, *2017 Update on the Status of Tribal Consultation Recommendations* (2017).

[228] S. 227. https://www.congress.gov/116/bills/s227/BILLS-116s227enr.pdf https://www.congress.gov/116/crpt/srpt206/CRPT-116srpt206.pdf

[229] Savanna's Act, S. 1942 introduced Oct. 7, 2017, and companion bill H.R 4485 introduced Nov. 29, 2017.

The Not Invisible Act[230] was first introduced in 2019 and aims to address the crisis of missing, murdered, and trafficked Native people by engaging law enforcement, tribal leaders, federal partners, and service providers and improving coordination across federal agencies. The Not Invisible Act established an advisory commission of local, tribal, and federal stakeholders to make recommendations to the U.S. DOI and U.S. DOJ on best practices to combat the epidemic of disappearances, homicide, violent crime, and trafficking of Native Americans and Alaska Natives.

Connecting Reforms to Increase Safety to Accountability

"Many villages, while lacking the resources to fully develop western justice systems do have village traditional justice approaches that can be strengthened or be reestablished to create protections for women in the village."[231]—Mike Jackson, Keeper of the Circle Organized Village of Kake, Retired State Justice Magistrate

Addressing the MMIW crisis requires increasing village responses to domestic violence to support the victims and also hold abusers accountable. Increasingly, villages are turning to traditional customary law and healing practices as important tools to address these offenses in a holistic manner. Murder can be attributed to failed domestic violence laws and policies of the United States that have a significant fatal impact on our communities.

The MMIW crisis reaches beyond domestic violence abusers, and safety requires the accountability of predators. Research on convicted rapists shows that criminals prey on vulnerable women and girls. In his research, Dr. David Lisak simply states: "undetected rapists represent the vast majority of rapists, and account for the vast majority of rapes."[232] "However, their crimes are characterized by extensive planning and premeditation…"[233] The lack of accountability emboldens perpetrators to perpetuate the violence. Predators—sex traffickers, rapists, murderers—are intentional in their actions and target vulnerable victims. The efforts to increase safety through protections and accountability must extend to the full range of violence committed against Native women. These crimes are often intertwined and woven together. From

---

[230] S. 982. https://www.congress.gov/116/bills/s982/BILLS-116s982enr.pdf. https://www.congress.gov/116/crpt/srpt214/CRPT-116srpt214.pdf

[231] Mike Jackson, AKNWRC MMIW Awareness Card (2019).

[232] Dr. David Lisak, Researcher Sexual Abuse in Men, Consultant, OVW U.S. DOJ. *See also* David Lisak & Paul M Miller, *Repeat Rape and Multiple Offending Among Undetected Rapist*, Violence & Victims, Vol. 17, No. 1, at 81 (2002). https://time.com/wp-content/uploads/2014/09/repeat_rape.pdf

[233] Dr. David Lisak, *Understanding the Predatory Nature of Sexual Violence*, University of Boston. https://www.middlebury.edu/media/view/240951/original

a tribal perspective, increased protections and accountability are needed where such crimes occur—in villages.

For decades, mothers, family members, Indian tribes, and advocates for Native women in Alaska have spoken loudly about the urgent need to respond to cases of women who have gone missing or who have been murdered. As a national movement, the effort to address the MMIW crisis requires broad public education and awareness. In strengthening the village-based response, it is essential to develop specific protocols or action plans for both reports of a missing person and for cases of murder.

Clearly, in cases of missing Native women, urgent emergency assistance and support to locate the woman are the priority. This response aims to find the woman alive and provide assistance so she can remain alive. The National Indigenous Women's Resource Center has developed an MMIW Toolkit that can assist villages in developing an MMIW protocol.[234] AKNWRC, with our regional partners, developed an Alaska focused toolkit entitled "Missing and Murdered Indigenous Women: An Action Plan for Alaska Native Communities."[235] In 2022 the NIWRC released "Reconnecting with Native Teachings and Creating Healing Spaces with and for 2S+/LGBTQ+ Victim-Survivors of Domestic Violence – A Toolkit for Family and Friends."[236]

One other resource that is a useful tool for Alaska Native communities and organizations to have on hand when developing effective strategies for responding to domestic violence, sexual assault and MMIP incidents is the "Murdered and Missing Indigenous Persons Service Delivery Guide" published in May 2022 by the Association of Village Council Presidents.[237] This document combines response readiness with culturally based prevention services and practices.

In responding to cases of murder, the investigation and accountability of the murderer are the focus. While the investigation and accountability of the murderer will not bring the loved one back, it can hopefully protect others, including family, community, and possible future victims. The focus of the village also turns to those left behind, particularly children who have lost their mothers. In these cases, access by the village government to federal resources to support these surviving victims is essential. The Victims of Crime Act is the largest federal grant program providing funds to support victims of crime, and

---

[234] http://www.niwrc.org/resources/tribal-community-response-when-woman-missing-toolkit-action

[235] https://www.aknwrc.org/resources/aknwrc-resources/mmiw-resources/

[236] https://www.niwrc.org/resources/toolkit/reconnecting-native-teachings-and-creating-healing-spaces-and-2slgbtq-victim

[237] https://www.avcp.org/2022/05/04/avcp-responds-to-mmip/

a dedicated tribal funding stream is available.[238] Unfortunately, the tribal set aside funding has not been made permanent.

Federal Systems Reporting of Missing and Murdered Native Women

The federal government funds two systems concerning cases of missing persons. One system is a federal criminal justice system used nationally by recognized law enforcement agencies to report missing person cases. A second system is federally funded but provided to the public to assist in identifying the remains of missing persons.

The first system is the FBI Criminal Justice Information Services Systems missing persons database. It is housed within the U.S. DOJ, National Crime Information Center (NCIC), containing twenty-one national data files. "The National Crime Information Center, or NCIC, has been called the lifeline of law enforcement—an electronic clearinghouse of crime data that can be tapped into by virtually every criminal justice agency nationwide, 24 hours a day, 365 days a year."[239] All state and some tribal law enforcement agencies have access to enter missing person reports into this federal criminal justice database. Currently, only one tribe in Alaska, Metlakatla, has direct access to NCIC through the U.S. DOJ Tribal Access Program (TAP). The TAP program expanded over the years to offer access to some of these databases through a revised program to Tribes without law enforcement. Since then, there have been two Alaska Tribes selected for deployment of equipment: Central Council of Tlingit and Haida Indian Tribes of Alaska and Kenaitze Indian Tribe.

In 2005, Congress reauthorized VAWA to include an amendment to address this lack of tribal access to NCIC.[240] It directed the U.S. Attorney General to provide Indian law enforcement agencies full direct access to NCIC, in cases of domestic violence, dating violence, sexual assault, and stalking. It provided the authority for Indian law enforcement agencies to enter information into, and obtain information from, the federal criminal information databases.

Congress included a similar mandate under the Tribal Law and Order Act of 2010. It mandated that "the Attorney General shall ensure that tribal law enforcement officials that meet applicable federal or state requirements be permitted access to national crime information databases."[241] Unfortunately, the

---

[238] https://ovc.ojp.gov/program/tribal/tribal-victim-services-set-aside#:~:text=In%20February%202019%2C%20Congress%20authorized, the%20Victims%20of%20Crime%20Act

[239] https://www.fbi.gov/services/cjis/ncic

[240] VAWA 2005, § 905(a), Tracking of Violence Against Indian Women, 119 Stat. 3079.

[241] Tribal Law and Order Act of 2010, Pub. L. No. 111-211, Title II, 124 Stat. 2279, §233(b)(1), 28 U.S.C. §534(d).

TLOA limited the provision by including an Indian country requirement, which effectively excluded tribes in Alaska.

> Tribal law enforcement access to federal criminal databases is a foundational element of an effective law enforcement response to tribal victims of domestic violence, sexual assault, and other VAWA-related crimes. The NCIC maintains 21 national data files, many of which are directly related to the emergency response of tribal law enforcement to assist victims. Law enforcement responding to a domestic violence incident who have NCIC access can verify a protection order, determine whether the suspect is a convicted sex offender in violation of registration requirements, or if the suspect is prohibited from possessing firearms, has an outstanding warrant, or is in violation of terms of parole.[242]

This lack of access or restriction placed on Alaska tribes to NCIC has placed Alaska Native women, girls, and families in greater danger as well as the law enforcement officers that respond to domestic violence situations.

The U.S. DOJ houses a second electronic system for public usage to locate the remains and determine the identities of missing persons called National Missing and Unidentified Persons Systems (NamUs).[243] It is a national information clearinghouse and resource center. NamUs was established to match unidentified human remains with people who were reported missing and offers all services at no cost to agencies or families. Entering a missing Native woman into the system is one tool available to villages and family members to locate their loved ones' remains. However, it is not a criminal justice law enforcement system for investigating or locating people's whereabouts to help save their lives.

The federal government's criminal justice response is inadequate in the face of the life-threatening safety crisis facing Indian tribes in Alaska. This inadequate federal response is one reason why Indian tribes must strengthen village-based responses to violence against women. This violence occurs in many forms, and cases of those Native women who are missing or murdered are a reflection of one end of the spectrum. MMIW is a crisis in human lives that is preventable with the will, resources, and removal of legal barriers preventing safety and justice for Alaska Native women.

In July 2020, the U.S. Attorney for the District of Alaska named E. Ingrid Cumberlidge as the District's MMIP Coordinator. She was tasked to gather reliable MMIP data; work with Alaska tribal villages to develop community

---

[242] Jacqueline Agtuca, *Safety for Native Women: VAWA and American Indian Tribes*, at 66 (Dorma Sahneyah, ed., 2014).

[243] https://www.namus.gov/

action plans; and form a working group of tribal, municipal, state, and federal law enforcement to share information and to create MMIP protocols and procedures.

At the end of 2021, the Alaska governor's office launched the People First Initiative aimed at addressing five major interconnected public safety issues: domestic violence and sexual assault; missing and murdered Indigenous persons; human and sex trafficking; foster care; and homelessness. The MMIP commission has been set up and is beginning to formulate specific strategies and recommendations to the state government.

> Violence against women is not traditional. It is a manifestation of colonization, sexism, and racism, and it erodes our sovereignty. Together we can help bring about a more effective and structural approach to justice that not only gathers data on the missing, but solves murders and helps prevent them in the first place.[244]
>
> —Pamela Stearns, Tlingit and Haida Violence Against Women Task Force

State Systems Reporting of Missing and Murdered Native Women

The calls for justice and accountability for the federal and state failure to respond to numerous cases of missing or murdered Alaska Native women have resulted in increased awareness nationally and within Alaska. This increased attention by the federal government is long overdue. In 2020, three bills were introduced in the Alaska State Senate with companion bills in the State House. While these three bills failed to pass the legislature, momentum continues to build throughout the state government that the MMIP crisis needs to be addressed.

MMIP Missing Persons Clearinghouse

The Missing Persons Clearinghouse (MPC) falls under the Alaska Bureau of Investigation (ABI) and tracks all missing persons cases reported within Alaska.[245] The MPC serves as the central repository for records regarding both juvenile and adult victims and serves as the gateway into various national missing persons databases. The MPC manages both hard copy files and several computer-assisted programs that aid in the centralization of MPC information regarding missing and unidentified human remains.

---

[244] Pamela Sterns, *Tlingit and Haida VAW Task Force to Gather Community Response to Address Missing and Murdered Indigenous Women in Alaska,* Restoration Magazine, Vol. 15, Issue 3, at 35 (2018).

[245] https://dps.alaska.gov/AST/ABI/MissingPerson

Strengthening the Local Tribal Response to Missing and Murdered Alaska Native Women

Addressing the crisis of missing and murdered Alaska Native women and girls requires restoring and enhancing local, tribal governmental capacity to respond to violence against women to provide for greater local control, safety, and accountability. These crimes are far removed from the reach of the state or federal governments. From this local approach, we create the possibilities of safer communities and a pathway for long-lasting justice. Villages offer the hope and possibility of preventing Alaska Native women from going missing or being murdered.

We know that our chances of finding a person are much better when our communities are alerted to the situation as soon as possible. Tribes can take matters into their own hands and utilize the Federal Emergency Management Agency (FEMA) Integrated Public Alert and Warning System (IPAWS) to create a process to alert the community to the missing person. The IPAWS is an alert system offered by FEMA. It is free to any tribe, community, city, or state in the country. The IPAWS system operates through the internet, cell phone, and radio. IPAWS, once it is set up, allows the community to put out an alert to residents in a defined area, about a missing person or any other tribal governmental issue of importance including health concerns, resource availability, weather alerts, etc. The alert can be a cell phone call or text, or an announcement on the local TV or radio station. As mentioned, the emergency 'event' is determined by the community and can be a missing child, vulnerable adult, elder, or anyone under any situation determined by the community's protocols. Communities can implement policies to ensure that the missing person is not voluntarily missing but is unexpectedly gone. The only costs are optional infrastructure improvements and the telecom software (the more special features, the higher the cost) such as a computer, software to implement IPAWS, and other voluntary options.

The AKNWRC is working with the NCAI Task Force and National Indigenous Women's Resource Center to educate Congress to strengthen tribal authority to respond to the MMIW crisis. We are also working to ensure the availability of resources to support such increased tribal responses. Efforts at all levels of tribal, state, and federal government are required to begin making the changes needed. Important to this continued progress is the ongoing MMIW public awareness efforts by Alaska Natives families, tribal leaders, and advocates. One example of these public awareness efforts is the Memorial Qaspeq created by Amber Webb.

The main inspiration for the qaspeq was the disappearance of Val Sifsof in July of 2012 from Granite Creek campground. She was a family friend. It was also the awareness of the pattern of deaths and disappearances that I didn't hear people talking about but that I'd been aware of since I was about 8 years old. They are all our relatives. The goal of the project is to humanize the issue and find a way to make people feel it. I wanted to make the qaspeq large to represent the space that the grief occupies within Native communities. It was done to honor the memory of our relatives and remind the world that it shouldn't be up to Native women to prove their innocence before crimes against them are investigated. It was also about healing myself and sparking healing for all Native women. I carry these stories, but they are not mine. The project has its own energy, and my job is just to facilitate its movement. I can't undo these crimes, but if we can open conversations about the root causes of violence that are honest and do not minimize the effects of violence, then the project is worth doing. The project has been ongoing for the last 18 months. With the larger qaspeq, I'm hoping that my efforts will also honor the advocacy work happening all over North America. This work has been driven by the efforts of Native women and it's important to acknowledge that. Visibility is a step toward changing social attitudes. It has been featured on Alaska channels 2 and 11, the Juneau Empire, First Alaskans magazine, First Americans magazine, and was present during testimony in Juneau for H.R. 10 in support of Savanna's Act and continued funding for VAWA. The resolution passed unanimously.[246]

—Amber Webb, Yup'ik Artist, Creator of the Memorial Qaspeq

---

[246] Amber Webb, *Individual Action: Shifting the Cultural Balance to Respect and Awareness*, Restoration Magazine, Vol. 17, Issue 1, at 44-45 (2020). Photo courtesy of Loren Holmes / AND).

National Day of Awareness for Missing and Murdered Indigenous Women

Respect is the foundation of safety for Alaska Native women. To end the crisis of missing and murdered Alaska Native women, respect must be restored. Efforts to restore the respect of Native women can take many paths, including increased public awareness efforts. Tribal efforts across the United States and internationally have brought this crisis into the public's eye. This increase in awareness is reflected in the annual National Day of Awareness for Missing and Murdered Indigenous Women with social justice actions on May 5. AKNWRC actively supported and participated in national and state awareness efforts.

The U.S. Congressional effort was launched in 2017 by the Senators from Montana after the murder of Hanna Harris on the Northern Cheyenne Reservation and other abductions and killings of Native women. The 2017 Senate Resolution calling for a National Day of Awareness for Missing and Murdered Native Women and Girls marked the first Congressional recognition of MMIW as a national issue.

Every year since 2017, a resolution recognizing May 5, as a National Day of Awareness for Missing and Murdered Native Women and Girls has been passed in the Senate. It is the hope of national policymakers and Indian tribes across the country that the National Day of Awareness activities will support further reforms to address the crisis of MMIW.[247] The mother of Hanna Harris and other families of MMIW are very active in organizing these National Day of Awareness social justice actions.

> As a mother, nothing will replace the loss of my daughter, but I know that by organizing today's walk and working to support the National Day of Awareness, this will create changes that will help others. And Hanna and so many others will not be forgotten.[248]
>
> —Malinda Limberhand, Mother of Hanna Harris

State governments are also beginning to recognize and respond to the crisis of MMIW. These changes are reflected in actions by city, county, state, and national legislative bodies. They have introduced and passed legislation such as establishing an MMIW Task Force to respond, creating and funding state positions to monitor MMIW cases within the state, proclamations recognizing

---

[247] https://www.congress.gov/116/bills/sres144/BILLS-116sres144ats.pdf.

[248] Malinda Limberhand, *A Mother's Walk for Justice,* Restoration Magazine, Vol. 15, Issue 2, at 23-26 (2018).

the National Day of Awareness, authorizing and funding a study, and other actions. The state of Alaska issued a statewide MMIP proclamation in 2022.[249]

These actions are urgently needed at the tribal, state, and national levels. Legislative reforms hold the potential to save the lives of Native women and girls vulnerable to such violence as these changes support the cultural norms of respect for women.

> This morning, as we witnessed the posting of the colors, I saw that POW-MIA flag, and a thought occurred to me that it's about time we start posting that red flag for MMIW. Many women die in the battlefields and warzones of their everyday lives. I would also like to encourage that we begin to use the Women's Warrior Song when we start meetings such as this.[250]
> —Catherine Edwards, Vice President (one of six), Central Council of Tlingit and Haida Indian Tribes of Alaska

Fatality Risk Factors to Consider in Developing a Tribal Response

The murders of Alaska Native women are statements of the potential lethality and danger of domestic violence. From these cases, we understand that murder is part of the spectrum of domestic violence that can hopefully be prevented with recognition and resources to strengthen tribal responses. In developing a tribal domestic violence response, the potential dangers should be considered and included in safety planning for the victim, her loved ones, and her community.

Reviewing the list of domestic violence fatality risk factors developed nationally and with Canadian First Nations women is helpful to understanding the potential lethality of domestic violence cases.[251] Comparing an abuser's behavior to the list below might help victims realize their safety is at risk. But, the presence or absence of any or all these factors is not a guarantee of lethality or safety. These risk factors are not ranked in any order.

- Threats of homicide or suicide
- Stalking

---

[249] https://gov.alaska.gov/newsroom/2022/05/05/missing-and-murdered-indigenous-people-awareness-day/

[250] *Statement Central Council Tlingit and Haida Indian Tribes of Alaska,* U.S. DOJ 2018 Violence Against Women Annual Consultation, Restoration Magazine, Vol. 15, Issue 3, at 42 (2018).

[251] Alberta Council of Women's Shelters with Dr. Jacquelyn Campbell, *Walking the Path Together Tools: Danger Assessment,* 2012. https://nursing.jhu.edu/faculty_research/research/projects/DA-I/Walking_the_Path_DA.pdf. Pennsylvania Coalition Against Domestic Violence, *Lethality Assessment,* 2018. http://www.pcadv.org/Learn-More/Domestic-Violence-Topics/Fatalities/DV-Fatality-Risk-Factors/

- Previous physical assaults
- Access to firearms
- Separation/estrangement
- Strangulation during previous assaults
- Access to victims
- Public display of violence toward the victim
- History of sexual violence
- Destruction of property
- Jealousy and possessiveness
- Controlling of the victim's daily activities and contact with others
- Drug or alcohol consumption
- Prior calls to the police
- Pet abuse
- Lack of respect for the law
- Obsessed with partner or family
- Intimidation/threats
- Witnessed intimate partner abuse as a child
- Depression or other acute mental health problems
- Unemployment
- Victim has children who are not the abuser's

Tribal Recommendations to Address the MMIW Crisis

- Tribal Access Program (TAP) is available for tribes to access NCIC. Entering and accessing information from NCIC is essential in utilizing the information contained in NCIC.
- Report MMIW cases to local law enforcement and the National Missing and Unidentified Persons Systems (NamUs) database.
- Support the inclusion of fatality reviews in the case of domestic violence homicides.
- Support and include access to advocacy services in domestic violence cases and sexual assault cases.
- If the tribe has a sexual assault code, carefully review it to ensure it reflects the community's values and standards.
- Review federal programs available to support developing and strengthening the tribe's response to domestic violence, such as the Tribal Victim of Crime Act.
- Explore utilizing the Federal Emergency Management Agency's Integrated Public Alert and Warning System (IPAWS) to create alerts.

Quick Facts
Homicide and American Indian and Alaska Native Women

In 2020, Alaska:

- had the highest homicide rate in the United States for female victims killed by male offenders for the seventh year in a row, and
- has ranked either first or second for 10 years in a row.[252]

In 2020, the rate of American Indian/Alaska Native women killed in Alaska was:

- 12.63 per 100,000 women, which is three and a half times the rate of all women in Alaska, and
- 10 times the rate for white women in Alaska.[253]

From 2011-2020, American Indian/Alaska Native women in Alaska had the highest rate of homicide across racial groups, 20.4 per 100,000 persons.[254]

In 2017, homicide was the sixth leading cause of death among American Indian and Alaska females between 1 and 44 years of age.[255]

From 2003-2008, Alaska Native women were 39.8% of the violent deaths[256] and 38% of homicide victims.[257]

Alaska is one of five states with the highest number of MMIW cases.[258]

Federal agencies do not have a consistent way to collect data on the MMIW crisis, as is demonstrated below by the data from different federal government agencies. However, one thing we know for sure is that the rate is disproportionately high, especially in Alaska, and there is concern that there is

---

[252] *When Men Murder Women, An Analysis of 2020 Homicide Data*, at 6, Violence Policy Center (2022). https://vpc.org/studies/wmmw2022.pdf

[253] *Id.*

[254] *AKVDRS Homicide Victim Update—Alaska, 2011-2020*, at 3, State of Alaska Epidemiology (2023). http://www.epi.alaska.gov/bulletins/docs/rr2023_01.pdf?utm_medium=email&utm_source=govdelivery

[255] *Leading Causes of Death – Female by Age Group – Non-Hispanic American Indian or Alaska Native – United States, 2018*, at 1, Centers for Disease Control and Prevention (2018). *https://www.cdc.gov/women/lcod/2018/nonhispanic-native/index.htm#age-group*

[256] *Alaska Violent Death Reporting System 2003-2008,* at 4, Table 1.2: Victim Count, Percent, and Rate of Violent Death by Gender Race and Ethnicity (2011). http://dhss.alaska.gov/dph/Epi/injury/Documents/akvdrs/assets/AKVDRS.pdf

[257] *Id.* at 17, Table 3.2.

[258] Annita Lucchesi and Abigail Echo-Hawk, *Missing and Murdered Indigenous Women & Girls, A snapshot of data from 71 urban cities in the United States*, at 10, Urban Indian Health Institute (2018). http://www.uihi.org/wp-content/uploads/2018/11/Missing-and-Murdered-Indigenous-Women-and-Girls-Report.pdf

an underreporting of actual cases given the corresponding public safety crisis in Alaska.[259]

The FBI reports 5,712 cases of missing and murdered Indigenous women were reported in the United States as of 2016.[260]

BIA statistics show nationally that approximately 1,500 American Indian and Alaska Native missing persons have been entered into the National Crime Information Center. Approximately 2,700 cases of Murder and Nonnegligent Homicide Offenses have been reported to the federal government's Uniform Crime Reporting Program. In total, BIA estimates there are about 4,200 missing and murdered cases that have gone unsolved.[261]

The disparity between the number of known MMIW cases and the number reported in the federal crime systems, as demonstrated by the above references, is an ongoing concern raised continuously by tribal leaders.

---

[259] attorney-general-william-p-barr-announces-emergency-funding-address-public-safety-crisis

[260] National Crime Information Center (2018). Federal Bureau of Investigation.

[261] https://www.bia.gov/service/mmu/missing-and-murdered-indigenous-people-crisis

Did you know?

1. Under VAWA 2005, Congress recognized the importance of understanding the crisis of violence against Native women and provided for research on the murder of Native women under a national baseline study. It directed the National Institute of Justice to develop a program of research on violence against American Indian women, and the statute lists "murder" as an area to be studied.

2. In 2017, and every year since, the U.S. Senate passed a resolution calling for a National Day of Awareness for Missing and Murdered Native Women and Girls. The hope of national policymakers and Indian tribes across the country is that the National Day of Awareness activities will support further reforms to address the crisis of MMIW. The mother of Hanna Harris and other families of MMIW are very active in organizing these National Day of Awareness social justice actions.

3. In 2020, the U.S. Congress passed the Savanna's Act in response to the murder of Savanna LaFontaine-Greywind. The Act aims to improve tribal access to federal crime information databases, such as the NCIC. It requires data collection on missing and murdered Native people. The Act also calls on the U.S. DOJ to develop law enforcement and justice protocols to address missing persons. Finally, it requires an annual report to Congress.

4. In 2020, the U.S. Congress passed the Not Invisible Act (NIA) to address the crisis of missing, murdered, and trafficked Native people by engaging law enforcement, tribal leaders, federal partners, and service providers and improving coordination across federal agencies. The NIA established an advisory commission of local, tribal, and federal stakeholders to make recommendations to the U.S. DOI and U.S. DOJ on best practices to combat the epidemic of disappearances, homicide, violent crime, and trafficking of Native Americans and Alaska Natives.

Questions to consider:

1. Villages are often frustrated with state law enforcement's slow response to missing and murdered Alaska Native women. What changes are needed to improve the state's response to reports of missing and murdered Native women?

2. The actual number of missing and murdered Native women in Alaska is unknown. What changes are needed to create a system to accurately gather and understand the number of missing Alaska Native women?

3. As a movement, we are not only concerned about the state's response after a woman goes missing or is murdered. We want to make changes to prevent a woman from going missing or being killed. Will increased advocacy services—both advocacies designed by and for Native victims and designed by non-Native for Native victims—for domestic violence victims help prevent future disappearances and murders? What changes or services can villages offer to prevent women from going missing or being murdered?

Chapter 9
VAWA 2022 and Alaska Tribal Public Safety

> *At this moment, we acknowledge that it takes a "village to raise a child," and Congress has heard the voices of those harmed by centuries of injustices from failed laws and policies that have created a crisis in our tribal communities. With the inclusion of the Alaska Tribal Public Safety Empowerment section, the new law recognizes the inherent authority of Alaska Native tribes. It provides much-needed resources to protect our citizens from domestic violence and other related crimes under certain conditions. While there is much work to be done, we want to take this moment to pause and celebrate what this law can mean to our communities.* [262]
>
> *—Tami Truett Jerue, Executive Director, AKNWRC*

Overview of VAWA 2022

The Violence Against Women Act Reauthorization Act of 2022 (VAWA 2022) was signed into law by President Biden on March 15, 2022.[263] The Act consists of many important provisions for tribal governments nationally and a dedicated new section for those in Alaska, including amendments to the scope of jurisdiction that can be exercised over non-Indian offenders.

The VAWA 2022 contains provisions that Tribal leaders, advocates, and communities have raised for decades. Tribes have highlighted these issues since the beginning of annual consultations addressing violence against Indian women mandated under VAWA 2005. These provisions are changes to federal law needed to increase the safety of Native women. The Tribal Title of VAWA 2022[264] continues to follow previous VAWA reauthorizations by addressing the legal barriers denying tribal victims access to the same laws and services others receive from state governments. VAWA 2022 also increases access to federal criminal justice data systems and additional resources for American Indian and Alaska Native tribes implementing the jurisdiction.

> Our tribal title closes loopholes, builds upon the success of the 2013 reauthorization, and includes specific solutions to protect Alaska Native people. The tribal title will further restore and improve the implementation of the special tribal criminal jurisdiction over non-Indians who commit violent crimes in Native communities. And it

---

[262] Tami Truett Jerue, Executive Director, Alaska Native Women's Resource Center.

[263] Consolidated Appropriations Act, 2022, H.R. 2741–792. https://www.congress.gov/117/bills/hr2471/BILLS-117hr2471enr.pdf

[264] VAWA 2022, Title VIII, Division W, Safety for Indian Women, 847-862, Tribal jurisdictional provisions of H.R. 2471, codified into 25 U.S.C. 25 U.S.C.§§ 1304.

would do so by allowing Tribes who exercise this special jurisdiction to charge defendants with crimes that co-occur with domestic violence, such as violence against children or assault on law enforcement.[265]—Senator Lisa Murkowski

VAWA was enacted in 1994 and has been reauthorized four times since—in 2000, 2005, 2013, and 2022. Each time VAWA has been reauthorized, it has included new provisions to address the high rates of violence against Native women. VAWA 2022 includes two tribal subtitles. The first, Subtitle A–Tools to Enhance Public Safety for Indian Tribes, addresses amendments for tribal governments in general. The second, Subtitle B–Alaska Tribal Public Safety Empowerment, addresses and applies to only tribal governments in Alaska. The two subtitles are summarized below.

Summary Key Provisions of Subtitle A–Tools to Enhance Public Safety for Indian Tribes

Sec. 801. Findings and purposes. This section takes note of the very high rates of violence against Native women and the need for additional efforts on the part of Federal, State, Tribal, and local governments to address this violence.

Sec. 802. Tribal Access Program. This section provides formal authorization for the U.S. DOJ Tribal Access Program (TAP) and authorizes $6 million annually through 2027 to support it. TAP aims to facilitate tribal access to the federal criminal information databases for criminal justice and other authorized purposes. It also amends 34 USC 41101 to empower Tribes to enact laws authorizing access to Federal Bureau of Investigation (FBI) criminal history record information for tribally-authorized background check purposes.[266]

Sec. 803. Bureau of Prisons Tribal Prisoner Program. This section permanently authorizes the former Bureau of Prisons (BOP) Pilot Program that required the federal BOP to house certain inmates sentenced in tribal court. To be eligible for the program, the offender must have been sentenced to more than one year for a violent crime. The program is limited to 100 tribally-sentenced inmates at any time and includes a provision directing BOP to notify Congress if tribal demand exceeds 100 inmates. VAWA 2022 directs the BOP to establish the program within 120 days of the date of enactment of VAWA 2022, which was March 15, 2022. Indian tribes in Alaska will now have the option of housing inmates sentenced to more than one year in a federal BOP facility.

---

[265] Senator Lisa Murkowski, press release on Dec. 12, 2021. https://www.murkowski.senate.gov/press/release/murkowski-commits-to-vawa-reauthorization-

[266] As of FY 2021, three tribes in Alaska are in progress with the Tribal Access Program (TAP). https://www.justice.gov/file/1433651/download

Sec. 804. Tribal jurisdiction over covered crimes. This section includes amendments to 25 USC 1304, which was initially enacted as part of VAWA 2013 and reaffirmed tribal jurisdiction over certain non-Indian offenders. These VAWA 2022 amendments will apply to Indian tribes in Alaska that are participating tribes under the Alaska Pilot Program discussed below. The amendments that will take effect on October 1, 2022, include:

- Replacement of the term special domestic violence criminal jurisdiction (SDVCJ) with the term special tribal criminal jurisdiction (STCJ);
- New categories of criminal conduct that Indian tribes can prosecute against non-Indians of sexual violence, stalking, sex trafficking, child violence, obstruction of justice, and assaults against justice personnel;
- Amendment of definitions of "domestic violence" and "dating violence" to give deference to how these terms may be defined in tribal law
- Clarification that for cases involving obstruction of justice or assaults against tribal justice personnel by a non-Indian, the tribe has jurisdiction even if the victim is also non-Indian;
- Remove the prior requirements under VAWA 2013 that the non-Indian live or work in the Indian country of the tribe or is in a qualifying relationship with a member of the tribe or non-member Indian resident;
- A new requirement that notice to defendants of their habeas corpus rights must be made in writing;
- Codify the requirement that defendants must exhaust their tribal court remedies before seeking habeas relief in federal court unless certain exceptions are met. This requirement is similar to habeas petitions arising out of state court proceedings under 18 USC 2254.

Section 804 also addresses tribal concerns regarding the essential resources Indian tribes need to fund the implementation of STCJ over non-Indian offenders. Section 804(h), titled Reimbursement and Grants to Tribal Governments, states the U.S. DOJ Attorney General may reimburse tribal governments for expenses incurred in exercising STCJ. Indian tribes participating in the Alaska Pilot Project are eligible to apply for reimbursement of funds under section 804(h). In addition, the Section provides a list of expenses eligible for reimbursement. Given the general need, tribal governments in Alaska have to develop and maintain services, these new resources are essential for tribal governments to implement STCJ over non-Indian offenders. U.S. DOJ is directed to consult with Indian tribes and promulgate rules for the reimbursement program before March 15, 2023. In addition, Congress increased the authorization of reimbursable funding to support the implementation of the STCJ from $5 million to $25 million. The Attorney General has one year from enactment to create a reimbursement program for eligible expenses to exercise STCJ.

Summary Subtitle B–Alaska Tribal Public Safety Empowerment

The VAWA 2022 reauthorization recognizes the challenges and disproportionate rate of sexual assault and domestic violence against Alaska Natives. It includes provisions specific to Alaska tribal governments.

The Alaska Tribal Subtitle is intended to increase safety for Alaska Native women by addressing jurisdictional barriers preventing Alaska Native women from full access to justice resources and safety. The sections in Subtitle B–Alaska Tribal Public Safety Empowerment, Sections 811- 813, addresses the systemic jurisdictional barriers faced by Alaska Native Villages created by federal law.

Congress, through this Subtitle, reaffirms the inherent authority of Alaska Indian tribes to address civil and criminal matters, including protection orders, involving all Indian persons in the village. Second, it created a pilot program for Alaska Native tribes to implement STCJ to exercise jurisdiction over non-Indians who commit the covered crimes within the specific area of the participating tribe. Third, it created two statutory mandates that provide for the inclusion of Indian tribes and accountability of the U.S. DOJ in implementing the Alaska Subtitle. The U.S. DOJ is mandated to establish an Alaska Tribal Public Safety Advisory Committee and submit to Congress a report describing the results of the Alaska Pilot Program for STCJ. In addition, Alaska tribes will be able to participate in funding that is included for the overall tribal title. The sections of the subtitle are summarized below in more detail, along with the statutory language.

Sec. 811 (a) Findings

The section provides Congressional findings that, for the first time since the original passage of VAWA 1995, specifically addresses Alaska Native women. The findings represent a clear congressional statement that violence against Alaska Native women is a national concern. The findings justify the creation of Subtitle B–Alaska Tribal Public Safety Empowerment in response to the disproportionate rates of domestic and sexual violence committed against Alaska Native women. The findings also recognize Alaska tribal governments are best positioned to effectively arrest, prosecute, and punish, and they should have the authority to do so or to work out voluntary agreements with each other and with local governments and the state on mutually beneficial terms. These findings reaffirm the unique legal relationship of the United States to Indian tribes and recognizes the federal trust responsibility to assist tribal governments in safeguarding the lives of Indian women.

Sec. 811(a) FINDINGS.—Congress finds that—

(1) according to the report of the Indian Law and Order Commission established by section 15 of the Indian Law Enforcement Reform Act (25 U.S.C. 2812), Alaska Native women—

(A) are overrepresented in the domestic violence victim population by 250 percent;

(B) in the State of Alaska, comprise—(i) 19 percent of the population of the State; but (ii) 47 percent of reported rape victims in the State; and

(C) as compared to the populations of other Indian Tribes, suffer the highest rates of domestic and sexual violence;

(2) most Alaska Native villages are located in remote areas that—

(A) are often inaccessible by road; and

(B) have no local law enforcement presence;

(3) the Commission referred to in paragraph (1)

(A) determined that the Alaska Department of Public Safety—(i) has primary responsibility for law enforcement in rural Alaska; but (ii) provides only 1 to 1.4 field officers per 1,000,000 acres; and

(B) recommended that "devolving authority to Alaska Native communities is essential for addressing local crime. Their governments are best positioned to effectively arrest, prosecute, and punish, and they should have the authority to do so-or to work out voluntary agreements with each other, and with local governments and the State on mutually beneficial terms"; and

(4) the unique legal relationship of the United States to Indian Tribes creates a Federal trust responsibility to assist Tribal governments in safeguarding the lives of Indian women.

Sec. 811 (b) Statutory Purposes

The stated statutory purposes reaffirm inherent tribal sovereignty and clarify the responsibilities of tribal, federal, and state officials to respond to these cases of violence against Alaska Native women. In addition, this section states that tribes in Alaska should be empowered to address and respond to these violent crimes against Native women. The purpose areas provide clarity for implementing the Subtitle linking the two purpose areas of increased coordination among tribal, state, and federal law enforcement to the empowerment of Indian tribes to effectively respond to the list of violent crimes.

> Sec. 811. (b) PURPOSES.—The purposes of this subtitle are—
> (1) to increase coordination and communication among Federal, State, Tribal, and local law enforcement agencies; and
> (2) to empower Indian Tribes to effectively respond to cases of domestic violence, dating violence, stalking, sex trafficking, sexual violence, and missing or murdered Alaska Natives through the exercise of special Tribal criminal jurisdiction.

Sec. 812. Definitions

The definitions section provides a statement of the meaning of the terms used in the Alaska Subtitle. Many of the terms used for the Alaska STCJ Pilot Program have the same meaning and reference as the Indian Civil Rights Act of 1968 (ICRA).[267] For example the terms assault of tribal justice personnel, covered crime, obstruction of justice, protection order, and violation of a protection order have the same meanings given to these terms under ICRA. Another example is the term "Village" means "the Alaska Native Village Statistical Area covering all or any portion of a Native village (as defined in section 3 of the Alaska Native Claims Settlement Act (43 U.S.C. 1602)), as depicted on the applicable Tribal Statistical Area Program Verification map of the Bureau of the Census."[268]

Sec. 813. Tribal Jurisdiction in Alaska

The "Tribal Jurisdiction in Alaska" section contains eight critical areas. While the "Alaska Pilot Program" is often the most frequently discussed, this section includes necessary legal clarifications reaffirming sovereignty and providing essential resources to implement the Alaska Tribal Subtitle. It requires the creation of an Alaska Tribal Public Safety Advisory Committee who is required to submit a report to Congress on the results of the Pilot Program five years after the passage of VAWA 2022. The various sections are summarized below.

Sec. 813(a) General.
In Section 813(a), Congress clarified any confusion regarding the authority of Indian tribes in Alaska over all Indians present in the respective village. The statute states, "Congress recognizes and affirms the inherent authority of any Indian tribe occupying a Village in the State to exercise criminal and civil jurisdiction over all Indians present in the Village."[269]

---

[267] 25 U.S.C. 1304(a).
[268] https://www.census.gov/geographies/reference-maps/2010/geo/tsap-verification-maps.html
[269] Sec. 813(a).

Sec. 813(b) Tribal Civil Jurisdiction to Enforce Protection Orders.
Since passage of VAWA in 1994 various local and state government agencies have challenged the authority of a tribal court to issue an order of protection, in some cases refusing to recognize the validity of an order of protection issued by a tribal court. Congress addressed this confusion by reaffirming tribal authority regarding orders of protection. Sec. 813(b) clearly states:

> (1) A court of any Indian tribe in the State shall have full civil jurisdiction to issue and enforce protection orders involving any person in matters—
> (A) arising within the Village of the Indian Tribe; or
> (B) otherwise within the authority of the Indian tribe.
>
> (2) The full civil jurisdiction to issue and enforce protection orders under paragraph (1) includes the authority to enforce protection orders through—
> (A) civil contempt proceedings;
> (B) exclusion of violators from the Village of the Indian tribe; and
> (C) other appropriate mechanisms.

Sec. 813(c) Special Tribal Criminal Jurisdiction (STCJ).
Under VAWA 2013, Alaska Indian tribes were excluded from exercising jurisdiction over non-Indians due to the Indian country requirement. In this section, Congress took steps to remove this legal barrier by recognizing and affirming the inherent power of self-government of Indian tribes participating in the Alaska Pilot Program to exercise STCJ over a non-Indian defendant. This jurisdictional authority is shared with the United States and the State. However, this tribal authority does not exist in cases where the victim is also a non-Indian. Fortunately, Congress created two exceptions to this rule when the non-Indian offense involves obstruction of justice or assault of tribal justice personnel.

Sec. 813(d) Pilot Program For STCJ Over Persons Who Are Not Indian.
Under this section, Congress created the vehicle by which an Indian tribe can exercise STCJ over non-Indian defendants in cases of covered crimes by creating the STCJ Pilot Program. The VAWA 2013 also provided a similar pilot program for SDVCJ that resulted in developing an inter-tribal working group by which tribes shared lessons and challenges concerning SDVCJ. Indian tribes, however, were not mandated to participate in the pilot to exercise SDVCJ over non-Indians, and it was not limited to a set number of tribes. It should be noted that this subsection does not alter or diminish the Alaska tribe's authority to exercise general jurisdiction over its citizens for other than the designated domestic violence crimes. In this pilot program section, Congress authorized the designation of up to five Alaska Tribes per year to be participating tribes.

An Indian tribe can request to be designated as a participating tribe in the program. Indian tribes have the option to form inter-tribal partnerships to participate jointly in the pilot program and will be considered as a single tribe.

This section requires the U.S. Attorney General to consult with affected Indian tribes and the Secretary of the U.S. DOI to develop the process to designate participating tribes. The U.S. DOJ must give pilot designation preference to Indian tribes occupying villages with a predominantly Indian population that lack a permanent state law enforcement physical presence. Again, like VAWA 2013 SDVCJ, it requires the U.S. DOJ to verify that for each Indian tribe seeking pilot designation their criminal justice system has adequate safeguards to protect defendants' rights in compliance with Indian Civil Rights Act (ICRA). The U.S. Attorney General will review the applications and select up to five tribes each year. This section limits participation in the pilot program to a total of 30 Indian tribes unless the U.S. DOJ submits an appropriate public and Congressional notice of its intention to designate additional Indian tribes as pilot participants.

Sec. 813(e) Sentences.
In this section, while recognizing alternative tribal forms of punishment, Congress provided three additional options for participating tribes to consider in cases of the sentence being more than one year. The expense of incarceration was one concern of Indian tribes in implementing VAWA 2013 SDVCJ, and these options partially address this concern. For sentences of more than one year, the tribal court may require the non-Indian defendant to serve a sentence at a tribal correctional facility approved by the BIA, at the expense of the U.S. Bureau of Prisons (BOP) at the nearest federal facility, or at the cost of the tribe but reimbursable at a facility approved by the state. Tribes can impose an alternative form of punishment as determined by tribal law.

Sec. 813(f) Memoranda of Agreement.
The section authorizes the U.S. DOJ and DOI to enter into a memoranda of agreement (MOA) with Indian Tribes participating in the pilot program and the state of Alaska. The agreement may include coordinating law enforcement activities and sharing resources, establishing cross-deputization arrangements, and addressing any other matters that will facilitate the successful implementation of the Alaska STCJ pilot program. The MOA can address other matters including incarceration of defendants, coordinating investigations, and prosecutions.

Sec. 813(g) Alaska Tribal Public Safety Advisory Committee.
This section requires the U.S. DOJ to establish an Alaska Tribal Public Safety Advisory Committee that will focus on improving the justice systems, crime prevention, and victim services of Indians Tribes and Alaska Natives. In the past, VAWA included the establishment of an advisory committee to ensure the direct involvement of Indian tribes in the guidance and development of ways to address priority issues. This committee will be a way for tribal leaders to voice their opinions on improving justice systems, crime prevention, and victim services for Native villages. In addition, it is intended to work to increase coordination among applicable law enforcement agencies. The committee will be composed of Indian tribes participating or aspiring to participate in the pilot project, tribal victim services programs, and tribal, state, and federal law enforcement departments. The travel expenses of committee members will be paid. The U.S. DOJ must establish the committee in consultation with the DOI, affected Indian Tribes, and the state of Alaska. Congress authorized funds to be appropriated for the committee's expenses, as necessary, for the fiscal years 2023 through 2027.

Sec. 813(h) Report to Congress.
This Section requires that not later than five years after the passage of VAWA 2022, the U.S. Attorney General submits to Congress a report describing the results of the Alaska pilot program for STCJ. The report must include any modifications to the law needed to improve law enforcement in villages. The report is to be drafted and submitted in consultation with "affected Indian tribes" and the Secretary of the Interior. VAWA was signed into law on March 15, 2022, and the report will be due no later than March 15, 2027.

Sec. 813(i) Applicability.
This section reaffirms that the Alaska STCJ pilot program maintains the jurisdictional authorities of the U.S., the State of Alaska, and Indian Tribes in Alaska. It states that the program does not limit, alter, expand, or diminish the civil or criminal jurisdiction of the U.S., the State of Alaska, or any Indian Tribe in Alaska. In addition, it does not create or eliminate any federal or state criminal jurisdiction over a village; or affect the U.S. authority (or any authority delegated by the U.S. to the State of Alaska) to investigate and prosecute a criminal violation in a village.

> Our goal with VAWA is to ensure that women are safe and that every victim has a path to justice. I'm proud that our legislation – which we crafted on a strong bipartisan basis – will soon become federal law. Due to the work of countless advocates and survivors, I'm confident it will improve lives and increase safety for women across the country.

In 2020, more than half of the women surveyed in Alaska had experienced intimate partner violence, sexual violence, or both in their lifetime. We know we have to address the ongoing crisis of violence – and now, the necessary resources are on the way to create safer communities for all women.[270]— Senator Lisa Murkowski

[270] Senator Murkowski, as quoted in press release, *Senate Passes Bipartisan Violence Against Women Act Reauthorization*, March 10, 2022. https://www.feinstein.senate.gov/public/index.cfm/press-releases?id=5227CD1D-A168-4A2D-A0A1-443F39FE109B

Did you know?

1. The findings of the Tribal Title of VAWA 2022 recognize Alaska tribal governments are best positioned to effectively arrest, prosecute, and punish, and they should have the authority to do so or to work out voluntary agreements with each other and with local governments and the state on mutually beneficial terms.

2. The second purpose of the Alaska Tribal Public Safety Empowerment Subtitle is to empower Indian Tribes to effectively respond to cases of domestic violence, dating violence, stalking, sex trafficking, sexual violence, and missing or murdered Alaska Natives through the exercise of special tribal criminal jurisdiction.

3. Under VAWA 2022, Congress took steps to recognize and affirm the inherent power of self-government of Indian tribes participating in the Alaska Pilot Program to exercise STCJ over a non-Indian defendant.

Questions to Consider:

1. How can the STCJ provision under VAWA 2022 support your tribal government in further addressing domestic violence and restoring the well-being of your village?

2. How can exercising STCJ further support survivors and increase safety for the whole community?

3. What support is needed to further understand and exercise STCJ in your village?

April 2020, Native Village of Emmonak, AK, Takurngailngq (Joann Horn), Executive Director of the Emmonak Women's Shelter, prepares for the May 5th, 2020, National Day of Awareness for Missing and Indigenous Women.

Chapter 10
Organizing to Restore the Safety of Native Women Through the Sovereignty of Indian Tribes in Alaska

> *Change will come from within our village, not the outside world. Yup'ik people, and other Alaska Natives, have lived here for thousands of years based on our belief of respect for all things. Domestic violence is the opposite of this belief we hold as Indigenous people.* [271]
>
> —*Nugange (Lenora "Lynn" Hootch)*
> *Executive Director, Yup'ik Women's Coalition*

Throughout the centuries, the Native peoples of Alaska have viewed the world from a position of respect for all things. From these Alaska Native worldviews, their beliefs, languages, teachings, cultural practices, and customary law developed over centuries and generations. The safety of Native women rested on this way of being.

> In the recovery framework "Honoring Our Strengths," culture is understood as the "outward expression of spirit," and revitalization of the spirit is a vital best practice to ensure health and well-being among Indigenous people. Recognition of the importance of ceremony, language and traditions help to focus on strengths and reconnection with oneself, their history, family, community, and land.[272]

Tribal leaders, advocates, and survivors are working in their villages to make the changes needed for villages as governments to develop a strong and immediate local response to domestic violence. As those who are committed to creating safety for themselves, their daughters, sisters, and mothers in their villages, they have established over the years, a close working relationship to achieve this goal. In this sense, their efforts to increase awareness, inform, and provide training on domestic violence to create the changes needed within villages is a social justice movement. The path forward for our movement has rested on an organizing strategy of increasing safety through strengthening the sovereignty of Indian tribes to protect women within their villages. For many, this social justice movement is the only public acknowledgement that the abuse is wrong; the only response to the violence they or a loved one has suffered.

---

[271] AKNWRC, *Increasing Safety for Alaska Native Women,* at 25 (2016).

[272] Donna M. Klingspohn, *The Importance of Culture in Addressing Domestic Violence for First Nation's Women,* 9 Front. Psychol., Article 872 (June 2018).

"Our villages can and have for centuries taken responsibility, and now is the time to let us do so again. The federal and state governments need to recognize that the old laws of the past need to be changed so villages can do so again." [273]
—Michael Williams Sr., Secretary/Treasurer, Akiak Native Community

"Our laws are in our hearts."[274]—Nettie Warbelow, Advocate, Village of Tetlin

While village-based responses are steadily developing, change is coming too slowly as lives are lost, and most abusers face no consequences for domestic violence and other crimes against Native women. The challenges created by history and current federal and state legal barriers continue to stall progress toward addressing the violence at the village level. Although the state and federal governments are more informed today than in the past, both continue to resist supporting the fundamental changes needed. The gauge of this resistance is seen in the ongoing reality that state troopers, as official first responders, are not available to immediately or adequately respond to domestic violence victims in most off-road rural Alaska villages. Even when available, such a response falls short of addressing safety and accountability from Alaska Native worldviews.

---

[273] Michael Williams Sr., Secretary/Treasurer, *Statement of the Akiak Native Community,* U.S. DOJ 2019 Violence Against Women Annual Government-to-Government Consultation (2019) (on file with AKNWRC).

[274] Tribal Court Roundtable, Fairbanks, Alaska (Nov. 2019) (transcript on file with the AKNWRC).

"Our children often are the first responders in many villages. We need to acknowledge this for change to happen."[275]—the late Shirley Moses, former Founder and Director, Healing Native Hearts Coalition

Recognizing the Right of Native Villages to Protect Women

"At the village level, we must address these issues because for most villages we are the only ones standing between a woman, or girl, and violence."[276]

—Tami Truett Jerue, Executive Director, AKNWRC

The foundation for the changes needed are the efforts within villages to understand domestic violence in the context of their own lived experience as a people—their specific history, teachings, beliefs, and customary laws. From this perspective, each village must decide what changes to make to create safety to respond to domestic violence and protect women. This understanding can be reached through a process of each village engaging from within itself as a people and as a tribal government.

Sovereignty is broadly defined as the right to govern oneself as a people. The Indigenous peoples of Alaska, in the face of foreign domination, never relinquished their authority as governments to protect their citizens. Over the years of aggression by outside governments, Russia, and the United States, the Indigenous peoples suffered devastating losses in lives, diminishment of their governments, destruction of their beliefs, loss of their languages, and attacks upon their traditional ways of life. Despite this history, Indigenous peoples who existed before the establishment of the United States continue to persevere and defend their authority to protect women and the right to self-government.

"We have an unending commitment to organize our movement and empower the messenger with resolve and hope to educate and create change at the federal and state level."—Michelle Demmert, Law and Policy Director, AKNWRC

Responding to Domestic Violence as Tribal Governments

The U.S. Supreme Court defined the nature of the relationship between Indian tribes and the United States early in U.S. history. In 1830, the Chief Justice of the Supreme Court recognized the internal sovereignty of Indian tribes writing in his opinion that they are "distinct, independent, political communities."[277]

---

275 Paula Julian, *Indigenous Organizing Approaches*, Restoration Magazine, Vol. 14, Issue 3, at 40 (2017).

276 *Id.* at 40.

277 *Worcester v. Georgia,* 31 U.S. (6 Pet.) 559-560 (1830).

While many changes have occurred since this early decision of the Supreme Court, this recognition of tribal sovereignty continues as a foundation of federal Indian law. It extends to all federally recognized Indian tribes, including the 229 Indian tribes in Alaska. Indian tribes, like state governments and the federal government, are recognized as sovereign governments. Alaska Native villages, as Tribal governments often without the needed resources that state and federal governments are afforded, have the authority to respond to domestic violence according to the decisions of their respective governments and worldview.

The U.S. Congress, since the passage of the Violence Against Women Act in 1994, has consistently recognized the authority and essential role of Alaska Indian tribes as governments to respond to violence against Native women. Through competitive and limited grant funding, the U.S. DOJ has provided funding to Alaska Indian tribes to exercise this authority and determine for themselves what responses to develop, including tribal justice systems consistent with Alaska Native customs and traditions, including but not limited to tribal courts and village police. Unfortunately, historically this funding has been inadequate.

Congress has appropriated limited funds under the annual budgets specifically to support Indian tribes in Alaska to enhance core components of their governmental response to domestic violence. The design of the village response is determined by each village government. If a tribe chooses to develop a western-based system, federal funds can support the hiring of advocates and the development of shelter and safe houses, tribal police, prosecutors, and judges, to assist domestic violence victims and hold abusers accountable. Funding is also available to support traditional tribal responses such as traditional advocates, Circles, Elders Councils, and other community-based processes that focus on the person or persons harmed, including community members, and repairing the harm while correcting the abusive behavior. The OVW funded 40 tribal governments of the 574 tribes in 2022.[278]

In addition, Congress under the Family Violence Prevention and Services Act (FVPSA), funds Indian tribes in Alaska as governments to support shelter and supportive services.[279] In 2018, Congress for the first time created a dedicated tribal program and appropriated 3%, totaling around $133 million, of the funding under the Crime Victims Fund for Indian tribes to assist victims of crime.[280] There are other federal statutes providing resources supporting the

[278] https://www.justice.gov/ovw/awards/fy-2021-ovw-grant-awards-program
[279] Family Violence Prevention and Services Act, 42 U.S.C. Ch. 110 § 10409. https://uscode.house.gov/view.xhtml?path=/prelim@title42/chapter110&edition=prelim
[280] Commerce, Justice, Science, and Related Agencies Appropriations Act, 2018, sec. 510. See also https://ovc.ojp.gov/sites/g/files/xyckuh226/files/media/document/tribalset-asideinformationalpaperfinal508.pdf

sovereign authority of Alaska Native villages to respond to domestic violence as governments.

Increased recognition of village authority to address violence against women and funding to support such efforts are the result of a strong village-based network of tribal advocates and leaders working in partnership to increase the safety of women. This movement of survivors, their families, advocates, and tribal leaders have worked hard to educate lawmakers and governmental entities on domestic violence and the crisis of violence against Alaska Native women. Their compelling testimonies and stories have resulted in legislative reforms amending federal law and creating new laws. These reforms reflect Congress' changing understanding of its responsibility and commitment to assist Indian tribes in Alaska in responding to violence against Native women.

Domestic violence is threatening the lives of Native women and their children. Advocates and tribal leaders understand villages have survived because of their teachings and beliefs that bind them together as Native people. The movement is working to increase safety using the teachings, laws, languages, and voices of survivors and advocates—all of which rests on respect. As a result, it also threatens the future stability of entire villages by undermining the traditional belief of respect for all things.

The reality that domestic violence is a pattern of intimate partner abuse based on power and control by the abuser, and disrespect and a learned belief that violence is a right of the abuser because of his personal relationship to his victim—I can use violence because she is mine—is in direct conflict with our Native way of life respecting all things. This view is destructive to our future existence as Indigenous peoples. It is much more than a crime. It is cultural genocide.

Because of the complicated jurisdictional structures created by federal laws, there is often no immediate response available for the immediate safety of the victim, her family, and the entire village. Domestic violence happens daily, and the state and federal public safety responses are not located in most villages. Existing outside of the villages, the state and federal governments are literally absent. They cannot provide an immediate response to domestic violence or other, often life-threatening, crimes of violence.

> As a government, we have the responsibility for the well-being of our people. For women, this includes being safe in their homes and in public. Like many villages depending upon the weather, entry into and out of our village by airline travel may be severely restricted for days or even weeks. I share this so you as federal representatives will understand the Asa'carsarmiut Tribe is typically in a position of being

> the only government in the geographic area to respond to crime. The state and the federal governments are not present to respond when a rape, domestic violence, murder, or other crime is committed.[281]
>
> —Catherine Moses, Asa'carsarmiut Indian Tribe

Developing Village-Based Responses to Protect Women

The path to increasing the safety of Native women is challenging because it requires the full participation of each village based on the authority of the village as a government. Often these governments lack the necessary resources available to more urban populations.[282] In our organizing to enhance village-based responses to domestic violence, certain core principles have emerged to provide the direction for the changes needed.

These principles include maintaining a focus on safety for Alaska Native women, holding abusers responsible for the abuse, and asserting the sovereign right of Alaska Native villages to respond to and protect victims of domestic violence from abusers. The hope for change rests in our knowledge as Alaska Natives that our teachings, languages, values, and laws reject abuse and violence as part of human life. Domestic violence and violence toward women have no place in our traditions as Indigenous peoples.

Creating changes to address domestic violence must come from within each village. A village as a government can create its own plan to address domestic violence. A village plan must be based on the reality of the village, not the outside world, state or federal governments, or western approaches that are not present in the village.

Village plans must address barriers facing the village such as lack of resources to fund employees, lack of law enforcement or justice or victim services, and rural isolation. For over a decade, tribal leadership during annual consultations with the United States has asked for the recognition and support needed to protect women in the villages from the violence of abusers and predators—but waiting for the outside world to protect a Native woman has never worked.

The AKNWRC through our experience has learned that increasing safety for Native women in villages is achieved through village engagement from within the community. The AKNWRC offers three actions for villages and advocates to consider in efforts to increase the village response to domestic violence.

---

[281] Catherine Moses, Tribal Administrator, *Statement of the Asa'carsarmiut Indian Tribe of Alaska*, U.S. DOJ 2018 Violence Against Women Annual Government-to-Government Consultation (on file with AKNWRC).

[282] André B. Rosay, *Violence Against American Indian and Alaska Native Women and Men*, at 50.

First, we seek to engage the village in the process of understanding domestic violence in the context of intimate partner violence.

Second, we work to develop prevention and public awareness materials based on the needs of the specific village using tribal values.

Third, we help craft an enhanced response to domestic violence based on the unique history, teachings, voices, language, law, and circumstances of each village.

"We are tribal citizens first and must work together to take care of ourselves."[283]
—Isabel Mills, Domestic Violence Program Coordinator
Organized Village of Kake, and Board Member, AKNWRC

Many survivors, their families, and communities have righteous anger regarding the state and federal justice systems' failure to protect Native women. The survivors, children who have lost their mothers, mothers and fathers who have lost daughters, and loved ones impacted by domestic violence, have common stories of grief and a lack of justice.

Violence against Native women is not the exception; it is a collective shared experience of trauma impacting all families with multiple victims. Many, the vast

[283] Paula Julian, *Indigenous Organizing Approaches*, Restoration Magazine, Vol. 14, Issue 3, at 40 (2017).

majority, have no closure to the grief caused by the abuse and violence. Public recognition of the crisis of violence may be their only comfort or recognition that the violence is beyond their individual actions. To these thousands of people, their righteous anger is a powerful call for justice that must be acknowledged and requires a response for accountability and healing.

The AKNWRC looks to the future with the hope of increasing the safety of Native women through a vision of increasing our understanding and organizing from within Indian tribes in Alaska to create the changes needed to restore respect and safety for Native women. The AKNWRC recognizes that many villages lack the resources to address domestic violence on their own. The state has failed to address domestic violence, and many believe nothing will ever be done even if they report the violence.

> There are three of us up here presenting; myself as state court magistrate, an Alaska State Trooper, and our Emmonak Women's Shelter Director. Look around the room at everyone here from the villages. There are more of you than there are of us. This is the reality. The solutions lie in all of you working with us to solve our problems and end domestic and sexual violence.[284]
>
> —Darlene Johnson, Alaska State Court Magistrate, Yup'ik Women's Coalition Sexual Assault Conference, April 25, 2017

The AKNWRC offers solutions to this crisis by determining and prioritizing reforms based on its engagement with villages. It organizes actions based on sharing what other tribes and villages have accomplished within their nations at the national and international levels and helps villages develop a tribal response. The solutions to address domestic violence at the village level must come from our tribal nations.

---

[284] Video, *Yup'ik Women's Coalition Sexual Assault Conference*, April 25, 2017.

"As a federally recognized Indian tribe we are the government representing our members. As a tribal government, we take responsibility for the safety and well-being regarding our 1,354 members such as health, education, and so many other things. The largest responsibility we have, in the context of this consultation, is to maintain a stable and safe community. Many of the challenges we faced as a tribe, and that we continue to face, are the legal barriers and challenges to our authority to fulfill these responsibilities."[285]

—Catherine Moses, Asa'carsarmiut Indian Tribe

Nancy Ellen Joe

The surface of your pain you have endured is a tale to tell.
The way your face would light up when you talked about what you love.
That is what people will forever remember.
That is the face you show the ones you love.
The pain you'd hide from others is a deep ocean in which not a soul shall know the pain.
Yet you smile as if yesterday's pain is something that is gone.
The days go on, the years, the centuries.
Yet, the generations after you will forever remember your strength.
Your picture bears a smile, which will never fade.

— Sadie Warbelow
Granddaughter of Nancy Ellen Joe, murdered in 1974

[285] Catherine Moses, Tribal Administrator, *Statement of the Asa'carsarmiut Indian Tribe*, U.S. DOJ 2018 Violence Against Women Annual Government-to-Government Consultation (on file with AKNWRC).

Did you know?

1. There are 229 federally recognized Indian tribes in Alaska, referred to as Alaska Native villages.

2. Alaska tribes never relinquished their sovereign authority of self-government to protect women.

3. Alaska Native villages as Indian tribes are eligible to receive federal funds to strengthen their response as governments to domestic violence. These efforts include support for indigenous and western justice approaches to hold abusers accountable, support domestic violence victims, increase community awareness, and enhance tribal response systems.

Questions to Consider:

1. How is your tribal government working to address domestic violence and to restore well-being in your village?

2. How are these efforts being organized to include survivors, elders, youth, and the community?

Timeline

Growth of a Movement for the Safety of Alaska Native and American Indian Women, 1977–2022*

1977

- The White Buffalo Calf Woman Society, a tribal women's advocacy organization on the Rosebud Sioux Indian reservation, establishes the first Native women's shelter on an American Indian reservation.[286]

1978

- The U.S. Commission on Civil Rights Consultation *Battered Women: Issues of Public Policy*, Jan. 30—31. Post-conference proceedings include over 700 pages of written and oral testimony to define the problems and address potential solutions, including the need for federal legislation. The document examines the need for a federal role in approaching domestic violence.[287] Tillie Black Bear testified during the hearings on wife-beating regarding domestic violence committed against Native women. She, and more than 600 persons who attended and observed the consultation formed the National Coalitions Against Domestic Violence.
- The National Coalition Against Domestic Violence is founded to provide advocacy and resources for victims of domestic violence.[288] Tillie Black Bear, Sicangu Lakota, serves as a founding mother and board member.

1979

- The first Alaska Native Village–based shelter, the Emmonak Women's Shelter, is founded in the Yukon Delta Region of Alaska.

1984

- The Family Violence Prevention and Services Act (FVPSA) is authorized, providing federal funding for the first time to help victims of domestic violence and their dependent children by providing support for shelters and related assistance.

1987

- The National Coalition Against Domestic Violence designates October as Domestic Violence Awareness Month.[289]

---

[286] About Us. (n.d.). *White Buffalo Calf Woman Society, Inc.* Retrieved September 4, 2012. http://www.wbcws.org/index_files/Page371.htm

[287] U.S. Commission on Civil Rights. (1978). *Battered Women: Issues of Public Policy.* Washington, DC: Government Printing Office. https://www.ojp.gov/pdffiles1/Digitization/53356NCJRS.pdf

[288] About NCADV. (n.d.). *National Coalition Against Domestic Violence.* Retrieved Sept. 4, 2012. https://ncadv.org/about-us

[289] Domestic Violence Awareness Month. (n.d.). *National Coalition Against Domestic Violence.* Accessed on Sept. 4, 2012. from http://www.ncadv.org/takeaction/DomesticViolenceAwarenessMonth.php

1990

- Senator Joe Biden introduces the first version of the VAWA to the Senate.

1991

- American Indians Against Abuse is incorporated as the first tribal coalition representing all 11 tribes of Wisconsin.

1993

- The United Nations adopted the Declaration on Elimination of Violence Against Women, the first international instrument explicitly addressing violence against women, to strengthen and complement the UN Convention on the Elimination of All Forms of Discrimination Against Women with a provision "Concerned that some groups of women, such as ... indigenous women ... are especially vulnerable to violence."[290]

1994

- VAWA is reintroduced in Congress, enacted with bipartisan support, and signed into law on September 13th by President Bill Clinton.
- The Inter-American Convention on the Prevention, Punishment, and Eradication of Violence Against Women is adopted during a Special Session of the General Assembly of the Organization of American States (OAS). To date, it has been ratified by 34 countries in the Americas.[291]

1995

- The Department of Justice creates the Violence Against Women Grants Office to implement VAWA grant programs and the Violence Against Women Policy Office. Alaska Native villages are included as eligible entities to receive funding under the new Grants to Indian Tribes Program.[292]
- The United Nations 4th World Conference on Women is held in Beijing, China. The Beijing Declaration included the goal to "prevent and eliminate all forms of violence against women and girls."[293]

2000

- VAWA is reauthorized in a bipartisan manner and signed into law by President Clinton. It creates the first federal funding stream for Tribal Domestic Violence and Sexual Assault Coalitions.

2003

- Based on discussions with Sacred Circle, Clan Star, Inc. and tribal domestic violence and sexual assault coalitions, the National Congress of American Indians establishes a National Task Force on Violence Against Native Women.

---

[290] https://digitallibrary.un.org/record/179739?ln=en

[291] Inter-American Convention on the Prevention, Punishment and Eradication of Violence Against Women (1994). http://www.oas.org/juridico/english/treaties/a-61.html

[292] *The History of the Violence Against Women Act* (2009), USDOJ, Office on Violence Against Women (2009). http://www.ovw.usdoj.gov/docs/history-vawa.pdf

[293] United Nations Fourth World Conference on Women (1995). http://www.un.org/womenwatch/daws/beijing/platform/index.html

- Clan Star, Inc. organized a delegation of tribal domestic violence and sexual assault coalitions and hosted a cultural exchange with Māori advocates in Wellington and Rotorua, Aotearoa (New Zealand), including meetings with the Ministry of Women's Affairs, and Māori Members of Parliament.

2005

- VAWA is reauthorized in a bipartisan manner by Congress and signed into law by President George Bush on January 5, 2006. It includes the first title dedicated to Indian Women's safety, including the statutory authority and duties of a Tribal Deputy Director.

2007

- A coalition of indigenous organizations and individuals submits a collaborative report to the UN Committee on the Elimination of Racial Discrimination (CERD) on the United States' obligations to indigenous peoples, raising the fact that Native women in the U.S. are victims of rape and sexual violence at much higher rates than any other group of women in this country, that most assailants are non-Indians, and that the current criminal jurisdictional scheme created by U.S. law impedes the ability of Indian nations to protect their citizens.[294] The United States ratified the International Convention for the Elimination of All Forms of Racial Discrimination (CERD Convention) in 1994.
- The UN General Assembly adopted the UN Declaration on the Rights of Indigenous Peoples on September 13, 2007, with four countries opposing the Declaration, including the United States.

2008

- A delegation of Native women leaders and other experts[295] attend the February session of CERD in Geneva to highlight the shocking rates of violence against Native women in the United States, and the United States' failure to provide basic law enforcement services in many Native communities.
- CERD responds by issuing Concluding Observations and Recommendations, expressing concern about the high incidence of violence experienced by American Indian and Alaska Native women, and urging the United States to increase its efforts to prevent and punish violence and abuse against Native women in particular.
- Indian organizations, Native women's organizations, tribes, and others working to end violence against Native women file an amicus brief with the Inter-American Commission on Human Rights in support of the plaintiff

---

[294] *Report of the Working Group on Indigenous Peoples*, submitted to CERD in December 2007 as part of a national report by non-governmental organizations.

[295] The delegation included Vikki Shirley, Navajo Nation First Lady and Navajo Nation Domestic Violence Task Force, Juana Majel Dixon, Pauma Band of Mission Indians and Co-Chair of the NCAI Task Force on Violence Against Native Women, Terri Henry, Director of Clan Star, Inc., and a member of the NCAI Task Force on Violence Against Native Women, and Virginia Davis, Associate Counsel for the NCAI.

in *Jessica Lenahan (Gonzales) v. United States,* the first individual case brought by a victim of domestic violence against the United States for international human rights violations.[296]

2009

- President Obama declares April as Sexual Assault Awareness Month.
- The United States signs into law the Apology to Native Americans recognizing the "years of official depredations, ill-conceived policies, ... many instances of violence, maltreatment, and neglect inflicted on Native peoples."

2010

- The National Indigenous Women's Resource Center is founded.
- President Obama announces the United States' support for the UN Declaration on the Rights of Indigenous Peoples, which is no longer opposed by any country. The Declaration is a powerful affirmation of indigenous rights, including the rights of Native women, as individuals and members of indigenous communities, to gender equality, security of the person, and access to justice. Article 22 of the Declaration is significant for Native women, calling on countries to pay "particular attention" to their special needs and rights in implementing the Declaration and to "take measures, in conjunction with indigenous peoples, to ensure that indigenous women and children enjoy the full protection and guarantees against all forms of violence and discrimination."
- The La Jolla Band of Luiseno Indians Avellaka Domestic Violence Program's video on violence against Native women as human rights violations to the Testify Project is shown as part of the Universal Periodic Review of the U.S.' human rights record of violations in Geneva, Switzerland.

2011

- A UN Special Rapporteur on Violence Against Women, Its Causes and Consequences, visits the Eastern Band of Cherokee Indians to examine violence against American Indian women, marking the first visit on tribal lands in the United States,[297] and presents her final report to the UN General Assembly recommending how the United States should prevent and remedy the epidemic of violence against Native women, including restoring tribal authority over all perpetrators who commit acts of sexual or domestic violence on tribal lands.

---

[296] The Indian Law Resource Center and Sacred Circle National Resource Center to End Violence Against Native Women filed the amicus brief with the Inter-American Commission on Human Rights in support of the plaintiff in *Jessica Lenahan (Gonzales) v. United States* on behalf of numerous nonprofit organizations and tribal governments working to end violence against Native women.

[297] The visit was co-hosted by NCAI, Clan Star, Inc., Indian Law Resource Center, and Sacred Circle National Resource Center to End Violence Against Native Women.

- At the request of Native women and Indian organizations,[298] the Inter-American Commission on Human Rights holds a first-ever thematic hearing in Washington, DC, on violence against Native women in the United States. The Commission issued an annex to the press release noting its receipt of troubling information about violence against indigenous women and urging countries to diligently address all forms of violence against women.
- The Inter-American Commission on Human Rights issues a landmark decision in *Jessica Lenahan (Gonzales) v. United States*, the first women's human rights case involving domestic violence brought against the United States. The Commission found the United States violated its obligations under international human rights laws by failing to protect Ms. Lenahan and her daughters from violence by her estranged husband. The Commission's decision acknowledges that domestic violence has a disproportionate impact on Native women and takes notice of the amicus brief filed by Indian and Native women's organizations on behalf of many nonprofit organizations and tribal governments.[299]
- The NCAI Task Force on Violence Against Native Women, Sacred Circle National Resource Center to End Violence Against Native Women, and the Indian Law Resource Center submit comments to the State Department on violence against Native women to inform the United States' next report to CERD on its compliance.
- The Senate Committee on Indian Affairs held a hearing on "Setting the Standard: Domestic Policy Implications of the UN Declaration on the Rights of Indigenous Peoples."
- Senate Committee Indian Affairs Chairman Daniel K. Akaka (D-HI) introduces S. 1763, the Stand Against Violence and Empower Native Women (SAVE Native Women) Act.

2012

- The UN Permanent Forum on Indigenous Issues holds an International Expert Group Meeting in New York City on violence against indigenous women and girls addressing mandates under Article 22 of the UN Declaration on the Rights of Indigenous Peoples. As an invited international Indigenous expert, Terri Henry, Tribal Councilwoman for Eastern Band of Cherokee Indians, and Co-Chair of the NCAI Task Force on Violence Against Native Women, discusses the epidemic of violence against Native women in the U.S. and how the United States is failing to

[298] The request for the hearing was filed by the Indian Law Resource Center, on behalf of itself, the NCAI Task Force on Violence Against Native Women, Clan Star, Inc., and the National Indigenous Women's Resource Center.

[299] The Indian Law Resource Center and Sacred Circle National Resource Center to End Violence Against Native Women filed an amicus brief with the Inter-American Commission on Human Rights in support of the plaintiff in *Jessica Lenahan (Gonzales) v. United States*, on behalf of numerous nonprofit organizations and tribal governments working to end violence against Native women.

meet its human rights obligations under the Declaration.

- VAWA 2011 is debated in Congress. Different versions of VAWA passed in the Senate and in the House of Representatives. Congress failed to reauthorize VAWA, and the Act remained expired for over 500 days due in part to opposition to restoring limited criminal jurisdiction to Indian tribes over non-Indians committing domestic violence, dating violence, and violating an order of protection on tribal lands.
- A Special Rapporteur on the Rights of Indigenous Peoples conducts the first mission to the United States and issues a report to the UN Human Rights Council acknowledging the alarmingly high rates of violence against Native women in this country and recommending that the U.S. Congress place an immediate priority on legislation, such as VAWA.
- The UN General Assembly adopts a resolution calling for the organization of a high-level plenary meeting to be known as the World Conference on Indigenous Peoples, held on September 22–23, 2014, in New York.

2013

- Two international human rights experts call on the United States to reauthorize the Violence Against Women Act, following the Senate's passing of a strengthened bipartisan bill.[300] Rashida Manjoo, Special Rapporteur on Violence Against Women, Its Causes, and Consequences, and James Anaya, Special Rapporteur on the Rights of Indigenous Peoples, emphasize the need for tribal provisions that would enhance protections for Native American and Alaska Native women.
- The UN Permanent Forum on Indigenous Issues releases documents for its 12th Session, including an advance unedited version of a study "on the extent of violence against indigenous women and girls in terms of Article 22(2) of the UN Declaration on the Rights of Indigenous Peoples."[301] The study adopts recommendations issued by the Permanent Forum's international expert group meeting, held in 2012, on violence against indigenous women and girls.
- President Obama signs into law the Violence Against Women Reauthorization Act of 2013, on March 7, 2013, restoring limited criminal jurisdiction of certain Indian tribes over non-Indians in cases of domestic violence and other important tribal amendments.
- The Indian Law and Order Commission issues "A Roadmap for Making Native America Safer, Report to the President & Congress of the United States" with a specific chapter dedicated to Alaska tribal issues as a national

---

[300] *USA: UN rights experts call on Congress to reauthorize the Violence Against Women Act*, United Nations Human Rights, Office of the High Commissioner for Human Rights (Feb. 19, 2013). http://www.ohchr.org/EN/NewsEvents/Pages/DisplayNews.aspx?NewsID=13012&LangID=E

[301] *Study on the extent of violence against indigenous women and girls in terms of article 22(2) of the UN Declaration on the Rights of Indigenous Peoples.* http://www.un.org/esa/socdev/unpfii/documents/2013/E_C19_2013_9.pdf

concern.[302]

- Advocates and tribal leaders have joined together during the Alaska Federation of Natives (AFN) to share, inform, and develop a joint response to address violence against women. The annual convention of AFN is a meeting point for the largest number of Indian tribes in Alaska. In 2013, violence against women received focused attention by AFN with the passage of the Protect Native Women resolution.[303]

2014

- President Obama signs into law the Repeal of Sec. 910, Title IX, VAWA, that limited Alaska Indian tribes, except one for one tribe, from exercising the expanded domestic violence criminal jurisdiction under VAWA 2013.

2016

- The Alaska Native Women's Resource Center is founded.
- The Healing Native Hearts Coalition is founded as a tribal coalition addressing domestic violence and sexual assault to serve the 37 Alaska Native villages and Native non-profits in Interior Alaska. HNHCoalition.org

2017

- The governor of Alaska recognized Indian tribes, but it has yet to be codified in Alaska law. "The law is clear. There are 229 Alaska tribes, and they are separate sovereigns with inherent sovereignty and subject matter jurisdiction over certain matters. Indian country is not a prerequisite for Alaska Tribe's inherent sovereignty or subject matter jurisdiction, but it may impact the extent of that jurisdiction."[304]

2020

- On Oct. 10, 2020, the Not Invisible Act of 2019 is signed into law to address the crisis of missing, murdered, and trafficked Native people by engaging law enforcement, tribal leaders, federal partners, and service providers and improving coordination across federal agencies. The Not Invisible Act established an advisory commission of local, tribal, and federal stakeholders to make recommendations to the U.S. DOI and U.S. DOJ on best practices to combat the epidemic of disappearances, homicide, violent crime, and trafficking of Native Americans and Alaska Natives. It is the first bill in history to be introduced and passed by four U.S. congressional members enrolled in their respective federally recognized Tribes, led by Secretary Deb Haaland during her time in Congress.[305]

---

302 Indian Law and Order Commission, *A Roadmap for Making Native America Safer: Report to the President and Congress of the United States* (2013). http://www.aisc.ucla.edu/iloc/report

303 Alaska Federation of Natives, 2013 Annual Convention, *Protect Native Women Resolution 12-14*, submitted by the Village of Tetlin, Kenaitze Indian Tribe, Village of Dot Lake, and the Village of Anvik.

304 State of Alaska Attorney General, *Opinion Letter Legal Status of Tribal Governments in Alaska* (Oct. 19, 2017). http://www.law.state.ak.us/pdf/opinions/opinions_2017/17-004_JU20172010.pdf

305 Not Invisible Act, S. 982. https://www.congress.gov/116/bills/s982/BILLS-116s982enr.pdf. https://www.congress.gov/116/crpt/srpt214/CRPT-116srpt214.pdf

- On Oct. 10, 2020, Savanna's Act is signed into law to improve the federal response to missing or murdered indigenous persons (MMIP), including by increasing coordination among federal, state, tribal, and local law enforcement agencies.[306]

2022

- Reauthorization of the Violence Against Women's Act with an Alaska specific title.[307]
- Not Invisible Act Commission begins active advisory role in combating violence against Native People.
- Alaska legislation passed into law acknowledging Alaska tribes are federally recognized.

*This expanded timeline was originally developed by the National Indigenous Women's Resource Center and published in *Safety for Indian Women: VAWA and American Indian Tribes* (2014).

---

306 Savanna's Act, S. 227. https://www.congress.gov/116/bills/s227/BILLS-116s227enr.pdf. https://www.congress.gov/116/crpt/srpt206/CRPT-116srpt206.pdf

307 VAWA 2022, Title VIII, Division W, Safety for Indian Women, 847-862, Tribal jurisdictional provisions of H.R. 2471, codified into 25 U.S.C. 25 U.S.C.§§ 1304.

Appendix A
Family Violence Prevention Services Act (FVPSA)
42 U.S.C. Chapter 110
Sections 10401-10414

December 20, 2010

42 U.S.C.
Title 42 - THE PUBLIC HEALTH AND WELFARE
CHAPTER 110 - FAMILY VIOLENCE PREVENTION AND SERVICES

§10401. Short title; purpose

(a) Short title. This chapter may be cited as the "Family Violence Prevention and Services Act".

(b) Purpose. It is the purpose of this chapter to—

(1) assist States and Indian tribes in efforts to increase public awareness about, and primary and secondary prevention of, family violence, domestic violence, and dating violence;

(2) assist States and Indian tribes in efforts to provide immediate shelter and supportive services for victims of family violence, domestic violence, or dating violence, and their dependents;

(3) provide for a national domestic violence hotline;

(4) provide for technical assistance and training relating to family violence, domestic violence, and dating violence programs to States and Indian tribes, local public agencies (including law enforcement agencies, courts, and legal, social service, and health care professionals in public agencies), nonprofit private organizations (including faith-based and charitable organizations, community-based organizations, and voluntary associations), tribal organizations, and other persons seeking such assistance and training.

(Pub. L. 98–457, title III, §301, as added Pub. L. 111–320, title II, §201, Dec. 20, 2010, 124 Stat. 3484.)

§10402. Definitions. In this chapter:

(1) Alaska Native. The term "Alaska Native" has the meaning given the term "Native" in section 1602 of title 43.

(2) Dating violence. The term "dating violence" has the meaning given such term in section 13925(a) of this title.

(3) Domestic violence. The term "domestic violence" has the meaning given such term in section 13925(a) of this title.

(4) Family violence. The term "family violence" means any act or threatened act of violence, including any forceful detention of an individual, that—

(A) results or threatens to result in physical injury; and

(B) is committed by a person against another individual (including an elderly individual) to or with whom such person—

(i) is related by blood;

(ii) is or was related by marriage or is or was otherwise legally related; or

(iii) is or was lawfully residing.

(5) Indian; Indian tribe; tribal organization. The terms "Indian", "Indian tribe", and "tribal organization" have the meanings given such terms in section 450b of title 25.

(6) Native Hawaiian. The term "Native Hawaiian" has the meaning given the term in section 7517 of title 20.

(7) Personally identifying information. The term "personally identifying information" has the meaning given the term in section 13925(a) of this title.

(8) Secretary. The term "Secretary" means the Secretary of Health and Human Services.

(9) Shelter. The term "shelter" means the provision of temporary refuge and supportive services in compliance with applicable State law (including regulation) governing the provision, on a regular basis, of shelter, safe homes, meals, and supportive services to victims of family violence, domestic violence, or dating violence, and their dependents.

(10) State. The term "State" means each of the several States, the District of Columbia, the Commonwealth of Puerto Rico, and, except as otherwise provided, Guam, American Samoa, the United States Virgin Islands, and the Commonwealth of the Northern Mariana Islands.

(11) State Domestic Violence Coalition. The term "State Domestic Violence Coalition" means a statewide nongovernmental nonprofit private domestic violence organization that—

(A) has a membership that includes a majority of the primary-purpose domestic violence service providers in the State;

(B) has board membership that is representative of primary-purpose domestic violence service providers, and which may include representatives of the communities in which the services are being provided in the State;

(C) has as its purpose to provide education, support, and technical assistance to such service providers to enable the providers to establish and maintain shelter and supportive services for victims of domestic violence and their dependents; and

(D) serves as an information clearinghouse, primary point of contact, and resource center on domestic violence for the State and supports the development of polices, protocols, and procedures to enhance domestic violence intervention and prevention in the State.

(12) Supportive services. The term "supportive services" means services for adult and youth victims of family violence, domestic violence, or dating violence, and dependents exposed to family violence, domestic violence, or dating violence, that are designed to—

(A) meet the needs of such victims of family violence, domestic violence, or dating violence, and their dependents, for short-term, transitional, or long-term safety; and

(B) provide counseling, advocacy, or assistance for victims of family violence, domestic violence, or dating violence, and their dependents.

(13) Tribally designated official. The term "tribally designated official" means an individual designated by an Indian tribe, tribal organization, or nonprofit private organization authorized by an Indian tribe, to administer a grant under section 10409 of this title.

(14) Underserved populations. The term "underserved populations" has the meaning given the term in section 13925(a) of this title. For the purposes of this chapter, the Secretary has the same authority to determine whether a population is an underserved population as the Attorney General has under that section 13925(a) [1] of this title.

(Pub. L. 98–457, title III, §302, as added Pub. L. 111–320, title II, §201, Dec. 20, 2010, 124 Stat. 3484; amended Pub. L. 114–95, title IX, §9215(ii), Dec. 10, 2015, 129 Stat. 2175.)

§10404. Authority of Authorization

(a) Formula grants to States

(1) In general. There is authorized to be appropriated to carry out sections 10401 through 10412 of this title, $175,000,000 for each of fiscal years 2011 through 2015.

(2) Allocations

(A) Formula grants to States

(i) Reservation of funds. For any fiscal year for which the amounts appropriated under paragraph (1) exceed $130,000,000, not less than 25 percent of such excess funds shall be made available to carry out section 10412 of this title.

(ii) Formula grants. Of the amounts appropriated under paragraph (1) for a fiscal year and not reserved under clause (i), not less than 70 percent shall be used for making grants under section 10406(a) of this title.

(B) Grants to tribes. Of the amounts appropriated under paragraph (1) for a fiscal year and not reserved under subparagraph (A)(i), not less than 10 percent shall be used to carry out section 10409 of this title.

(C) Technical assistance and training centers. Of the amounts appropriated under paragraph (1) for a fiscal year and not reserved under subparagraph (A)(i), not less than 6 percent shall be used by the Secretary for making grants under section 10410 of this title.

(D) Grants for State Domestic Violence Coalitions. Of the amounts appropriated under paragraph (1) for a fiscal year and not reserved under subparagraph (A)(i), not less than 10 percent of such amounts shall be used by the Secretary for making grants under section 10411 of this title.

(E) Administration, evaluation and monitoring. Of the amount appropriated under paragraph (1) for a fiscal year and not reserved under subparagraph (A)(i), not more than 2.5 percent shall be used by the

Secretary for evaluation, monitoring, and other administrative costs under this chapter.

(b) National domestic violence hotline. There is authorized to be appropriated to carry out section 10413 of this title $3,500,000 for each of fiscal years 2011 through 2015.

(c) Domestic Violence Prevention Enhancement and Leadership Through Alliances. There is authorized to be appropriated to carry out section 10414 of this title $6,000,000 for each of fiscal years 2011 through 2015.

(Pub. L. 98–457, title III, §303, as added Pub. L. 111–320, title II, §201, Dec. 20, 2010, 124 Stat. 3486.)

§10404. Authority of Secretary

(a) Authorities. In order to carry out the provisions of this chapter, the Secretary is authorized to—

(1) appoint and fix the compensation of such personnel as are necessary;

(2) procure, to the extent authorized by section 3109 of title 5, such temporary and intermittent services of experts and consultants as are necessary;

(3) make grants to eligible entities or enter into contracts with for-profit or nonprofit nongovernmental entities and establish reporting requirements for such grantees and contractors;

(4) prescribe such regulations and guidance as are reasonably necessary in order to carry out the objectives and provisions of this chapter, including regulations and guidance on implementing new grant conditions established or provisions modified by amendments made to this chapter by the CAPTA Reauthorization Act of 2010, to ensure accountability and transparency of the actions of grantees and contractors, or as determined by the Secretary to be reasonably necessary to carry out this chapter; and

(5) coordinate programs within the Department of Health and Human Services, and seek to coordinate those programs with programs administered by other Federal agencies, that involve or affect efforts to prevent family violence, domestic violence, and dating violence or the provision of assistance for adult and youth victims of family violence, domestic violence, or dating violence.

(b) Administration. The Secretary shall—

(1) assign 1 or more employees of the Department of Health and Human Services to carry out the provisions of this chapter, including carrying out evaluation and monitoring under this chapter, which employees shall, prior to such appointment, have expertise in the field of family violence and domestic violence prevention and services and, to the extent practicable, have expertise in the field of dating violence;

(2) provide technical assistance in the conduct of programs for the prevention and treatment of family violence, domestic violence, and dating violence;

(3) provide for and coordinate research into the most effective approaches to the intervention in and prevention of family violence, domestic violence, and dating violence, by—

(A) consulting with experts and program providers within the family violence, domestic violence, and dating violence field to identify gaps in research and knowledge, establish research priorities, and disseminate research findings;

(B) collecting and reporting data on the provision of family violence, domestic violence, and dating violence services, including assistance and programs supported by Federal funds made available under this chapter and by other governmental or nongovernmental sources of funds; and

(C) coordinating family violence, domestic violence, and dating violence research efforts within the Department of Health and Human Services with relevant research administered or carried out by other Federal agencies and other researchers, including research on the provision of assistance for adult and youth victims of family violence, domestic violence, or dating violence; and

(4) support the development and implementation of effective policies, protocols, and programs within the Department and at other Federal agencies that address the safety and support needs of adult and youth victims of family violence, domestic violence, or dating violence.

(c) Reports. Every 2 years, the Secretary shall review and evaluate the activities conducted by grantees, subgrantees, and contractors under this chapter and the effectiveness of the programs administered pursuant to this chapter, and submit a report containing the evaluation to the Committee on Education and Labor of the House of Representatives and the Committee on Health, Education, Labor, and Pensions of the Senate. Such report shall also include a summary of the documentation provided to the Secretary through performance reports submitted under section 10406(d) of this title. The Secretary shall make publicly available on the Department of Health and Human Services website the evaluation reports submitted to Congress under this subsection, including the summary of the documentation provided to the Secretary under section 10406(d) of this title.

(Pub. L. 98–457, title III, §304, as added Pub. L. 111–320, title II, §201, Dec. 20, 2010, 124 Stat. 3487.)

§10405. Allotment of funds

(a) In general. From the sums appropriated under section 10403 of this title and available for grants to States under section 10406(a) of this title for any fiscal year—

(1) Guam, American Samoa, the United States Virgin Islands, and the Commonwealth of the Northern Mariana Islands shall each be allotted not less than 1/8 of 1 percent of the amounts available for grants under section 10406(a) of this title for the fiscal year for which the allotment is made; and

(2) each State shall be allotted for a grant under section 10406(a) of this title, $600,000, with the remaining funds to be allotted to each State in an amount that bears the same ratio to such remaining funds as the population of such State bears to the population of all States.

(b) Population. For the purpose of this section, the population of each State, and the total population of all the States, shall be determined by the Secretary on the basis of the most recent census data available to the Secretary, and the Secretary shall use for such purpose, if available, the annual interim current census data produced by the Secretary of Commerce pursuant to section 181 of title 13.

(c) Ratable reduction. If the sums appropriated under section 10403 of this title for any fiscal year and available for grants to States under section 10406(a) of this title are not sufficient to pay in full the total amounts that all States are entitled to receive under subsection (a) for such fiscal year, then the maximum amounts that all States are entitled to receive under subsection (a) for such fiscal year shall be ratably reduced. In the event that additional funds become available for making such grants for any fiscal year during which the preceding sentence is applicable, such reduced amounts shall be increased on the same basis as they were reduced.

(d) Reallotment. If, at the end of the sixth month of any fiscal year for which sums are appropriated under section 10403 of this title, the amount allotted to a State has not been made available to such State in a grant under section 10406(a) of this title because of the failure of such State to meet the requirements for such a grant, then the Secretary shall reallot such amount to States that meet such requirements.

(e) Continued availability of funds. All funds allotted to a State for a fiscal year under this section, and made available to such State in a grant under section 10406(a) of this title, shall remain available for obligation by the State until the end of the following fiscal year. All such funds that are not obligated by the State by the end of the following fiscal year shall be made available to the Secretary for discretionary activities under section 10414 of this title. Such funds shall remain available for obligation, and for expenditure by a recipient of the funds under section

10414 of this title, for not more than 1 year from the date on which the funds are made available to the Secretary.

(f) Definition. In subsection (a)(2), the term "State" does not include any jurisdiction specified in subsection (a)(1).

(Pub. L. 98–457, title III, §305, as added Pub. L. 111–320, title II, §201, Dec. 20, 2010, 124 Stat. 3488.)

§10406. Formula grants to States

(a) Formula grants to States. The Secretary shall award grants to States in order to assist in supporting the establishment, maintenance, and expansion of programs and projects—

(1) to prevent incidents of family violence, domestic violence, and dating violence;

(2) to provide immediate shelter, supportive services, and access to community-based programs for victims of family violence, domestic violence, or dating violence, and their dependents; and

(3) to provide specialized services for children exposed to family violence, domestic violence, or dating violence, underserved populations, and victims who are members of racial and ethnic minority populations.

(b) Administrative expenses

(1) Administrative costs. Each State may use not more than 5 percent of the grant funds for State administrative costs.

(2) Subgrants to eligible entities. The State shall use the remainder of the grant funds to make subgrants to eligible entities for approved purposes as described in section 10408 of this title.

(c) Grant conditions

(1) Approved activities. In carrying out the activities under this chapter, grantees and subgrantees may collaborate with and provide information to Federal, State, local, and tribal public officials and agencies, in accordance with limitations on disclosure of confidential or private information as described in paragraph (5), to develop and implement policies to reduce or eliminate family violence, domestic violence, and dating violence.

(2) Discrimination prohibited

(A) Application of civil rights provisions

For the purpose of applying the prohibitions against discrimination on the basis of age under the Age Discrimination Act of 1975 (42 U.S.C. 6101 et seq.), on the basis of disability under section 504 of the Rehabilitation Act of 1973 (29 U.S.C. 794), on the basis of sex under title IX of the Education Amendments of 1972 (20 U.S.C. 1681 et seq.), or on the basis of race, color, or national origin under title VI of the Civil Rights Act of 1964 (42 U.S.C. 2000d et seq.), programs and activities funded in whole or in part with funds made available under this chapter are considered to be programs and activities receiving Federal financial assistance.

(B) Prohibition on discrimination on basis of sex, religion

(i) In general. No person shall on the ground of sex or religion be excluded from participation in, be denied the benefits of, or be subject to discrimination under, any program or activity funded in whole or in part with funds made available under this chapter. Nothing in this chapter shall require any such program or activity to include any individual in any program or activity without taking into consideration that individual's sex in those certain instances where sex is a bona fide occupational qualification or programmatic factor reasonably necessary to the normal or safe operation of that particular program or activity.

(ii) Enforcement. The Secretary shall enforce the provisions of clause (i) in accordance with section 602 of the Civil Rights Act of 1964 (42 U.S.C. 2000d–1). Section 603 of such Act (42 U.S.C. 2000d–2) shall apply with respect to any action taken by the Secretary to enforce such clause.

(iii) Construction. This subparagraph shall not be construed as affecting any legal remedy provided under any other provision of law.

(C) Enforcement authorities of Secretary. Whenever the Secretary finds that a State, Indian tribe, or other entity that has received financial assistance under this chapter has failed to comply with a provision of law referred to in subparagraph (A), with subparagraph (B), or with an applicable regulation (including one prescribed to carry out subparagraph (B)), the Secretary shall notify the chief executive officer of the State involved or the tribally designated official of the tribe involved and shall request such officer or official to secure compliance. If, within a reasonable period of time, not to exceed 60 days, the chief executive officer or official fails or refuses to secure compliance, the Secretary may—

(i) refer the matter to the Attorney General with a recommendation that an appropriate civil action be instituted;

(ii) exercise the powers and functions provided by title VI of the Civil Rights Act of 1964 (42 U.S.C. 2000d et seq.), the Age Discrimination Act of 1975 (42 U.S.C. 6101 et seq.), sections 504 and 505 of the Rehabilitation Act of 1973 [29 U.S.C. 794, 794a], or title IX of the Education Amendments of 1972 (20 U.S.C. 1681 et seq.), as may be applicable; or

(iii) take such other action as may be provided by law.

(D) Enforcement authority of Attorney General. When a matter is referred to the Attorney General pursuant to subparagraph (C)(i), or whenever the Attorney General has reason to believe that a State, an Indian tribe, or an entity described in subparagraph (C) is engaged in a pattern or practice in violation of a provision of law referred to in subparagraph (A) or in violation of subparagraph (B), the Attorney General may bring a civil action in any appropriate district court of the United States for such relief as may be appropriate, including injunctive relief.

(3) Income eligibility standards. No income eligibility standard may be imposed upon individuals with respect to eligibility for assistance or services supported with funds appropriated to carry out this chapter. No fees may be levied for assistance or services provided with funds appropriated to carry out this chapter.

(4) Match. No grant shall be made under this section to any entity other than a State or an Indian tribe unless the entity agrees that, with respect to the costs to be incurred by the entity in carrying out the program or project for which the grant is awarded, the entity will make available (directly or through donations from public or private entities) non-Federal contributions in an amount that is not less than $1 for every $5 of Federal funds provided under the grant. The non-Federal contributions required under this paragraph may be in cash or in kind.

(5) Nondisclosure of confidential or private information

(A) In general. In order to ensure the safety of adult, youth, and child victims of family violence, domestic violence, or dating violence, and their families, grantees and subgrantees under this chapter shall protect the confidentiality and privacy of such victims and their families.

(B) Nondisclosure. Subject to subparagraphs (C), (D), and (E), grantees and subgrantees shall not—

(i) disclose any personally identifying information collected in connection with services requested (including services utilized or denied), through grantees' and subgrantees' programs; or

(ii) reveal personally identifying information without informed, written, reasonably time-limited consent by the person about whom information is sought, whether for this program or any other Federal or State grant program, which consent—

(I) shall be given by—

(aa) the person, except as provided in item (bb) or (cc);

(bb) in the case of an unemancipated minor, the minor and the minor's parent or guardian; or

(cc) in the case of an individual with a guardian, the individual's guardian; and

(II) may not be given by the abuser or suspected abuser of the minor or individual with a guardian, or the abuser or suspected abuser of the other parent of the minor.

(C) Release. If release of information described in subparagraph (B) is compelled by statutory or court mandate—

(i) grantees and subgrantees shall make reasonable attempts to provide notice to victims affected by the release of the information; and

(ii) grantees and subgrantees shall take steps necessary to protect the privacy and safety of the persons affected by the release of the information.

(D) Information sharing. Grantees and subgrantees may share—

(i) nonpersonally identifying information, in the aggregate, regarding services to their clients and demographic nonpersonally identifying information in order to comply with Federal, State, or tribal reporting, evaluation, or data collection requirements;

(ii) court-generated information and law enforcement-generated information contained in secure, governmental registries for protective order enforcement purposes; and

(iii) law enforcement- and prosecution-generated information necessary for law enforcement and prosecution purposes.

(E) Oversight. Nothing in this paragraph shall prevent the Secretary from disclosing grant activities authorized in this chapter to the Committee on Education and Labor of the House of Representatives and the Committee on Health, Education, Labor, and Pensions of the Senate and exercising congressional oversight authority. In making all such disclosures, the Secretary shall protect the confidentiality of individuals and omit personally identifying information, including location information about individuals and shelters.

(F) Statutorily permitted reports of abuse or neglect. Nothing in this paragraph shall prohibit a grantee or subgrantee from reporting abuse and neglect, as those terms are defined by law, where mandated or expressly permitted by the State or Indian tribe involved.

(G) Preemption. Nothing in this paragraph shall be construed to supersede any provision of any Federal, State, tribal, or local law that provides greater protection than this paragraph for victims of family violence, domestic violence, or dating violence.

(H) Confidentiality of location. The address or location of any shelter facility assisted under this chapter that otherwise maintains a confidential location shall, except with written authorization of the person or persons responsible for the operation of such shelter, not be made public.

(6) Supplement not supplant. Federal funds made available to a State or Indian tribe under this chapter shall be used to supplement and not supplant other Federal, State, tribal, and local public funds expended to provide services and activities that promote the objectives of this chapter.

(d) Reports and evaluation. Each grantee shall submit an annual performance report to the Secretary at such time as shall be reasonably required by the Secretary. Such performance report shall describe the grantee and subgrantee activities that have been carried out with grant funds made available under subsection (a) or section 10409 of this title, contain an evaluation of the effectiveness of such activities, and provide such additional information as the Secretary may reasonably require. (Pub. L. 98–457, title III, §306, as added Pub. L. 111–320, title II, §201, Dec. 20, 2010, 124 Stat. 3489.)

§10407. State application

(a) Application

(1) In general. The chief executive officer of a State seeking funds under section 10406(a) of this title or a tribally designated official seeking funds under section 10409(a) of this title shall submit an application to the Secretary at such time and in such manner as the Secretary may reasonably require.

(2) Contents. Each such application shall—

(A) provide a description of the procedures that have been developed to ensure compliance with the provisions of sections 10406(c) and 10408(d) of this title;

(B) provide, with respect to funds described in paragraph (1), assurances that—

(i) not more than 5 percent of such funds will be used for administrative costs;

(ii) the remaining funds will be distributed to eligible entities as described in section 10408(a) of this title for approved activities as described in section 10408(b) of this title; and

(iii) in the distribution of funds by a State under section 10408(a) of this title, the State will give special emphasis to the support of community-based projects of demonstrated effectiveness, that are carried out by nonprofit private organizations and that—

(I) have as their primary purpose the operation of shelters for victims of family violence, domestic violence, and dating violence, and their dependents; or

(II) provide counseling, advocacy, and self-help services to victims of family violence, domestic violence, and dating violence, and their dependents;

(C) in the case of an application submitted by a State, provide an assurance that there will be an equitable distribution of grants and grant funds within the State and between urban and rural areas within such State;

(D) in the case of an application submitted by a State, provide an assurance that the State will consult with and provide for the participation of the State Domestic Violence Coalition in the planning and monitoring of the distribution of grants to eligible entities as described in section 10408(a) of this title and the administration of the grant programs and projects;

(E) describe how the State or Indian tribe will involve community-based organizations, whose primary purpose is to provide culturally appropriate services to underserved populations, including how such community-based organizations can assist the State or Indian tribe in addressing the unmet needs of such populations;

(F) describe how activities and services provided by the State or Indian tribe are designed to reduce family violence, domestic violence, and dating violence, including how funds will be used to provide shelter, supportive services, and prevention services in accordance with section 10408(b) of this title;

(G) specify the State agency or tribally designated official to be designated as responsible for the administration of programs and activities relating to family violence, domestic violence, and dating violence, that are carried out by the State or Indian tribe under this chapter, and for coordination of related programs within the jurisdiction of the State or Indian tribe;

(H) provide an assurance that the State or Indian tribe has a law or procedure to bar an abuser from a shared household or a household of the abused person, which may include eviction laws or procedures, where appropriate; and

(I) meet such requirements as the Secretary reasonably determines are necessary to carry out the objectives and provisions of this chapter.

(b) Approval of application

(1) In general. The Secretary shall approve any application that meets the requirements of subsection (a) and section 10406 of this title. The Secretary shall not disapprove any application under this subsection unless the Secretary gives the applicant reasonable notice of the Secretary's intention to disapprove and a 6-month period providing an opportunity for correction of any deficiencies.

(2) Correction of deficiencies. The Secretary shall give such notice, within 45 days after the date of submission of the application, if any of the provisions of subsection (a) or section 10406 of this title have not been satisfied in such application. If the State or Indian tribe does not correct the deficiencies in such application within the 6-month period following the receipt of the Secretary's notice, the Secretary shall withhold payment of any grant funds under section 10406 of this title to such State or under section 10409 of this title to such Indian tribe until such date as the State or Indian tribe provides documentation that the deficiencies have been corrected.

(3) State or tribal Domestic Violence Coalition participation in determinations of compliance. State Domestic Violence Coalitions, or comparable coalitions for Indian tribes, shall be permitted to participate in determining whether grantees for corresponding States or Indian tribes are in compliance with subsection (a) and section 10406(c) of this title, except that no funds made available under section 10411 of this title shall be used to challenge a determination about whether a grantee is in compliance with, or to seek the enforcement of, the requirements of this chapter.

(4) Failure to report; nonconforming expenditures. The Secretary shall suspend funding for an approved application if the applicant fails to submit an annual performance report under section 10406(d) of this title, or if funds are expended for purposes other than those set forth in section 10406(b) of this title, after following the procedures set forth in paragraphs (1), (2), and (3).

(Pub. L. 98–457, title III, §307, as added Pub. L. 111–320, title II, §201, Dec. 20, 2010, 124 Stat. 3493.)

§10408. Subgrants and uses of funds

(a) Subgrants. A State that receives a grant under section 10406(a) of this title shall use grant funds described in section 10406(b)(2) of this title to provide subgrants to eligible entities for programs and projects within such State, that is [1] designed to prevent incidents of family violence, domestic violence, and dating violence by providing immediate shelter and supportive services for adult and youth victims of family violence, domestic violence, or dating violence (and their dependents), and that may provide prevention services to prevent future incidents of family violence, domestic violence, and dating violence.

(b) Use of funds

(1) In general. Funds awarded to eligible entities under subsection (a) shall be used to provide shelter, supportive services, or prevention services to adult and youth victims of family violence, domestic violence, or dating violence, and their dependents, which may include—

(A) provision, on a regular basis, of immediate shelter and related supportive services to adult and youth victims of family violence, domestic violence, or dating violence, and their dependents, including paying for the operating and administrative expenses of the facilities for such shelter;

(B) assistance in developing safety plans, and supporting efforts of victims of family violence, domestic violence, or dating violence to make decisions related to their ongoing safety and well-being;

(C) provision of individual and group counseling, peer support groups, and referral to community-based services to assist family violence, domestic violence, and dating violence victims, and their dependents, in recovering from the effects of the violence;

(D) provision of services, training, technical assistance, and outreach to increase awareness of family violence, domestic violence, and dating violence and increase the accessibility of family violence, domestic violence, and dating violence services;

(E) provision of culturally and linguistically appropriate services;

(F) provision of services for children exposed to family violence, domestic violence, or dating violence, including age-appropriate counseling, supportive services, and services for the nonabusing parent that support that parent's role as a caregiver, which may, as appropriate, include services that work with the nonabusing parent and child together;

(G) provision of advocacy, case management services, and information and referral services, concerning issues related to family violence, domestic violence, or dating violence intervention and prevention, including—

(i) assistance in accessing related Federal and State financial assistance programs;

(ii) legal advocacy to assist victims and their dependents;

(iii) medical advocacy, including provision of referrals for appropriate health care services (including mental health, alcohol, and drug abuse treatment), but which shall not include reimbursement for any health care services;

(iv) assistance locating and securing safe and affordable permanent housing and homelessness prevention services;

(v) provision of transportation, child care, respite care, job training and employment services, financial literacy services and education, financial planning, and related economic empowerment services; and

(vi) parenting and other educational services for victims and their dependents; and

(H) prevention services, including outreach to underserved populations.

(2) Shelter and supportive services. Not less than 70 percent of the funds distributed by a State under subsection (a) shall be distributed to entities for the primary purpose of providing immediate shelter and supportive services to adult and youth victims of family violence, domestic violence, or dating violence, and their dependents, as described in paragraph (1)(A). Not less than 25 percent of the funds distributed by a State under subsection (a) shall be distributed to entities for the purpose of providing supportive services and prevention services as described in subparagraphs (B) through (H) of paragraph (1).

(c) Eligible entities. To be eligible to receive a subgrant from a State under this section, an entity shall be—

(1) a local public agency, or a nonprofit private organization (including faith-based and charitable organizations, community-based organizations, tribal organizations, and voluntary associations), that assists victims of family violence, domestic violence, or dating violence, and their dependents, and has a documented history of effective work concerning family violence, domestic violence, or dating violence; or

(2) a partnership of 2 or more agencies or organizations that includes—

(A) an agency or organization described in paragraph (1); and

(B) an agency or organization that has a demonstrated history of serving populations in their communities, including providing culturally appropriate services.

(d) Conditions

(1) Direct payments to victims or dependents

No funds provided under this chapter may be used as direct payment to any victim of family violence, domestic violence, or dating violence, or to any dependent of such victim.

(2) Voluntarily accepted services

Receipt of supportive services under this chapter shall be voluntary. No condition may be applied for the receipt of emergency shelter as described in subsection (b)(1)(A).

(Pub. L. 98–457, title III, §308, as added Pub. L. 111–320, title II, §201, Dec. 20, 2010, 124 Stat. 3494.)

§10409. Grants for Indian tribes

(a) Grants authorized. The Secretary, in consultation with tribal governments pursuant to Executive Order No. 13175 (25 U.S.C. 450 note) and in accordance with section 14045d of this title, shall continue to award grants for Indian tribes from amounts appropriated under section 10403(a)(2)(B) of this title to carry out this section.

(b) Eligible entities. To be eligible to receive a grant under this section, an entity shall be an Indian tribe, or a tribal organization or nonprofit private organization authorized by an Indian tribe. An Indian tribe shall have the option to authorize a tribal organization or a nonprofit private organization to submit an application and administer the grant funds awarded under this section.

(c) Conditions. Each recipient of such a grant shall comply with requirements that are consistent with the requirements applicable to grantees under section 10406 of this title.

(d) Grantee application. To be eligible to receive a grant under this section, an entity shall submit an application to the Secretary under section 10407 of this title at such time, in such manner, and containing such information as the Secretary determines to be essential to carry out the objectives and provisions of this chapter. The Secretary shall approve any application that meets requirements consistent with the requirements of section 10406(c) of this title and section 10407(a) of this title.

(e) Use of funds. An amount provided under a grant to an eligible entity shall be used for the services described in section 10408(b) of this title.

(Pub. L. 98–457, title III, §309, as added Pub. L. 111–320, title II, §201, Dec. 20, 2010, 124 Stat. 3496.)

§10410. National resource centers and training and technical assistance centers

(a) Purpose and grants authorized

(1) Purpose. The purpose of this section is to provide resource information, training, and technical assistance relating to the objectives of this chapter to improve the capacity of individuals, organizations, governmental entities, and communities to prevent family violence, domestic violence, and dating violence and to provide effective intervention services.

(2) Grants authorized. From the amounts appropriated under this chapter and reserved under section 10403(a)(2)(C) of this title, the Secretary—

(A) shall award grants to eligible entities for the establishment and maintenance of—

(i) 2 national resource centers (as provided for in subsection (b)(1)); and

(ii) at least 7 special issue resource centers addressing key areas of domestic violence, and intervention and prevention (as provided for in subsection (b)(2)); and

(B) may award grants, to—

(i) State resource centers to reduce disparities in domestic violence in States with high proportions of Indian (including Alaska Native) or Native Hawaiian populations (as provided for in subsection (b)(3)); and

(ii) support training and technical assistance that address emerging issues related to family violence, domestic violence, or dating violence, to entities demonstrating related expertise.

(b) Domestic violence resource centers

(1) National resource centers. In accordance with subsection (a)(2), the Secretary shall award grants to eligible entities for—

(A) a National Resource Center on Domestic Violence, which shall—

(i) offer a comprehensive array of technical assistance and training resources to Federal, State, and local governmental agencies, domestic violence service providers, community-based organizations, and other professionals and interested parties, related to domestic violence service programs and research, including programs and research related to victims and their children who are exposed to domestic violence; and

(ii) maintain a central resource library in order to collect, prepare, analyze, and disseminate information and statistics related to—

(I) the incidence and prevention of family violence and domestic violence; and

(II) the provision of shelter, supportive services, and prevention services to adult and youth victims of domestic violence (including services to prevent repeated incidents of violence); and

(B) a National Indian Resource Center Addressing Domestic Violence and Safety for Indian Women, which shall—

(i) offer a comprehensive array of technical assistance and training resources to Indian tribes and tribal organizations, specifically designed to enhance the capacity of the tribes and organizations to respond to domestic violence and the findings of section 901 of the Violence Against Women and Department of Justice Reauthorization Act of 2005 (42 U.S.C. 3796gg–10 note);

(ii) enhance the intervention and prevention efforts of Indian tribes and tribal organizations to respond to domestic violence and increase the safety of Indian women in support of the purposes of section 902 of the Violence Against Women and Department of Justice Reauthorization Act of 2005 [42 U.S.C. 3796gg–10 note]; and

(iii) coordinate activities with other Federal agencies, offices, and grantees that address the needs of Indians (including Alaska Natives), and Native Hawaiians that experience domestic violence, including the Office of Justice Services at the Bureau of Indian Affairs, the Indian Health Service of the Department of Health and Human Services, and the Office on Violence Against Women of the Department of Justice.

(2) Special issue resource centers. In accordance with subsection (a)(2)(A)(ii), the Secretary shall award grants to eligible entities for special issue resource centers, which shall be national in scope and shall provide information, training, and technical assistance to State and local domestic violence service providers. Each special issue resource center shall focus on enhancing domestic violence intervention and prevention efforts in at least one of the following areas:

(A) The response of the criminal and civil justice systems to domestic violence victims, which may include the response to the use of the self-defense plea by domestic violence victims and the issuance and use of protective orders.

(B) The response of child protective service agencies to victims of domestic violence and their dependents and child custody issues in domestic violence cases.

(C) The response of the interdisciplinary health care system to victims of domestic violence and access to health care resources for victims of domestic violence.

(D) The response of mental health systems, domestic violence service programs, and other related systems and programs to victims of domestic violence and to their children who are exposed to domestic violence.

(E) In the case of 3 specific resource centers, enhancing domestic violence intervention and prevention efforts for victims of domestic violence who are members of racial and ethnic minority groups, to enhance the cultural and linguistic relevancy of service delivery, resource utilization, policy, research, technical assistance, community education, and prevention initiatives.

(3) State resource centers to reduce tribal disparities

(A) In general. In accordance with subsection (a)(2), the Secretary may award grants to eligible entities for State resource centers, which shall provide statewide information, training, and technical assistance to Indian tribes, tribal organizations, and local domestic violence service organizations serving Indians (including Alaska Natives) or Native Hawaiians, in a culturally sensitive and relevant manner.

(B) Requirements. An eligible entity shall use a grant provided under this paragraph—

(i) to offer a comprehensive array of technical assistance and training resources to Indian tribes, tribal organizations, and providers of services to Indians (including Alaska Natives) or Native Hawaiians, specifically designed to enhance the capacity of the tribes, organizations, and providers to respond to domestic violence, including offering the resources in States in which the population of Indians (including Alaska Natives) or Native Hawaiians exceeds 2.5 percent of the total population of the State;

(ii) to coordinate all projects and activities with the national resource center described in paragraph (1)(B), including projects and activities that involve working with nontribal State and local governments to enhance their capacity to understand the unique needs of Indians (including Alaska Natives) and Native Hawaiians; and

(iii) to provide comprehensive community education and domestic violence prevention initiatives in a culturally sensitive and relevant manner.

(c) Eligibility

(1) In general. To be eligible to receive a grant under subsection (b)(1)(A) or subparagraph (A), (B), (C), or (D) of subsection (b)(2), an entity shall be a nonprofit private organization that focuses primarily on domestic violence and that—

(A) provides documentation to the Secretary demonstrating experience working directly on issues of domestic violence, and (in the case of an entity seeking a grant under subsection (b)(2)) demonstrating experience working directly in the corresponding specific special issue area described in subsection (b)(2);

(B) includes on the entity's advisory board representatives who are from domestic violence service programs and who are geographically and culturally diverse; and

(C) demonstrates the strong support of domestic violence service programs from across the Nation for the entity's designation as a national resource center or a special issue resource center, as appropriate.

(2) National Indian Resource Center. To be eligible to receive a grant under subsection (b)(1)(B), an entity shall be a tribal organization or a nonprofit private organization that focuses primarily on issues of domestic violence within Indian tribes and that submits documentation to the Secretary demonstrating—

(A) experience working with Indian tribes and tribal organizations to respond to domestic violence and the findings of section 901 of the Violence Against Women and Department of Justice Reauthorization Act of 2005 (42 U.S.C. 3796gg–10 note);

(B) experience providing Indian tribes and tribal organizations with assistance in developing tribally-based prevention and intervention services addressing domestic violence and safety for Indian women consistent with the purposes of section 902 of the Violence Against Women and Department of Justice Reauthorization Act of 2005 (42 U.S.C. 3796gg–10 note);

(C) strong support for the entity's designation as the National Indian Resource Center Addressing Domestic Violence and Safety for Indian Women from advocates working within Indian tribes to address domestic violence and the safety of Indian women;

(D) a record of demonstrated effectiveness in assisting Indian tribes and tribal organizations with prevention and intervention services addressing domestic violence; and

(E) the capacity to serve Indian tribes (including Alaska Native villages and regional and village corporations) across the United States.

(3) Special issue resource centers concerned with racial and ethnic minority groups.

To be eligible to receive a grant under subsection (b)(2)(E), an entity shall be an entity that—

(A) is a nonprofit private organization that focuses primarily on issues of domestic violence in a racial or ethnic community, or is a public or private nonprofit educational institution that has a domestic violence institute, center, or program related to culturally specific issues in domestic violence; and

(B)(i) has documented experience in the areas of domestic violence prevention and services, and experience relevant to the specific racial or ethnic population to which information, training, technical assistance, and outreach would be provided under the grant;

(ii) demonstrates the strong support, of advocates from across the Nation who are working to address domestic violence; and

(iii) has a record of demonstrated effectiveness in enhancing the cultural and linguistic relevancy of service delivery.

(4) State resource centers to reduce tribal disparities. To be eligible to receive a grant under subsection (b)(3), an entity shall—

(A)(i) be located in a State in which the population of Indians (including Alaska Natives) or Native Hawaiians exceeds 10 percent of the total population of the State; or

(ii) be an Indian tribe, tribal organization, or Native Hawaiian organization that focuses primarily on issues of domestic violence among Indians or Native Hawaiians, or an institution of higher education; and

(B) demonstrate the ability to serve all regions of the State, including underdeveloped areas and areas that are geographically distant from population centers.

(d) Reports and evaluation. Each entity receiving a grant under this section shall submit a performance report to the Secretary annually and in such manner as shall be reasonably required by the Secretary. Such performance report shall describe the activities that have been carried out with such grant funds, contain an evaluation of the effectiveness of the activities, and provide such additional information as the Secretary may reasonably require.

(Pub. L. 98–457, title III, §310, as added Pub. L. 111–320, title II, §201, Dec. 20, 2010, 124 Stat. 3497.)

§10411. Grants to State Domestic Violence Coalitions

(a) Grants. The Secretary shall award grants for the funding of State Domestic Violence Coalitions.

(b) Allotment of funds

(1) In general. From the amount appropriated under section 10403(a)(2)(D) of this title for each fiscal year, the Secretary shall allot to each of the 50 States, the District of Columbia, the Commonwealth of Puerto Rico, and each of the covered territories an amount equal to 1/56 of the amount so appropriated for such fiscal year.

(2) Definition. For purposes of this subsection, the term "covered territories" means Guam, American Samoa, the United States Virgin Islands, and the Commonwealth of the Northern Mariana Islands.

(c) Application. Each State Domestic Violence Coalition desiring a grant under this section shall submit an application to the Secretary at such time, in such manner, and containing such information as the Secretary determines to be essential to carry out the objectives of this section. The application submitted by the coalition for the grant shall provide documentation of the coalition's work, satisfactory to the Secretary, demonstrating that the coalition—

(1) meets all of the applicable requirements set forth in this chapter; and

(2) demonstrates the ability to conduct appropriately all activities described in this section, as indicated by—

(A) documented experience in administering Federal grants to conduct the activities described in subsection (d); or

(B) a documented history of active participation in the activities described in paragraphs (1), (3), (4), and (5) of subsection (d) and a demonstrated capacity to conduct the activities described in subsection (d)(2).

(d) Use of funds. A coalition that receives a grant under this section shall use the grant funds for administration and operations to further the purposes of family violence, domestic violence, and dating violence intervention and prevention, through activities that shall include—

(1) working with local family violence, domestic violence, and dating violence service programs and providers of direct services to encourage appropriate and comprehensive responses to family violence, domestic violence, and dating violence against adults or youth within the State involved, including providing training and technical assistance and conducting State needs assessments;

(2) participating in planning and monitoring the distribution of subgrants and subgrant funds within the State under section 10408(a) of this title;

(3) working in collaboration with service providers and community-based organizations to address the needs of family violence, domestic violence, and dating violence victims, and their dependents, who are members of racial and ethnic minority populations and underserved populations;

(4) collaborating with and providing information to entities in such fields as housing, health care, mental health, social welfare, or business to support the development and implementation of effective policies, protocols, and programs that address the safety and support needs of adult and youth victims of family violence, domestic violence, or dating violence;

(5) encouraging appropriate responses to cases of family violence, domestic violence, or dating violence against adults or youth, including by working with judicial and law enforcement agencies;

(6) working with family law judges, criminal court judges, child protective service agencies, and children's advocates to develop appropriate responses to child custody and visitation issues in cases of child exposure to family violence, domestic violence, or dating violence and in cases in which—

(A) family violence, domestic violence, or dating violence is present; and

(B) child abuse is present;

(7) providing information to the public about prevention of family violence, domestic violence, and dating violence, including information targeted to underserved populations; and

(8) collaborating with Indian tribes and tribal organizations (and corresponding Native Hawaiian groups or communities) to address the needs of Indian (including Alaska Native) and Native Hawaiian victims

of family violence, domestic violence, or dating violence, as applicable in the State.

(e) Limitation on use of funds. A coalition that receives a grant under this section shall not be required to use funds received under this chapter for the purposes described in paragraph (5) or (6) of subsection (d) if the coalition provides an annual assurance to the Secretary that the coalition is—

(1) using funds received under section 2001(c)(1) of the Omnibus Crime Control and Safe Streets Act of 1968 (42 U.S.C. 3796gg(c)(1)) for such purposes; and

(2) coordinating the activities carried out by the coalition under subsection (d) with the State's activities under part T of title I of the Omnibus Crime Control and Safe Streets Act of 1968 (42 U.S.C. 3796gg et seq.) that address those purposes.

(f) Prohibition on lobbying. No funds made available to entities under this section shall be used, directly or indirectly, to influence the issuance, amendment, or revocation of any executive order or similar promulgation by any Federal, State, or local agency, or to undertake to influence the passage or defeat of any legislation by Congress, or by any State or local legislative body, or State proposals by initiative petition, except that the representatives of the entity may testify or make other appropriate communication—

(1) when formally requested to do so by a legislative body, a committee, or a member of the body or committee; or

(2) in connection with legislation or appropriations directly affecting the activities of the entity.

(g) Reports and evaluation. Each entity receiving a grant under this section shall submit a performance report to the Secretary at such time as shall be reasonably required by the Secretary. Such performance report shall describe the activities that have been carried out with such grant funds, contain an evaluation of the effectiveness of such activities, and provide such additional information as the Secretary may reasonably require.

(h) Indian representatives. For purposes of this section, a State Domestic Violence Coalition may include representatives of Indian tribes and tribal organizations.

(Pub. L. 98–457, title III, §311, as added Pub. L. 111–320, title II, §201, Dec. 20, 2010, 124 Stat. 3501.)

§10412. Specialized services for abused parents and their children

(a) In general

(1) Program. The Secretary shall establish a grant program to expand the capacity of family violence, domestic violence, and dating violence service programs and community-based programs to prevent future domestic violence by addressing, in an appropriate manner, the needs of children exposed to family violence, domestic violence, or dating violence.

(2) Grants. The Secretary may make grants to eligible entities through the program established under paragraph (1) for periods of not more than 2 years. If the Secretary determines that an entity has received such a grant and been successful in meeting the objectives of the grant application submitted under subsection (c), the Secretary may renew the grant for 1 additional period of not more than 2 years.

(b) Eligible entities. To be eligible to receive a grant under this section, an entity shall be a local agency, a nonprofit private organization (including faith-based and charitable organizations, community-based organizations, and voluntary associations), or a tribal organization, with a demonstrated record of serving victims of family violence, domestic violence, or dating violence and their children.

(c) Application. An entity seeking a grant under this section shall submit an application to the Secretary at such time, in such manner, and containing such information as the Secretary may reasonably require, including—

(1) a description of how the entity will prioritize the safety of, and confidentiality of information about—

(A) victims of family violence, victims of domestic violence, and victims of dating violence; and

(B) children of victims described in subparagraph (A);

(2) a description of how the entity will provide developmentally appropriate and age-appropriate services, and culturally and linguistically appropriate services, to the victims and children; and

(3) a description of how the entity will ensure that professionals working with the children receive the training and technical assistance appropriate and relevant to the unique needs of children exposed to family violence, domestic violence, or dating violence.

(d) Use of funds. An entity that receives a grant under this section for a family violence, domestic violence, and dating violence service or community-based program described in subsection (a)—

(1) shall use the funds made available through the grant—

(A) to provide direct counseling, appropriate services consistent with subsection (c)(2), or advocacy on behalf of victims of family violence, domestic violence, or dating violence and their children, including coordinating services with services provided by the child welfare system;

(B) to provide services for nonabusing parents to support those parents' roles as caregivers and their roles in responding to the social, emotional, and developmental needs of their children; and

(C) where appropriate, to provide the services described in this subsection while working with such a nonabusing parent and child together; and

(2) may use the funds made available through the grant—

(A) to provide early childhood development and mental health services;

(B) to coordinate activities with and provide technical assistance to community-based organizations serving victims of family violence, domestic violence, or dating violence or children exposed to family violence, domestic violence, or dating violence; and

(C) to provide additional services and referrals to services for children, including child care, transportation, educational support, respite care, supervised visitation, or other necessary services.

(e) Reports and evaluation. Each entity receiving a grant under this section shall submit a performance report to the Secretary at such time as shall be reasonably required by the Secretary. Such performance report shall describe the activities that have been carried out with such grant funds, contain an evaluation of the effectiveness of such activities, and provide such additional information as the Secretary may reasonably require.

(Pub. L. 98–457, title III, §312, as added Pub. L. 111–320, title II, §201, Dec. 20, 2010, 124 Stat. 3503.)

§10413. National domestic violence hotline grant

(a) In general. The Secretary shall award a grant to 1 or more private entities to provide for the ongoing operation of a 24-hour, national, toll-free telephone hotline to provide information and assistance to adult and youth victims of family violence, domestic violence, or dating violence, family and household members of such victims, and persons affected by the victimization. The Secretary shall give priority to applicants with experience in operating a hotline that provides assistance to adult and youth victims of family violence, domestic violence, or dating violence.

(b) Term. The Secretary shall award a grant under this section for a period of not more than 5 years.

(c) Conditions on payment. The provision of payments under a grant awarded under this section shall be subject to annual approval by the Secretary and subject to the availability of appropriations for each fiscal year to make the payments.

(d) Application. To be eligible to receive a grant under this section, an entity shall submit an application to the Secretary that shall—

(1) contain such agreements, assurances, and information, be in such form, and be submitted in such manner, as the Secretary shall prescribe;

(2) include a complete description of the applicant's plan for the operation of a national domestic violence hotline, including descriptions of—

(A) the training program for hotline personnel, including technology training to ensure that all persons affiliated with the hotline are able to effectively operate any technological systems used by the hotline;

(B) the hiring criteria and qualifications for hotline personnel;

(C) the methods for the creation, maintenance, and updating of a resource database;

(D) a plan for publicizing the availability of the hotline;

(E) a plan for providing service to non-English speaking callers, including service through hotline personnel who have non-English language capability;

(F) a plan for facilitating access to the hotline by persons with hearing impairments; and

(G) a plan for providing assistance and referrals to youth victims of domestic violence and for victims of dating violence who are minors, which may be carried out through a national teen dating violence hotline;

(3) demonstrate that the applicant has recognized expertise in the area of family violence, domestic violence, or dating violence and a record of high quality service to victims of family violence, domestic violence, or dating violence, including a demonstration of support from advocacy groups and State Domestic Violence Coalitions;

(4) demonstrate that the applicant has the capacity and the expertise to maintain a domestic violence hotline and a comprehensive database of service providers;

(5) demonstrate the ability to provide information and referrals for callers, directly connect callers to service providers, and employ crisis interventions meeting the standards of family violence, domestic violence, and dating violence providers;

(6) demonstrate that the applicant has a commitment to diversity and to the provision of services to underserved populations, including to ethnic, racial, and non-English speaking minorities, in addition to older individuals and individuals with disabilities;

(7) demonstrate that the applicant complies with nondisclosure requirements as described in section 10406(c)(5) of this title and follows comprehensive quality assurance practices; and

(8) contain such other information as the Secretary may require.

(e) Hotline activities

(1) In general. An entity that receives a grant under this section for activities described, in whole or in part, in subsection (a) shall use funds made available through the grant to establish and operate a 24-hour, national, toll-free telephone hotline to provide information and assistance to adult and youth victims of family violence, domestic violence, or dating violence, and other individuals described in subsection (a).

(2) Activities. In establishing and operating the hotline, the entity—

(A) shall contract with a carrier for the use of a toll-free telephone line;

(B) shall employ, train (including providing technology training), and supervise personnel to answer incoming calls, provide counseling and referral services for callers on a 24-hour-a-day basis, and directly connect callers to service providers;

(C) shall assemble and maintain a database of information relating to services for adult and youth victims of family violence, domestic violence, or dating violence to which callers may be referred throughout the United States, including information on the availability of shelters and supportive services for victims of family violence, domestic violence, or dating violence;

(D) shall widely publicize the hotline throughout the United States, including to potential users;

(E) shall provide assistance and referrals to meet the needs of underserved populations and individuals with disabilities;

(F) shall provide assistance and referrals for youth victims of domestic violence and for victims of dating violence who are minors, which may be carried out through a national teen dating violence hotline;

(G) may provide appropriate assistance and referrals for family and household members of victims of family violence, domestic violence, or dating violence, and persons affected by the victimization described in subsection (a); and

(H) at the discretion of the hotline operator, may provide assistance, or referrals for counseling or intervention, for identified adult and youth perpetrators, including self-identified perpetrators, of family violence, domestic violence, or dating violence, but shall not be required to provide such assistance or referrals in any circumstance in which the hotline operator fears the safety of a victim may be impacted by an abuser or suspected abuser.

(f) Reports and evaluation. The entity receiving a grant under this section shall submit a performance report to the Secretary at such time as shall be reasonably required by the Secretary. Such performance report shall describe the activities that have been carried out with such grant funds, contain an evaluation of the effectiveness of such activities, and provide such additional information as the Secretary may reasonably require.

(Pub. L. 98–457, title III, §313, as added Pub. L. 111–320, title II, §201, Dec. 20, 2010, 124 Stat. 3504.)

Appendix B
Violence Against Women Reauthorization Act of 2022
Public Law 90-284

Subtitle B-Alaska Tribal Public Safety Empowerment

March 15, 2022

"(C) to ensure that, in criminal proceedings in which a participating tribe exercises special Tribal criminal jurisdiction, jurors are summoned, selected, and instructed in a manner consistent with all applicable requirements; and

"(D) to accord victims of covered crimes rights that are similar to the rights of a crime victim described in section 3771(a) of title 18, United States Code, consistent with Tribal law and custom.

"(i) SUPPLEMENT, NOT SUPPLANT.—Amounts made available under this section shall supplement and not supplant any other Federal, State, or local government amounts made available to carry out activities described in this section.

"(j) AUTHORIZATION OF APPROPRIATIONS.—

"(1) IN GENERAL.—There is authorized to be appropriated $25,000,000 for each of fiscal years 2023 through 2027—

"(A) to carry out subsection (h); and

"(B) to provide training, technical assistance, data collection, and evaluation of the criminal justice systems of participating tribes.

"(2) LIMITATIONS.—Of the total amount made available under paragraph (1) for each fiscal year, not more than 40 percent shall be used for reimbursements under subsection (h)(1).".

Subtitle B—Alaska Tribal Public Safety Empowerment

SEC. 811. FINDINGS; PURPOSES.

(a) FINDINGS.—Congress finds that—

(1) according to the report of the Indian Law and Order Commission established by section 15 of the Indian Law Enforcement Reform Act (25 U.S.C. 2812), Alaska Native women—

(A) are overrepresented in the domestic violence victim population by 250 percent;

(B) in the State of Alaska, comprise—

(i) 19 percent of the population of the State; but

(ii) 47 percent of reported rape victims in the State; and

(C) as compared to the populations of other Indian Tribes, suffer the highest rates of domestic and sexual violence;

(2) most Alaska Native villages are located in remote areas that—

(A) are often inaccessible by road; and

(B) have no local law enforcement presence;

(3) the Commission referred to in paragraph (1)—

(A) determined that the Alaska Department of Public Safety—

(i) has primary responsibility for law enforcement in rural Alaska; but

(ii) provides only 1 to 1.4 field officers per 1,000,000 acres; and

(B) recommended that "devolving authority to Alaska Native communities is essential for addressing local crime. Their governments are best positioned to effectively arrest, prosecute, and punish, and they should have the authority to do so-or to work out voluntary agreements with each other, and with local governments and the State on mutually beneficial terms"; and

(4) the unique legal relationship of the United States to Indian Tribes creates a Federal trust responsibility to assist Tribal governments in safeguarding the lives of Indian women.

(b) PURPOSES.—The purposes of this subtitle are—

(1) to increase coordination and communication among Federal, State, Tribal, and local law enforcement agencies; and

(2) to empower Indian Tribes to effectively respond to cases of domestic violence, dating violence, stalking, sex trafficking, sexual violence, and missing or murdered Alaska Natives through the exercise of special Tribal criminal jurisdiction.

SEC. 812. DEFINITIONS.

In this subtitle:

(1) ASSAULT OF TRIBAL JUSTICE PERSONNEL; COVERED CRIME; OBSTRUCTION OF JUSTICE; PROTECTION ORDER; VIOLATION OF A PROTECTION ORDER.—

(A) IN GENERAL.—The terms "assault of Tribal justice personnel", "covered crime", "obstruction of justice", "protection order", and "violation of a protection order" have the meanings given the terms in section 204(a) of Public Law 90–284 (25 U.S.C. 1304(a)) (commonly known as the "Indian Civil Rights Act of 1968").

(B) APPLICATION.—For purposes of the application of the definitions of "assault of Tribal justice personnel", "obstruction of justice", and "violation of a protection order", and for purposes of the application of the defined terms contained in the definition of "covered crime", under section 204(a) of Public Law 90–284 (25 U.S.C. 1304(a)) (commonly known as the "Indian Civil Rights Act of 1968") to the pilot program, the Attorney General shall modify any reference to "Indian country" to mean the Village of a participating Tribe.

(2) INDIAN; INDIAN COURT; INDIAN TRIBE; POWERS OF SELF-GOVERNMENT.—The terms "Indian", "Indian court", "Indian tribe", and "powers of self-government" have the meanings given the terms in section 201 of Public Law 90–284 (25 U.S.C. 1301) (commonly known as the "Indian Civil Rights Act of 1968").

(3) PARTICIPATING TRIBE.— The term "participating Tribe" means an Indian tribe that is designated under section 813(d)(1) as a participating Tribe to exercise special Tribal criminal jurisdiction.

(4) PILOT PROGRAM.—The term "pilot program" means the pilot program established by section 813(d)(1).

(5) SPECIAL TRIBAL CRIMINAL JURISDICTION.—The term "special Tribal criminal jurisdiction" means the criminal jurisdiction that a participating Tribe may exercise under this subtitle but could not otherwise exercise.

(6) STATE.—The term "State" means the State of Alaska.

(7) VILLAGE.—The term "Village" means the Alaska Native Village Statistical Area covering all or any portion of a Native village (as defined in section 3 of the Alaska Native Claims Settlement Act (43 U.S.C. 1602)), as depicted on the applicable

Tribal Statistical Area Program Verification map of the Bureau of the Census.

SEC. 813. TRIBAL JURISDICTION IN ALASKA.

(a) IN GENERAL.—Subject to title II of Public Law 90–284 (25 U.S.C. 1301 et seq.) (commonly known as the "Indian Civil Rights Act of 1968"), Congress recognizes and affirms the inherent authority of any Indian tribe occupying a Village in the State to exercise criminal and civil jurisdiction over all Indians present in the Village.

(b) TRIBAL CIVIL JURISDICTION TO ENFORCE PROTECTION ORDERS.—

(1) IN GENERAL.—A court of any Indian tribe in the State shall have full civil jurisdiction to issue and enforce protection orders involving any person in matters—

(A) arising within the Village of the Indian tribe; or

(B) otherwise within the authority of the Indian tribe.

(2) INCLUSIONS.—The full civil jurisdiction to issue and enforce protection orders under paragraph (1) includes the authority to enforce protection orders through—

(A) civil contempt proceedings;

(B) exclusion of violators from the Village of the Indian tribe; and

(C) other appropriate mechanisms.

(c) SPECIAL TRIBAL CRIMINAL JURISDICTION.—

(1) IN GENERAL.—Notwithstanding any other provision of law, in addition to all powers of self-government recognized and affirmed under subsection (a), the powers of self-government of a participating Tribe include the inherent power of the participating Tribe, which is hereby recognized and affirmed, to exercise special Tribal criminal jurisdiction over a defendant for a covered crime that occurs in the Village of the participating Tribe.

(2) CONCURRENT JURISDICTION.—The exercise of special Tribal criminal jurisdiction by a participating Tribe shall be concurrent with the jurisdiction of the United States, the State, or both.

(3) EXCEPTION IF VICTIM AND DEFENDANT ARE BOTH NON-INDIANS.—

(A) IN GENERAL.—A participating Tribe may not exercise special Tribal criminal jurisdiction over an alleged offense of a covered crime, other than obstruction of justice or assault of Tribal justice personnel, if neither the defendant nor the alleged victim is an Indian.

(B) DEFINITION OF VICTIM.—In this paragraph and with respect to a criminal proceeding in which a participating Tribe exercises special Tribal criminal jurisdiction based on a violation of a protection order, the term "victim" means a person specifically protected by the protection order that the defendant allegedly violated.

(d) PILOT PROGRAM FOR SPECIAL TRIBAL CRIMINAL JURISDICTION OVER PERSONS WHO ARE NOT INDIANS.—

(1) ESTABLISHMENT.—Subject to title II of Public Law 90–284 (25 U.S.C. 1301 et seq.) (commonly known as the "Indian Civil Rights Act of 1968"), there is established a pilot program under which the Attorney General, subject to paragraph (5), shall designate not more than 5 Indian tribes per calendar

year as participating Tribes to exercise the special Tribal criminal jurisdiction described in paragraph (6) over all persons present in the Village of the Indian tribe.

(2) PROCEDURE.—At any time during the 1-year period beginning on the date of enactment of this Act, and annually thereafter, an Indian tribe may request the Attorney General to designate the Indian tribe as a participating Tribe under paragraph (1).

(3) DESIGNATION OF PARTICIPATING TRIBES.—

(A) IN GENERAL.—The Attorney General, in consultation with the Secretary of the Interior and affected Indian tribes, shall establish a process to designate Indian tribes to participate in the pilot program, which process shall—

(i) require that preference shall be given to Indian tribes occupying Villages—

(I) the populations of which are predominantly Indian; and

(II) that lack a permanent State law enforcement physical presence;

(ii) require that for each Indian tribe requesting to be designated as a participating Tribe, the Attorney General makes a determination that the criminal justice system of the Indian tribe has adequate safeguards in place to protect defendants' rights, consistent with section 204(d) of Public Law 90–284 (25 U.S.C. 1304(d)) (commonly known as the "Indian Civil Rights Act of 1968"); and

(iii) be subject to such other criteria as the Attorney General considers to be appropriate to achieve the purposes of this subtitle.

(B) DESIGNATION.—The Attorney General shall designate Indian tribes to participate in the pilot program under paragraph (1) using the process established under subparagraph (A).

(4) INTERTRIBAL PARTICIPATION.—

(A) IN GENERAL.—2 or more participating Tribes (or the Tribal organization (as defined in section 4 of the Indian Self-Determination and Education Assistance Act (25 U.S.C. 5304)) of the participating Tribe, if the Tribal organization is exercising delegated authority from the participating Tribe)—

(i) may elect to participate jointly in the pilot program by providing shared resources to carry out the purposes of the pilot program; and

(ii) on making an election pursuant to clause (i), shall be considered to be a single participating Tribe for purposes of the maximum number of participating Tribes under paragraphs (1) and (5).

(B) ADDITIONAL PARTICIPATING TRIBES.—

(i) IN GENERAL.—Additional participating Tribes may elect to join an established intertribal partnership under subparagraph (A) at any time after the intertribal partnership is established.

(ii) APPLICATION.—An intertribal partnership that additional participating Tribes elect to join pursuant to clause (i) shall be considered to be a single participating Tribe for purposes of the maximum number of participating Tribes under paragraphs (1) and (5).

(5) MAXIMUM NUMBER OF PARTICIPATING TRIBES.—

(A) IN GENERAL.—Except as provided in subparagraph (B), the Attorney General may designate not more than 30 Indian tribes to participate in the pilot program.

(B) EXCEPTION.—The limitation under subparagraph (A) shall not apply if the Attorney General submits to the Committee on Indian Affairs of the Senate and the Committee on Natural Resources of the House of Representatives, and publishes in the Federal Register, a written notice of the intention to designate additional Indian tribes as participating Tribes, including the rationale for the designation, by not later than the date that is 180 days before the date of designation.

(6) DESCRIPTION OF JURISDICTION.—Congress recognizes and affirms that an Indian tribe selected to participate in the pilot program as a participating Tribe may exercise, subject to paragraph (7), special Tribal criminal jurisdiction with respect to covered crimes.

(7) RIGHTS OF DEFENDANTS.—In exercising special Tribal criminal jurisdiction under the pilot program, a participating Tribe shall provide to each defendant all rights described in section 204(d) of Public Law 90–284 (25 U.S.C. 1304(d)) (commonly known as the "Indian Civil Rights Act of 1968").

(e) SENTENCES.—In a criminal proceeding in which an Indian court of a participating Tribe, in exercising special Tribal criminal jurisdiction with respect to a covered crime, imposes a sentence of imprisonment of more than 1 year on a defendant pursuant to section 202(b) of Public Law 90–284 (25 U.S.C. 1302(b)) (commonly known as the "Indian Civil Rights Act of 1968"), the Indian court may require the defendant—

(1) to serve a sentence—

(A) in a Tribal correctional center that has been approved by the Bureau of Indian Affairs for long-term incarceration, in accordance with guidelines set by the Bureau of Indian Affairs;

(B) at the expense of the United States, in the nearest appropriate Federal facility pursuant to the Bureau of Prisons Tribal Prisoner Program established under section 234(c)(1) of the Tribal Law and Order Act of 2010 (25 U.S.C. 1302 note; Public Law 111–211); or

(C) at the expense of the participating Tribe and, subject to section 204(f)(1) of Public Law 90–284 (25 U.S.C. 1304(f)(1)) (commonly known as the "Indian Civil Rights Act of 1968"), reimbursable by the Attorney General, in a detention or correctional center approved by the State or a local government of the State pursuant to a memorandum of agreement between the participating Tribe and the State or local government of the State; or

(2) to serve another alternative form of punishment, as determined by the Indian court pursuant to Tribal law.

(f) MEMORANDA OF AGREEMENT.—The Attorney General and the Secretary of the Interior may enter into such memoranda of agreement with participating Tribes and the State as are necessary and appropriate—

(1) to coordinate respective law enforcement activities;
(2) to share equipment and other resources;
(3) to establish cross-deputization arrangements;
(4) to coordinate appropriate training activities; and
(5) to address any other matters that will facilitate the successful implementation of the pilot program, including intergovernmental agreements regarding—
(A) the incarceration of convicted persons; and
(B) cooperation in the investigation and prosecution of crimes.

(g) ALASKA TRIBAL PUBLIC SAFETY ADVISORY COMMITTEE.—
(1) ESTABLISHMENT.—Not later than 1 year after the date of enactment of this Act, the Attorney General, in consultation with the Secretary of the Interior, affected Indian tribes, and the State, shall establish a committee, to be known as the "Alaska Tribal Public Safety Advisory Committee" (referred to in this subsection as the "Committee").
(2) MEMBERSHIP.—The Committee shall consist of 1 or more representatives from—
(A) participating Tribes and Indian tribes aspiring to participate in the pilot program;
(B) Federal, Tribal, State, and local law enforcement; and
(C) Tribal nonprofit organizations providing victim services.
(3) DUTIES.—The Committee shall focus on—
(A) improving the justice systems, crime prevention, and victim services of Indian tribes and the State; and
(B) increasing coordination and communication among Federal, Tribal, State, and local law enforcement agencies.
(4) TRAVEL EXPENSES.—A member of the Committee shall be allowed travel expenses, including per diem in lieu of subsistence, at rates authorized for employees of agencies under subchapter I of chapter 57 of title 5, United States Code, while away from their homes or regular places of business in the performance of services for the Committee.
(5) NONAPPLICABILITY OF FACA.—The Federal Advisory Committee Act (5 U.S.C. App.) shall not apply to the Committee.
(6) AUTHORIZATION OF APPROPRIATIONS.—There are authorized to be appropriated to carry out this subsection such sums as may be necessary for the period of fiscal years 2023 through 2027, to remain available until expended.

(h) REPORT TO CONGRESS.—Not later than 5 years after the date of enactment of this Act, the Attorney General, in consultation with the Secretary of the Interior and affected Indian tribes, shall submit to Congress a report describing the results of the pilot program, including an explanation of any modifications to law necessary to facilitate improved law enforcement in Villages.

(i) APPLICABILITY.—Nothing in this subtitle—
(1) limits, alters, expands, or diminishes the civil or criminal jurisdiction of the United States, the State, any subdivision of the State, or any Indian tribe in the State;
(2) creates or eliminates any Federal or State criminal jurisdiction over a Village; or

(3) affects the authority of the United States or any authority delegated by the United States to the State to investigate and prosecute a criminal violation in a Village.

TITLE IX—OFFICE ON VIOLENCE AGAINST WOMEN

SEC. 901. ESTABLISHMENT OF OFFICE ON VIOLENCE AGAINST WOMEN.

(a) ESTABLISHMENT OF OFFICE ON VIOLENCE AGAINST WOMEN.—Section 2002 of title I of the Omnibus Crime Control and Safe Streets Act of 1968 (34 U.S.C. 10442) is amended—

(1) in the section heading, by striking "**VIOLENCE AGAINST WOMEN OFFICE**" and inserting "**OFFICE ON VIOLENCE AGAINST WOMEN**";

(2) in subsection (a), by striking "a Violence Against Women Office" and inserting "an Office on Violence Against Women";

(3) in subsection (b), by inserting ", not subsumed by any other office" after "within the Department of Justice"; and

(4) in subsection (c)(2), by striking "authorized or undertaken under the" and all that follows and inserting "authorized or undertaken under—

"(A) the Violence Against Women Act of 1994 (title IV of Public Law 103–322);

"(B) the Violence Against Women Act of 2000 (division B of Public Law 106–386);

"(C) the Violence Against Women and Department of Justice Reauthorization Act of 2005 (Public Law 109–162; 119 Stat. 2960);

"(D) the Violence Against Women Reauthorization Act of 2013 (Public Law 113–4; 127 Stat. 54); and

"(E) the Violence Against Women Act Reauthorization Act of 2022.".

(b) DIRECTOR OF THE OFFICE ON VIOLENCE AGAINST WOMEN.—Section 2003 of title I of the Omnibus Crime Control and Safe Streets Act of 1968 (34 U.S.C. 10443) is amended—

(1) in the section heading, by striking "**VIOLENCE AGAINST WOMEN OFFICE**" and inserting "**OFFICE ON VIOLENCE AGAINST WOMEN**";

(2) in subsection (a)—

(A) by striking "the Violence Against Women Office" and inserting "the Office on Violence Against Women"; and

(B) by striking "in this title referred to" and inserting "in this part referred to";

(3) in subsection (b)(2)—

(A) by striking "or the Violence" and inserting ", the Violence"; and

(B) by striking the period at the end and inserting ", the Violence Against Women and Department of Justice Reauthorization Act of 2005 (Public Law 109–162; 119 Stat. 2960), the Violence Against Women Reauthorization Act of 2013 (Public Law 113–4; 127 Stat. 54), or the Violence Against Women Act Reauthorization Act of 2022.".

(c) DUTIES AND FUNCTIONS OF DIRECTOR OF THE OFFICE ON VIOLENCE AGAINST WOMEN.—Section 2004 of title I of the Omnibus

Appendix C
Violence Against Women Reauthorization Act of 2013
Public Law 113-4

Title IX. Safety for Indian Women

March 7, 2013

VIOLENCE AGAINST WOMEN
REAUTHORIZATION ACT OF 2013
Pages 118 – 126

TITLE IX—SAFETY FOR INDIAN WOMEN

national security officials to be used solely for a national security purpose in a manner that protects the confidentiality of such information.".

(b) GUIDELINES.—Section 384(d) of the Illegal Immigration Reform and Immigrant Responsibility Act of 1996 (8 U.S.C. 1367(d)) is amended—

(1) by inserting ", Secretary of State," after "The Attorney General";

(2) by inserting ", Department of State," after "Department of Justice"; and

(3) by inserting "and severe forms of trafficking in persons or criminal activity listed in section 101(a)(15)(U) of the Immigration and Nationality Act (8 U.S.C. 1101(a)(15)(u))" after "domestic violence".

Deadline. Guidance. 8 USC 1367 note.

(c) IMPLEMENTATION.—Not later than 180 days after the date of the enactment of this Act, the Attorney General, the Secretary of State, and Secretary of Homeland Security shall provide the guidance required by section 384(d) of the Illegal Immigration Reform and Immigrant Responsibility Act of 1996 (8 U.S.C. 1367(d)), consistent with the amendments made by subsections (a) and (b).

8 USC 1367.

(d) CLERICAL AMENDMENT.—Section 384(a)(1) of the Illegal Immigration Reform and Immigrant Responsibility Act of 1986 is amended by striking "241(a)(2)" in the matter following subparagraph (F) and inserting "237(a)(2)".

TITLE IX—SAFETY FOR INDIAN WOMEN

SEC. 901. GRANTS TO INDIAN TRIBAL GOVERNMENTS.

Section 2015(a) of title I of the Omnibus Crime Control and Safe Streets Act of 1968 (42 U.S.C. 3796gg–10(a)) is amended—

(1) in paragraph (2), by inserting "sex trafficking," after "sexual assault,";

(2) in paragraph (4), by inserting "sex trafficking," after "sexual assault,";

(3) in paragraph (5), by striking "and stalking" and all that follows and inserting "sexual assault, sex trafficking, and stalking;";

(4) in paragraph (7)—

(A) by inserting "sex trafficking," after "sexual assault," each place it appears; and

(B) by striking "and" at the end;

(5) in paragraph (8)—

(A) by inserting "sex trafficking," after "stalking,"; and

(B) by striking the period at the end and inserting a semicolon; and

(6) by adding at the end the following:

"(9) provide services to address the needs of youth who are victims of domestic violence, dating violence, sexual assault, sex trafficking, or stalking and the needs of youth and children exposed to domestic violence, dating violence, sexual assault, or stalking, including support for the nonabusing parent or the caretaker of the youth or child; and

"(10) develop and promote legislation and policies that enhance best practices for responding to violent crimes against Indian women, including the crimes of domestic violence, dating violence, sexual assault, sex trafficking, and stalking.".

SEC. 902. GRANTS TO INDIAN TRIBAL COALITIONS.

Section 2001 of title I of the Omnibus Crime Control and Safe Streets Act of 1968 (42 U.S.C. 3796gg) is amended by striking subsection (d) and inserting the following:

"(d) TRIBAL COALITION GRANTS.—

"(1) PURPOSE.—The Attorney General shall award a grant to tribal coalitions for purposes of—

"(A) increasing awareness of domestic violence and sexual assault against Indian women;

"(B) enhancing the response to violence against Indian women at the Federal, State, and tribal levels;

"(C) identifying and providing technical assistance to coalition membership and tribal communities to enhance access to essential services to Indian women victimized by domestic and sexual violence, including sex trafficking; and

"(D) assisting Indian tribes in developing and promoting State, local, and tribal legislation and policies that enhance best practices for responding to violent crimes against Indian women, including the crimes of domestic violence, dating violence, sexual assault, sex trafficking, and stalking.

"(2) GRANTS.—The Attorney General shall award grants on an annual basis under paragraph (1) to—

"(A) each tribal coalition that—

"(i) meets the criteria of a tribal coalition under section 40002(a) of the Violence Against Women Act of 1994 (42 U.S.C. 13925(a));

"(ii) is recognized by the Office on Violence Against Women; and

"(iii) provides services to Indian tribes; and

"(B) organizations that propose to incorporate and operate a tribal coalition in areas where Indian tribes are located but no tribal coalition exists.

"(3) USE OF AMOUNTS.—For each of fiscal years 2014 through 2018, of the amounts appropriated to carry out this subsection—

"(A) not more than 10 percent shall be made available to organizations described in paragraph (2)(B), provided that 1 or more organizations determined by the Attorney General to be qualified apply; Applicability.

"(B) not less than 90 percent shall be made available to tribal coalitions described in paragraph (2)(A), which amounts shall be distributed equally among each eligible tribal coalition for the applicable fiscal year.

"(4) ELIGIBILITY FOR OTHER GRANTS.—Receipt of an award under this subsection by a tribal coalition shall not preclude the tribal coalition from receiving additional grants under this title to carry out the purposes described in paragraph (1).

"(5) MULTIPLE PURPOSE APPLICATIONS.—Nothing in this subsection prohibits any tribal coalition or organization described in paragraph (2) from applying for funding to address sexual assault or domestic violence needs in the same application.".

SEC. 903. CONSULTATION.

Section 903 of the Violence Against Women and Department of Justice Reauthorization Act of 2005 (42 U.S.C. 14045d) is amended—

(1) in subsection (a)—

(A) by striking "and the Violence Against Women Act of 2000" and inserting ", the Violence Against Women Act of 2000"; and

(B) by inserting ", and the Violence Against Women Reauthorization Act of 2013" before the period at the end;

(2) in subsection (b)—

(A) in the matter preceding paragraph (1), by striking "Secretary of the Department of Health and Human Services" and inserting "Secretary of Health and Human Services, the Secretary of the Interior,"; and

(B) in paragraph (2), by striking "and stalking" and inserting "stalking, and sex trafficking"; and

(3) by adding at the end the following:

"(c) ANNUAL REPORT.—The Attorney General shall submit to Congress an annual report on the annual consultations required under subsection (a) that—

"(1) contains the recommendations made under subsection (b) by Indian tribes during the year covered by the report;

"(2) describes actions taken during the year covered by the report to respond to recommendations made under subsection (b) during the year or a previous year; and

"(3) describes how the Attorney General will work in coordination and collaboration with Indian tribes, the Secretary of Health and Human Services, and the Secretary of the Interior to address the recommendations made under subsection (b).

Deadline.

"(d) NOTICE.—Not later than 120 days before the date of a consultation under subsection (a), the Attorney General shall notify tribal leaders of the date, time, and location of the consultation.".

SEC. 904. TRIBAL JURISDICTION OVER CRIMES OF DOMESTIC VIOLENCE.

Title II of Public Law 90–284 (25 U.S.C. 1301 et seq.) (commonly known as the "Indian Civil Rights Act of 1968") is amended by adding at the end the following:

25 USC 1304.

"SEC. 204. TRIBAL JURISDICTION OVER CRIMES OF DOMESTIC VIOLENCE.

"(a) DEFINITIONS.—In this section:

"(1) DATING VIOLENCE.—The term 'dating violence' means violence committed by a person who is or has been in a social relationship of a romantic or intimate nature with the victim, as determined by the length of the relationship, the type of relationship, and the frequency of interaction between the persons involved in the relationship.

"(2) DOMESTIC VIOLENCE.—The term 'domestic violence' means violence committed by a current or former spouse or intimate partner of the victim, by a person with whom the victim shares a child in common, by a person who is cohabitating with or has cohabitated with the victim as a spouse or intimate partner, or by a person similarly situated to a spouse of the victim under the domestic- or family- violence laws of an Indian tribe that has jurisdiction over the Indian country where the violence occurs.

"(3) INDIAN COUNTRY.—The term 'Indian country' has the meaning given the term in section 1151 of title 18, United States Code.

"(4) PARTICIPATING TRIBE.—The term 'participating tribe' means an Indian tribe that elects to exercise special domestic violence criminal jurisdiction over the Indian country of that Indian tribe.

"(5) PROTECTION ORDER.—The term 'protection order'—

"(A) means any injunction, restraining order, or other order issued by a civil or criminal court for the purpose of preventing violent or threatening acts or harassment against, sexual violence against, contact or communication with, or physical proximity to, another person; and

"(B) includes any temporary or final order issued by a civil or criminal court, whether obtained by filing an independent action or as a pendent lite order in another proceeding, if the civil or criminal order was issued in response to a complaint, petition, or motion filed by or on behalf of a person seeking protection.

"(6) SPECIAL DOMESTIC VIOLENCE CRIMINAL JURISDICTION.—The term 'special domestic violence criminal jurisdiction' means the criminal jurisdiction that a participating tribe may exercise under this section but could not otherwise exercise.

"(7) SPOUSE OR INTIMATE PARTNER.—The term 'spouse or intimate partner' has the meaning given the term in section 2266 of title 18, United States Code.

"(b) NATURE OF THE CRIMINAL JURISDICTION.—

"(1) IN GENERAL.—Notwithstanding any other provision of law, in addition to all powers of self-government recognized and affirmed by sections 201 and 203, the powers of self-government of a participating tribe include the inherent power of that tribe, which is hereby recognized and affirmed, to exercise special domestic violence criminal jurisdiction over all persons.

"(2) CONCURRENT JURISDICTION.—The exercise of special domestic violence criminal jurisdiction by a participating tribe shall be concurrent with the jurisdiction of the United States, of a State, or of both.

"(3) APPLICABILITY.—Nothing in this section—

"(A) creates or eliminates any Federal or State criminal jurisdiction over Indian country; or

"(B) affects the authority of the United States or any State government that has been delegated authority by the United States to investigate and prosecute a criminal violation in Indian country.

"(4) EXCEPTIONS.—

"(A) VICTIM AND DEFENDANT ARE BOTH NON-INDIANS.—

"(i) IN GENERAL.—A participating tribe may not exercise special domestic violence criminal jurisdiction over an alleged offense if neither the defendant nor the alleged victim is an Indian.

"(ii) DEFINITION OF VICTIM.—In this subparagraph and with respect to a criminal proceeding in which a participating tribe exercises special domestic violence criminal jurisdiction based on a violation of a protection order, the term 'victim' means a person specifically protected by a protection order that the defendant allegedly violated.

"(B) DEFENDANT LACKS TIES TO THE INDIAN TRIBE.—A participating tribe may exercise special domestic violence criminal jurisdiction over a defendant only if the defendant—

"(i) resides in the Indian country of the participating tribe;

"(ii) is employed in the Indian country of the participating tribe; or

"(iii) is a spouse, intimate partner, or dating partner of—

"(I) a member of the participating tribe; or

"(II) an Indian who resides in the Indian country of the participating tribe.

"(c) CRIMINAL CONDUCT.—A participating tribe may exercise special domestic violence criminal jurisdiction over a defendant for criminal conduct that falls into one or more of the following categories:

"(1) DOMESTIC VIOLENCE AND DATING VIOLENCE.—An act of domestic violence or dating violence that occurs in the Indian country of the participating tribe.

"(2) VIOLATIONS OF PROTECTION ORDERS.—An act that—

"(A) occurs in the Indian country of the participating tribe; and

"(B) violates the portion of a protection order that—

"(i) prohibits or provides protection against violent or threatening acts or harassment against, sexual violence against, contact or communication with, or physical proximity to, another person;

"(ii) was issued against the defendant;

"(iii) is enforceable by the participating tribe; and

"(iv) is consistent with section 2265(b) of title 18, United States Code.

"(d) RIGHTS OF DEFENDANTS.—In a criminal proceeding in which a participating tribe exercises special domestic violence criminal jurisdiction, the participating tribe shall provide to the defendant—

"(1) all applicable rights under this Act;

"(2) if a term of imprisonment of any length may be imposed, all rights described in section 202(c);

"(3) the right to a trial by an impartial jury that is drawn from sources that—

"(A) reflect a fair cross section of the community; and

"(B) do not systematically exclude any distinctive group in the community, including non-Indians; and

"(4) all other rights whose protection is necessary under the Constitution of the United States in order for Congress to recognize and affirm the inherent power of the participating tribe to exercise special domestic violence criminal jurisdiction over the defendant.

"(e) PETITIONS TO STAY DETENTION.—

"(1) IN GENERAL.—A person who has filed a petition for a writ of habeas corpus in a court of the United States under section 203 may petition that court to stay further detention of that person by the participating tribe.

"(2) GRANT OF STAY.—A court shall grant a stay described in paragraph (1) if the court—

"(A) finds that there is a substantial likelihood that the habeas corpus petition will be granted; and

"(B) after giving each alleged victim in the matter an opportunity to be heard, finds by clear and convincing evidence that under conditions imposed by the court, the petitioner is not likely to flee or pose a danger to any person or the community if released.

"(3) NOTICE.—An Indian tribe that has ordered the detention of any person has a duty to timely notify such person of his rights and privileges under this subsection and under section 203.

"(f) GRANTS TO TRIBAL GOVERNMENTS.—The Attorney General may award grants to the governments of Indian tribes (or to authorized designees of those governments)—

"(1) to strengthen tribal criminal justice systems to assist Indian tribes in exercising special domestic violence criminal jurisdiction, including—

"(A) law enforcement (including the capacity of law enforcement or court personnel to enter information into and obtain information from national crime information databases);

"(B) prosecution;

"(C) trial and appellate courts;

"(D) probation systems;

"(E) detention and correctional facilities;

"(F) alternative rehabilitation centers;

"(G) culturally appropriate services and assistance for victims and their families; and

"(H) criminal codes and rules of criminal procedure, appellate procedure, and evidence;

"(2) to provide indigent criminal defendants with the effective assistance of licensed defense counsel, at no cost to the defendant, in criminal proceedings in which a participating tribe prosecutes a crime of domestic violence or dating violence or a criminal violation of a protection order;

"(3) to ensure that, in criminal proceedings in which a participating tribe exercises special domestic violence criminal jurisdiction, jurors are summoned, selected, and instructed in a manner consistent with all applicable requirements; and

"(4) to accord victims of domestic violence, dating violence, and violations of protection orders rights that are similar to the rights of a crime victim described in section 3771(a) of title 18, United States Code, consistent with tribal law and custom.

"(g) SUPPLEMENT, NOT SUPPLANT.—Amounts made available under this section shall supplement and not supplant any other Federal, State, tribal, or local government amounts made available to carry out activities described in this section.

"(h) AUTHORIZATION OF APPROPRIATIONS.—There are authorized to be appropriated $5,000,000 for each of fiscal years 2014 through 2018 to carry out subsection (f) and to provide training, technical assistance, data collection, and evaluation of the criminal justice systems of participating tribes.".

SEC. 905. TRIBAL PROTECTION ORDERS.

Section 2265 of title 18, United States Code, is amended by striking subsection (e) and inserting the following:

"(e) TRIBAL COURT JURISDICTION.—For purposes of this section, a court of an Indian tribe shall have full civil jurisdiction to issue and enforce protection orders involving any person, including the authority to enforce any orders through civil contempt proceedings, to exclude violators from Indian land, and to use other appropriate mechanisms, in matters arising anywhere in the Indian country of the Indian tribe (as defined in section 1151) or otherwise within the authority of the Indian tribe.".

SEC. 906. AMENDMENTS TO THE FEDERAL ASSAULT STATUTE.

(a) IN GENERAL.—Section 113 of title 18, United States Code, is amended—

(1) in subsection (a)—

(A) by striking paragraph (1) and inserting the following:

"(1) Assault with intent to commit murder or a violation of section 2241 or 2242, by a fine under this title, imprisonment for not more than 20 years, or both.";

(B) in paragraph (2), by striking "felony under chapter 109A" and inserting "violation of section 2241 or 2242";

(C) in paragraph (3) by striking "and without just cause or excuse,";

(D) in paragraph (4), by striking "six months" and inserting "1 year";

(E) in paragraph (7)—

(i) by striking "substantial bodily injury to an individual who has not attained the age of 16 years" and inserting "substantial bodily injury to a spouse or intimate partner, a dating partner, or an individual who has not attained the age of 16 years"; and

(ii) by striking "fine" and inserting "a fine"; and

(F) by adding at the end the following:

"(8) Assault of a spouse, intimate partner, or dating partner by strangling, suffocating, or attempting to strangle or suffocate, by a fine under this title, imprisonment for not more than 10 years, or both."; and

(2) in subsection (b)—

(A) by striking "(b) As used in this subsection—" and inserting the following:

"(b) DEFINITIONS.—In this section—";

(B) in paragraph (1)(B), by striking "and" at the end;

(C) in paragraph (2), by striking the period at the end and inserting a semicolon; and

(D) by adding at the end the following:

"(3) the terms 'dating partner' and 'spouse or intimate partner' have the meanings given those terms in section 2266;

"(4) the term 'strangling' means intentionally, knowingly, or recklessly impeding the normal breathing or circulation of the blood of a person by applying pressure to the throat or neck, regardless of whether that conduct results in any visible injury or whether there is any intent to kill or protractedly injure the victim; and

"(5) the term 'suffocating' means intentionally, knowingly, or recklessly impeding the normal breathing of a person by covering the mouth of the person, the nose of the person, or both, regardless of whether that conduct results in any visible injury or whether there is any intent to kill or protractedly injure the victim.".

(b) INDIAN MAJOR CRIMES.—Section 1153(a) of title 18, United States Code, is amended by striking "assault with intent to commit murder, assault with a dangerous weapon, assault resulting in serious bodily injury (as defined in section 1365 of this title)" and inserting "a felony assault under section 113".

(c) REPEAT OFFENDERS.—Section 2265A(b)(1)(B) of title 18, United States Code, is amended by inserting "or tribal" after "State".

SEC. 907. ANALYSIS AND RESEARCH ON VIOLENCE AGAINST INDIAN WOMEN.

(a) IN GENERAL.—Section 904(a) of the Violence Against Women and Department of Justice Reauthorization Act of 2005 (42 U.S.C. 3796gg–10 note) is amended—

(1) in paragraph (1)—

(A) by striking "The National" and inserting "Not later than 2 years after the date of enactment of the Violence Against Women Reauthorization Act of 2013, the National"; and

(B) by inserting "and in Native villages (as defined in section 3 of the Alaska Native Claims Settlement Act (43 U.S.C. 1602))" before the period at the end;

(2) in paragraph (2)(A)—

(A) in clause (iv), by striking "and" at the end;

(B) in clause (v), by striking the period at the end and inserting "; and"; and

(C) by adding at the end the following:

"(vi) sex trafficking.";

(3) in paragraph (4), by striking "this Act" and inserting "the Violence Against Women Reauthorization Act of 2013"; and

(4) in paragraph (5), by striking "this section $1,000,000 for each of fiscal years 2007 and 2008" and inserting "this subsection $1,000,000 for each of fiscal years 2014 and 2015".

(b) AUTHORIZATION OF APPROPRIATIONS.—Section 905(b)(2) of the Violence Against Women and Department of Justice Reauthorization Act of 2005 (28 U.S.C. 534 note) is amended by striking "fiscal years 2007 through 2011" and inserting "fiscal years 2014 through 2018".

SEC. 908. EFFECTIVE DATES; PILOT PROJECT. 25 USC 1304 note.

(a) GENERAL EFFECTIVE DATE.—Except as provided in section 4 and subsection (b) of this section, the amendments made by this title shall take effect on the date of enactment of this Act.

(b) EFFECTIVE DATE FOR SPECIAL DOMESTIC-VIOLENCE CRIMINAL JURISDICTION.—

(1) IN GENERAL.—Except as provided in paragraph (2), subsections (b) through (d) of section 204 of Public Law 90–284 (as added by section 904) shall take effect on the date that is 2 years after the date of enactment of this Act.

(2) PILOT PROJECT.—

(A) IN GENERAL.—At any time during the 2-year period beginning on the date of enactment of this Act, an Indian tribe may ask the Attorney General to designate the tribe Time period.

as a participating tribe under section 204(a) of Public Law 90–284 on an accelerated basis.

(B) PROCEDURE.—The Attorney General may grant a request under subparagraph (A) after coordinating with the Secretary of the Interior, consulting with affected Indian tribes, and concluding that the criminal justice system of the requesting tribe has adequate safeguards in place to protect defendants' rights, consistent with section 204 of Public Law 90–284.

Consultation.
Deadline.

(C) EFFECTIVE DATES FOR PILOT PROJECTS.—An Indian tribe designated as a participating tribe under this paragraph may commence exercising special domestic violence criminal jurisdiction pursuant to subsections (b) through (d) of section 204 of Public Law 90–284 on a date established by the Attorney General, after consultation with that Indian tribe, but in no event later than the date that is 2 years after the date of enactment of this Act.

SEC. 909. INDIAN LAW AND ORDER COMMISSION; REPORT ON THE ALASKA RURAL JUSTICE AND LAW ENFORCEMENT COMMISSION.

(a) IN GENERAL.—Section 15(f) of the Indian Law Enforcement Reform Act (25 U.S.C. 2812(f)) is amended by striking "2 years" and inserting "3 years".

Consultation.

(b) REPORT.—The Attorney General, in consultation with the Attorney General of the State of Alaska, the Commissioner of Public Safety of the State of Alaska, the Alaska Federation of Natives and Federally recognized Indian tribes in the State of Alaska, shall report to Congress not later than one year after enactment of this Act with respect to whether the Alaska Rural Justice and Law Enforcement Commission established under Section 112(a)(1) of the Consolidated Appropriations Act, 2004 should be continued and appropriations authorized for the continued work of the commission. The report may contain recommendations for legislation with respect to the scope of work and composition of the commission.

18 USC 2265 note.
Applicability.

SEC. 910. SPECIAL RULE FOR THE STATE OF ALASKA.

(a) EXPANDED JURISDICTION.—In the State of Alaska, the amendments made by sections 904 and 905 shall only apply to the Indian country (as defined in section 1151 of title 18, United States Code) of the Metlakatla Indian Community, Annette Island Reserve.

(b) RETAINED JURISDICTION.—The jurisdiction and authority of each Indian tribe in the State of Alaska under section 2265(e) of title 18, United States Code (as in effect on the day before the date of enactment of this Act)—

(1) shall remain in full force and effect; and

(2) are not limited or diminished by this Act or any amendment made by this Act.

(c) SAVINGS PROVISION.—Nothing in this Act or an amendment made by this Act limits or diminishes the jurisdiction of the State of Alaska, any subdivision of the State of Alaska, or any Indian tribe in the State of Alaska.

Appendix D
Violence Against Women and Department of Justice Reauthorization Act
of 2005 and Technical Assistance Corrections
Public Law 109 – 162
Pages 3077 - 3084

January 5, 2006

VIOLENCE AGAINST WOMEN AND DEPARTMENT OF JUSTICE REAUTHORIZATION ACT OF 2005

Pages 3077 – 3084

TITLE IX—SAFETY FOR INDIAN WOMEN

from clients and petitioners by international marriage brokers, the Department of State, or the Department of Homeland Security;

(D) that examines, based on the information gathered, the extent to which persons with a history of violence are using either the K nonimmigrant visa process or the services of international marriage brokers, or both, and the extent to which such persons are providing accurate and complete information to the Department of State or the Department of Homeland Security and to international marriage brokers in accordance with subsections (a) and (d)(2)(B); and

(E) that assesses the accuracy and completeness of the criminal background check performed by the Secretary of Homeland Security at identifying past instances of domestic violence.

(2) REPORT.—Not later than 2 years after the date of enactment of this Act, the Comptroller General shall submit to the Committee on the Judiciary of the Senate and the Committee on the Judiciary of the House of Representatives a report setting forth the results of the study conducted under paragraph (1).

(3) DATA COLLECTION.—The Secretary of Homeland Security and the Secretary of State shall collect and maintain the data necessary for the Comptroller General of the United States to conduct the study required by paragraph (1).

(g) REPEAL OF MAIL-ORDER BRIDE PROVISION.—Section 652 of the Illegal Immigration Reform and Immigrant Responsibility Act of 1996 (division C of Public Law 104–208; 8 U.S.C. 1375) is hereby repealed.

SEC. 834. SHARING OF CERTAIN INFORMATION. 8 USC 1202 note.

Section 222(f) of the Immigration and Nationality Act (8 U.S.C. 1202(f)) shall not be construed to prevent the sharing of information regarding a United States petitioner for a visa under clause (i) or (ii) of section 101(a)(15)(K) of such Act (8 U.S.C. 1101(a)(15)(K)) for the limited purposes of fulfilling disclosure obligations imposed by the amendments made by section 832(a) or by section 833, including reporting obligations of the Comptroller General of the United States under section 833(f).

TITLE IX—SAFETY FOR INDIAN WOMEN

SEC. 901. FINDINGS. 42 USC 3796gg–10 note.

Congress finds that—

(1) 1 out of every 3 Indian (including Alaska Native) women are raped in their lifetimes;

(2) Indian women experience 7 sexual assaults per 1,000, compared with 4 per 1,000 among Black Americans, 3 per 1,000 among Caucasians, 2 per 1,000 among Hispanic women, and 1 per 1,000 among Asian women;

(3) Indian women experience the violent crime of battering at a rate of 23.2 per 1,000, compared with 8 per 1,000 among Caucasian women;

(4) during the period 1979 through 1992, homicide was the third leading cause of death of Indian females aged 15

to 34, and 75 percent were killed by family members or acquaintances;

(5) Indian tribes require additional criminal justice and victim services resources to respond to violent assaults against women; and

(6) the unique legal relationship of the United States to Indian tribes creates a Federal trust responsibility to assist tribal governments in safeguarding the lives of Indian women.

42 USC 3796gg–10 note.

SEC. 902. PURPOSES.

The purposes of this title are—

(1) to decrease the incidence of violent crimes against Indian women;

(2) to strengthen the capacity of Indian tribes to exercise their sovereign authority to respond to violent crimes committed against Indian women; and

(3) to ensure that perpetrators of violent crimes committed against Indian women are held accountable for their criminal behavior.

42 USC 14045d.

SEC. 903. CONSULTATION.

(a) IN GENERAL.—The Attorney General shall conduct annual consultations with Indian tribal governments concerning the Federal administration of tribal funds and programs established under this Act, the Violence Against Women Act of 1994 (title IV of Public Law 103–322; 108 Stat. 1902) and the Violence Against Women Act of 2000 (division B of Public Law 106–386; 114 Stat. 1491).

(b) RECOMMENDATIONS.—During consultations under subsection (a), the Secretary of the Department of Health and Human Services and the Attorney General shall solicit recommendations from Indian tribes concerning—

(1) administering tribal funds and programs;

(2) enhancing the safety of Indian women from domestic violence, dating violence, sexual assault, and stalking; and

(3) strengthening the Federal response to such violent crimes.

SEC. 904. ANALYSIS AND RESEARCH ON VIOLENCE AGAINST INDIAN WOMEN.

42 USC 3796gg–10 note.

(a) NATIONAL BASELINE STUDY.—

(1) IN GENERAL.—The National Institute of Justice, in consultation with the Office on Violence Against Women, shall conduct a national baseline study to examine violence against Indian women in Indian country.

(2) SCOPE.—

(A) IN GENERAL.—The study shall examine violence committed against Indian women, including—

(i) domestic violence;

(ii) dating violence;

(iii) sexual assault;

(iv) stalking; and

(v) murder.

(B) EVALUATION.—The study shall evaluate the effectiveness of Federal, State, tribal, and local responses to the violations described in subparagraph (A) committed against Indian women.

(C) RECOMMENDATIONS.—The study shall propose recommendations to improve the effectiveness of Federal, State, tribal, and local responses to the violation described in subparagraph (A) committed against Indian women.

(3) TASK FORCE.— Establishment.

(A) IN GENERAL.—The Attorney General, acting through the Director of the Office on Violence Against Women, shall establish a task force to assist in the development and implementation of the study under paragraph (1) and guide implementation of the recommendation in paragraph (2)(C).

(B) MEMBERS.—The Director shall appoint to the task force representatives from—

(i) national tribal domestic violence and sexual assault nonprofit organizations;

(ii) tribal governments; and

(iii) the national tribal organizations.

(4) REPORT.—Not later than 2 years after the date of enactment of this Act, the Attorney General shall submit to the Committee on Indian Affairs of the Senate, the Committee on the Judiciary of the Senate, and the Committee on the Judiciary of the House of Representatives a report that describes the study.

(5) AUTHORIZATION OF APPROPRIATIONS.—There is authorized to be appropriated to carry out this section $1,000,000 for each of fiscal years 2007 and 2008, to remain available until expended.

(b) INJURY STUDY.—

(1) IN GENERAL.—The Secretary of Health and Human Services, acting through the Indian Health Service and the Centers for Disease Control and Prevention, shall conduct a study to obtain a national projection of—

(A) the incidence of injuries and homicides resulting from domestic violence, dating violence, sexual assault, or stalking committed against American Indian and Alaska Native women; and

(B) the cost of providing health care for the injuries described in subparagraph (A).

(2) REPORT.—Not later than 2 years after the date of enactment of this Act, the Secretary of Health and Human Services shall submit to the Committee on Indian Affairs of the Senate, the Committee on the Judiciary of the Senate, and the Committee on the Judiciary of the House of Representatives a report that describes the findings made in the study and recommends health care strategies for reducing the incidence and cost of the injuries described in paragraph (1).

(3) AUTHORIZATION OF APPROPRIATIONS.—There is authorized to be appropriated to carry out this section $500,000 for each of fiscal years 2007 and 2008, to remain available until expended.

SEC. 905. TRACKING OF VIOLENCE AGAINST INDIAN WOMEN.

(a) ACCESS TO FEDERAL CRIMINAL INFORMATION DATABASES.—Section 534 of title 28, United States Code, is amended—

(1) by redesignating subsection (d) as subsection (e); and

(2) by inserting after subsection (c) the following:

"(d) INDIAN LAW ENFORCEMENT AGENCIES.—The Attorney General shall permit Indian law enforcement agencies, in cases of domestic violence, dating violence, sexual assault, and stalking, to enter information into Federal criminal information databases and to obtain information from the databases.".

28 USC 534 note. (b) TRIBAL REGISTRY.—

(1) ESTABLISHMENT.—The Attorney General shall contract with any interested Indian tribe, tribal organization, or tribal nonprofit organization to develop and maintain—

(A) a national tribal sex offender registry; and

(B) a tribal protection order registry containing civil and criminal orders of protection issued by Indian tribes and participating jurisdictions.

(2) AUTHORIZATION OF APPROPRIATIONS.—There is authorized to be appropriated to carry out this section $1,000,000 for each of fiscal years 2007 through 2011, to remain available until expended.

SEC. 906. GRANTS TO INDIAN TRIBAL GOVERNMENTS.

(a) IN GENERAL.—Part T of title I of the Omnibus Crime Control and Safe Streets Act of 1968 (42 U.S.C. 3796gg et seq.) is amended by adding at the end the following:

42 USC 3796gg–10. **"SEC. 2007. GRANTS TO INDIAN TRIBAL GOVERNMENTS.**

"(a) GRANTS.—The Attorney General may make grants to Indian tribal governments and tribal organizations to—

"(1) develop and enhance effective governmental strategies to curtail violent crimes against and increase the safety of Indian women consistent with tribal law and custom;

"(2) increase tribal capacity to respond to domestic violence, dating violence, sexual assault, and stalking crimes against Indian women;

"(3) strengthen tribal justice interventions including tribal law enforcement, prosecution, courts, probation, correctional facilities;

"(4) enhance services to Indian women victimized by domestic violence, dating violence, sexual assault, and stalking;

"(5) work in cooperation with the community to develop education and prevention strategies directed toward issues of domestic violence, dating violence, and stalking programs and to address the needs of children exposed to domestic violence;

"(6) provide programs for supervised visitation and safe visitation exchange of children in situations involving domestic violence, sexual assault, or stalking committed by one parent against the other with appropriate security measures, policies, and procedures to protect the safety of victims and their children; and

"(7) provide transitional housing for victims of domestic violence, dating violence, sexual assault, or stalking, including rental or utilities payments assistance and assistance with related expenses such as security deposits and other costs incidental to relocation to transitional housing, and support services to enable a victim of domestic violence, dating violence, sexual assault, or stalking to locate and secure permanent housing and integrate into a community.

"(b) COLLABORATION.—All applicants under this section shall demonstrate their proposal was developed in consultation with a nonprofit, nongovernmental Indian victim services program, including sexual assault and domestic violence victim services providers in the tribal or local community, or a nonprofit tribal domestic violence and sexual assault coalition to the extent that they exist. In the absence of such a demonstration, the applicant may meet the requirement of this subsection through consultation with women in the community to be served.

"(c) NONEXCLUSIVITY.—The Federal share of a grant made under this section may not exceed 90 percent of the total costs of the project described in the application submitted, except that the Attorney General may grant a waiver of this match requirement on the basis of demonstrated financial hardship. Funds appropriated for the activities of any agency of an Indian tribal government or of the Bureau of Indian Affairs performing law enforcement functions on any Indian lands may be used to provide the non-Federal share of the cost of programs or projects funded under this section.".

(b) AUTHORIZATION OF FUNDS FROM GRANTS TO COMBAT VIOLENT CRIMES AGAINST WOMEN.—Section 2007(b)(1) of the Omnibus Crime Control and Safe Streets Act of 1968 (42 U.S.C. 3796gg–1(b)(1)) is amended to read as follows:

"(1) Ten percent shall be available for grants under the program authorized in section 2007. The requirements of this part shall not apply to funds allocated for such program.".

(c) AUTHORIZATION OF FUNDS FROM GRANTS TO ENCOURAGE STATE POLICIES AND ENFORCEMENT OF PROTECTION ORDERS PROGRAM.—Section 2101 of the Omnibus Crime Control and Safe Streets Act of 1968 (42 U.S.C. 3796hh) is amended by striking subsection (e) and inserting the following:

"(e) Not less than 10 percent of the total amount available under this section for each fiscal year shall be available for grants under the program authorized in section 2007. The requirements of this part shall not apply to funds allocated for such program.".

(d) AUTHORIZATION OF FUNDS FROM RURAL DOMESTIC VIOLENCE AND CHILD ABUSE ENFORCEMENT ASSISTANCE GRANTS.—Subsection 40295(c) of the Violence Against Women Act of 1994 (42 U.S.C. 13971(c)(3)) is amended by striking paragraph (3) and inserting the following:

"(3) Not less than 10 percent of the total amount available under this section for each fiscal year shall be available for grants under the program authorized in section 2007 of the Omnibus Crime Control and Safe Streets Act of 1968. The requirements of this paragraph shall not apply to funds allocated for such program.".

(e) AUTHORIZATION OF FUNDS FROM THE SAFE HAVENS FOR CHILDREN PROGRAM.—Section 1301 of the Violence Against Women Act of 2000 (42 U.S.C. 10420) is amended by striking subsection (f) and inserting the following:

"(f) Not less than 10 percent of the total amount available under this section for each fiscal year shall be available for grants under the program authorized in section 2007 of the Omnibus Crime Control and Safe Streets Act of 1968. The requirements of this subsection shall not apply to funds allocated for such program.".

(f) AUTHORIZATION OF FUNDS FROM THE TRANSITIONAL HOUSING ASSISTANCE GRANTS FOR CHILD VICTIMS OF DOMESTIC VIOLENCE, STALKING, OR SEXUAL ASSAULT PROGRAM.—Section 40299(g) of the

Violence Against Women Act of 1994 (42 U.S.C. 13975(g)) is amended by adding at the end the following:

"(4) TRIBAL PROGRAM.—Not less than 10 percent of the total amount available under this section for each fiscal year shall be available for grants under the program authorized in section 2007 of the Omnibus Crime Control and Safe Streets Act of 1968. The requirements of this paragraph shall not apply to funds allocated for such program.".

(g) AUTHORIZATION OF FUNDS FROM THE LEGAL ASSISTANCE FOR VICTIMS IMPROVEMENTS PROGRAM.—Section 1201(f) of the Violence Against Women Act of 2000 (42 U.S.C. 3796gg–6) is amended by adding at the end the following:

"(4) Not less than 10 percent of the total amount available under this section for each fiscal year shall be available for grants under the program authorized in section 2007 of the Omnibus Crime Control and Safe Streets Act of 1968. The requirements of this paragraph shall not apply to funds allocated for such program.".

SEC. 907. TRIBAL DEPUTY IN THE OFFICE ON VIOLENCE AGAINST WOMEN.

Part T of title I of the Omnibus Crime Control and Safe Streets Act of 1968 (42 U.S.C. 3796gg et seq.), as amended by section 906, is amended by adding at the end the following:

42 USC 3796gg–11.

"SEC. 2008. TRIBAL DEPUTY.

"(a) ESTABLISHMENT.—There is established in the Office on Violence Against Women a Deputy Director for Tribal Affairs.

"(b) DUTIES.—

"(1) IN GENERAL.—The Deputy Director shall under the guidance and authority of the Director of the Office on Violence Against Women—

Grants. Contracts.

"(A) oversee and manage the administration of grants to and contracts with Indian tribes, tribal courts, tribal organizations, or tribal nonprofit organizations;

"(B) ensure that, if a grant under this Act or a contract pursuant to such a grant is made to an organization to perform services that benefit more than 1 Indian tribe, the approval of each Indian tribe to be benefitted shall be a prerequisite to the making of the grant or letting of the contract;

Guidelines.

"(C) coordinate development of Federal policy, protocols, and guidelines on matters relating to violence against Indian women;

"(D) advise the Director of the Office on Violence Against Women concerning policies, legislation, implementation of laws, and other issues relating to violence against Indian women;

"(E) represent the Office on Violence Against Women in the annual consultations under section 903;

"(F) provide technical assistance, coordination, and support to other offices and bureaus in the Department of Justice to develop policy and to enforce Federal laws relating to violence against Indian women, including through litigation of civil and criminal actions relating to those laws;

"(G) maintain a liaison with the judicial branches of Federal, State, and tribal governments on matters relating to violence against Indian women;

"(H) support enforcement of tribal protection orders and implementation of full faith and credit educational projects and comity agreements between Indian tribes and States; and

"(I) ensure that adequate tribal technical assistance is made available to Indian tribes, tribal courts, tribal organizations, and tribal nonprofit organizations for all programs relating to violence against Indian women.

"(c) AUTHORITY.—

"(1) IN GENERAL.—The Deputy Director shall ensure that a portion of the tribal set-aside funds from any grant awarded under this Act, the Violence Against Women Act of 1994 (title IV of Public Law 103–322; 108 Stat. 1902), or the Violence Against Women Act of 2000 (division B of Public Law 106–386; 114 Stat. 1491) is used to enhance the capacity of Indian tribes to address the safety of Indian women.

"(2) ACCOUNTABILITY.—The Deputy Director shall ensure that some portion of the tribal set-aside funds from any grant made under this part is used to hold offenders accountable through—

"(A) enhancement of the response of Indian tribes to crimes of domestic violence, dating violence, sexual assault, and stalking against Indian women, including legal services for victims and Indian-specific offender programs;

"(B) development and maintenance of tribal domestic violence shelters or programs for battered Indian women, including sexual assault services, that are based upon the unique circumstances of the Indian women to be served;

"(C) development of tribal educational awareness programs and materials;

"(D) support for customary tribal activities to strengthen the intolerance of an Indian tribe to violence against Indian women; and

"(E) development, implementation, and maintenance of tribal electronic databases for tribal protection order registries.".

SEC. 908. ENHANCED CRIMINAL LAW RESOURCES.

(a) FIREARMS POSSESSION PROHIBITIONS.—Section 921(33)(A)(i) of title 18, United States Code, is amended to read: "(i) is a misdemeanor under Federal, State, or Tribal law; and".

(b) LAW ENFORCEMENT AUTHORITY.—Section 4(3) of the Indian Law Enforcement Reform Act (25 U.S.C. 2803(3) is amended—

(1) in subparagraph (A), by striking "or";

(2) in subparagraph (B), by striking the semicolon and inserting ", or"; and

(3) by adding at the end the following:

"(C) the offense is a misdemeanor crime of domestic violence, dating violence, stalking, or violation of a protection order and has, as an element, the use or attempted use of physical force, or the threatened use of a deadly weapon, committed by a current or former spouse, parent, or guardian of the victim, by a person with whom the victim shares a child in common, by a person who is cohabitating with or has cohabited with the victim as a spouse, parent, or guardian, or by a person similarly situated to a spouse, parent or guardian of the victim, and the employee has reasonable grounds to believe that the person to be arrested has committed, or is committing the crime;".

SEC. 909. DOMESTIC ASSAULT BY AN HABITUAL OFFENDER.

Chapter 7 of title 18, United States Code, is amended by adding at the end the following:

"§ 117. Domestic assault by an habitual offender

"(a) IN GENERAL.—Any person who commits a domestic assault within the special maritime and territorial jurisdiction of the United States or Indian country and who has a final conviction on at least 2 separate prior occasions in Federal, State, or Indian tribal court proceedings for offenses that would be, if subject to Federal jurisdiction—

"(1) any assault, sexual abuse, or serious violent felony against a spouse or intimate partner; or

"(2) an offense under chapter 110A,

shall be fined under this title, imprisoned for a term of not more than 5 years, or both, except that if substantial bodily injury results from violation under this section, the offender shall be imprisoned for a term of not more than 10 years.

"(b) DOMESTIC ASSAULT DEFINED.—In this section, the term 'domestic assault' means an assault committed by a current or former spouse, parent, child, or guardian of the victim, by a person with whom the victim shares a child in common, by a person who is cohabitating with or has cohabitated with the victim as a spouse, parent, child, or guardian, or by a person similarly situated to a spouse, parent, child, or guardian of the victim.".

DNA Fingerprint Act of 2005.

TITLE X—DNA FINGERPRINTING

42 USC 13701 note.

SEC. 1001. SHORT TITLE.

This title may be cited as the "DNA Fingerprint Act of 2005".

SEC. 1002. USE OF OPT-OUT PROCEDURE TO REMOVE SAMPLES FROM NATIONAL DNA INDEX.

Section 210304 of the DNA Identification Act of 1994 (42 U.S.C. 14132) is amended—

(1) in subsection (a)(1)(C), by striking "DNA profiles" and all that follows through ", and";

(2) in subsection (d)(1), by striking subparagraph (A), and inserting the following:

Certification.

"(A) The Director of the Federal Bureau of Investigation shall promptly expunge from the index described in subsection (a) the DNA analysis of a person included in the index—

"(i) on the basis of conviction for a qualifying Federal offense or a qualifying District of Columbia offense (as determined under sections 3 and 4 of the DNA Analysis Backlog Elimination Act of 2000 (42 U.S.C. 14135a, 14135b), respectively), if the Director receives, for each conviction of the person of a qualifying offense,

PUBLIC LAW 109–271—AUG. 12, 2006

TECHNICAL CORRECTIONS TO
VIOLENCE AGAINST WOMEN AND DEPARTMENT OF JUSTICE
REAUTHORIZATION ACT OF 2005
Pages 763 – 766

TITLE IX—SAFETY FOR INDIAN WOMEN

(c) DEPORTABLE ALIENS.—Section 237(a)(1)(H)(ii) of such Act (8 U.S.C. 1227(a)(1)(H)(ii)) is amended to read as follows:

"(ii) is a VAWA self-petitioner.".

(d) REMOVAL.—Section 239(e)(2)(B) of such Act (8 U.S.C. 1229(e)(2)(B)) is amended by striking "(V)" and inserting "(U)".

(e) CANCELLATION OF REMOVAL.—Section 240A(b)(4)(B) of such Act (8 U.S.C. 1229b(b)(4)(B)) is amended by striking "they were applications filed under section 204(a)(1)(A)(iii), (A)(iv), (B)(ii), or (B)(iii) for purposes of section 245 (a) and (c)." and inserting "the applicants were VAWA self-petitioners.".

(f) ADJUSTMENT OF STATUS.—Section 245 of such Act (8 U.S.C. 1255) is amended—

(1) in subsection (a), by striking "under subparagraph (A)(iii), (A)(iv), (B)(ii), or (B)(iii) of section 204(a)(1) or" and inserting "as a VAWA self-petitioner"; and

(2) in subsection (c), by striking "under subparagraph (A)(iii), (A)(iv), (A)(v), (A)(vi), (B)(ii), (B)(iii), or (B)(iv) of section 204(a)(1)" and inserting "as a VAWA self-petitioner".

(g) IMMIGRATION OFFICERS.—Section 287 of such Act (8 U.S.C. 1357) is amended by redesignating subsection (i) as subsection (h).

(h) PENALTIES FOR DISCLOSURE OF INFORMATION.—Section 384(a)(2) of the Illegal Immigration Reform and Immigrant Responsibility Act of 1996 (8 U.S.C. 1367(a)(2)) is amended by striking "clause (iii) or (iv)" and all that follows and inserting "paragraph (15)(T), (15)(U), or (51) of section 101(a) of the Immigration and Nationality Act or section 240A(b)(2) of such Act.".

SEC. 7. TITLE IX—INDIAN WOMEN.

(a) OMNIBUS CRIME CONTROL AND SAFE STREETS.—

(1) GRANTS TO COMBAT VIOLENT CRIMES AGAINST WOMEN.—Part T of the Omnibus Crime Control and Safe Streets Act of 1968 is amended—

(A) by redesignating the second section 2007 (42 U.S.C. 3796gg–10) (relating to grants to Indian tribal governments), as added by section 906 of the Violence Against Women and Department of Justice Reauthorization Act of 2005, as section 2015;

(B) by redesignating the second section 2008 (42 U.S.C. 3796gg–11) (relating to a tribal deputy), as added by section 907 of the Violence Against Women and Department of Justice Reauthorization Act of 2005, as section 2016; and

(C) by moving those sections so as to appear at the end of the part.

(2) STATE GRANT AMOUNTS.—Section 2007(b) of the Omnibus Crime Control and Safe Streets Act of 1968 (42 U.S.C. 3796gg–1(b)), as amended by section 906(b) of the Violence Against Women and Department of Justice Reauthorization Act of 2005, is amended by striking paragraph (1) and inserting the following:

"(1) 10 percent shall be available for grants under the program authorized by section 2015, which shall not otherwise be subject to the requirements of this part (other than section 2008);".

(3) GRANTS TO INDIAN TRIBAL GOVERNMENTS.—Section 2015 of the Omnibus Crime Control and Safe Streets Act of 1968, as added by section 906 of the Violence Against Women and

Department of Justice Reauthorization Act of 2005 (as redesignated by paragraph (1)(A)), is amended—

42 USC 3796gg–10.

(A) in subsection (a)—

(i) in the matter preceding paragraph (1), by striking "and tribal organizations" and inserting "or authorized designees of Indian tribal governments";

(ii) in paragraph (6), by striking "and" at the end;

(iii) in paragraph (7), by striking the period at the end and inserting "; and"; and

(iv) by adding at the end the following:

"(8) provide legal assistance necessary to provide effective aid to victims of domestic violence, dating violence, stalking, or sexual assault who are seeking relief in legal matters arising as a consequence of that abuse or violence, at minimal or no cost to the victims."; and

(B) by striking subsection (c).

42 USC 3796gg–11.

(4) TRIBAL DEPUTY RESPONSIBILITIES.—Section 2016(b)(1)(I) of the Omnibus Crime Control and Safe Streets Act of 1968 (as redesignated by paragraph (1)(B)) is amended by inserting after "technical assistance" the following: "that is developed and provided by entities having expertise in tribal law, customary practices, and Federal Indian law".

(5) GRANTS TO ENCOURAGE ARREST POLICIES AND ENFORCEMENT OF PROTECTION ORDERS.—Section 2101 of the Omnibus Crime Control and Safe Streets Act of 1968 (42 U.S.C. 3796hh) is amended by striking subsection (e) and inserting the following:

"(e) ALLOTMENT FOR INDIAN TRIBES.—

"(1) IN GENERAL.—Not less than 10 percent of the total amount available under this section for each fiscal year shall be available for grants under the program authorized by section 2015.

"(2) APPLICABILITY OF PART.—The requirements of this part shall not apply to funds allocated for the program described in paragraph (1).".

(b) RURAL DOMESTIC VIOLENCE.—

(1) IN GENERAL.—Section 40295(d) of the Safe Homes for Women Act of 1994 (42 U.S.C. 13971(d)), as amended by section 306 of the Violence Against Women and Department of Justice Reauthorization Act of 2005, is amended by striking paragraph (1) and inserting the following:

"(1) ALLOTMENT FOR INDIAN TRIBES.—

"(A) IN GENERAL.—Not less than 10 percent of the total amount available under this section for each fiscal year shall be available for grants under the program authorized by section 2015 of the Omnibus Crime Control and Safe Streets Act of 1968 (42 U.S.C. 3796gg–10).

"(B) APPLICABILITY OF PART.—The requirements of this section shall not apply to funds allocated for the program described in subparagraph (A).".

(2) CONFORMING AMENDMENT.—Section 906 of the Violence Against Women and Department of Justice Reauthorization Act of 2005 is amended by—

42 USC 13971.

(A) striking subsection (d); and

42 USC 3796gg–6, 10420, 13975.

(B) redesignating subsections (e) through (g) as subsections (d) through (f), respectively.

(c) VIOLENCE AGAINST WOMEN ACT OF 1994.—

(1) TRANSITIONAL HOUSING ASSISTANCE.—Section 40299(g) of the Violence Against Women Act of 1994 (42 U.S.C. 13975(g)), as amended by sections 602 and 906 of the Violence Against Women and Department of Justice Reauthorization Act of 2005, is amended—

(A) in paragraph (3)(C), by striking clause (i) and inserting the following:

"(i) INDIAN TRIBES.—

"(I) IN GENERAL.—Not less than 10 percent of the total amount available under this section for each fiscal year shall be available for grants under the program authorized by section 2015 of the Omnibus Crime Control and Safe Streets Act of 1968 (42 U.S.C. 3796gg–10).

"(II) APPLICABILITY OF PART.—The requirements of this section shall not apply to funds allocated for the program described in subclause (I)."; and

(B) by striking paragraph (4).

(2) COURT TRAINING AND IMPROVEMENTS.—Section 41006 of the Violence Against Women Act of 1994 (42 U.S.C. 14043a–3), as added by section 105 of the Violence Against Women and Department of Justice Reauthorization Act of 2005, is amended by striking subsection (c) and inserting the following:

"(c) SET ASIDE.—

"(1) IN GENERAL.—Not less than 10 percent of the total amount available under this section for each fiscal year shall be available for grants under the program authorized by section 2015 of the Omnibus Crime Control and Safe Streets Act of 1968 (42 U.S.C. 3796gg–10).

"(2) APPLICABILITY OF PART.—The requirements of this section shall not apply to funds allocated for the program described in paragraph (1).".

(d) VIOLENCE AGAINST WOMEN ACT OF 2000.—

(1) LEGAL ASSISTANCE FOR VICTIMS.—Section 1201(f) of the Violence Against Women Act of 2000 (42 U.S.C. 3796gg–6(f)), as amended by sections 103 and 906 of the Violence Against Women and Department of Justice Reauthorization Act of 2005, is amended—

(A) in paragraph (2)—

(i) in subparagraph (A), by striking "10 percent" and inserting "3 percent";

(ii) by redesignating subparagraph (B) as subparagraph (C); and

(iii) by inserting after subparagraph (A) the following:

"(B) TRIBAL GOVERNMENT PROGRAM.—

"(i) IN GENERAL.—Not less than 7 percent of the total amount available under this section for each fiscal year shall be available for grants under the program authorized by section 2015 of the Omnibus Crime Control and Safe Streets Act of 1968 (42 U.S.C. 3796gg–10).

"(ii) APPLICABILITY OF PART.—The requirements of this section shall not apply to funds allocated for the program described in clause (i)."; and

(B) by striking paragraph (4).

(2) SAFE HAVENS FOR CHILDREN.—Section 1301 of the Violence Against Women Act of 2000 (42 U.S.C. 10420), as amended by sections 906 and 306 of the Violence Against Women and Department of Justice Reauthorization Act of 2005, is amended—

(A) in subsection (e)(2)—

(i) by striking subparagraph (A); and

(ii) by redesignating subparagraphs (B) and (C) as subparagraphs (A) and (B), respectively; and

(B) by striking subsection (f) and inserting the following:

"(f) ALLOTMENT FOR INDIAN TRIBES.—

Grants.

"(1) IN GENERAL.—Not less than 10 percent of the total amount available under this section for each fiscal year shall be available for grants under the program authorized by section 2015 of the Omnibus Crime Control and Safe Streets Act of 1968 (42 U.S.C. 3796gg–10).

"(2) APPLICABILITY OF PART.—The requirements of this section shall not apply to funds allocated for the program described in paragraph (1).".

SEC. 8. TITLE XI—DEPARTMENT OF JUSTICE.

(a) ORGANIZED RETAIL THEFT.—Section 1105(a)(3) of the Violence Against Women and Department of Justice Reauthorization Act of 2005 (28 U.S.C. 509 note) is amended by striking "The Attorney General through the Bureau of Justice Assistance in the Office of Justice may" and inserting "The Director of the Bureau of Justice Assistance of the Office of Justice Programs may".

(b) FORMULAS AND REPORTING.—Sections 1134 and 1135 of the Violence Against Women and Department of Justice Reauthorization Act of 2005 (Public Law 109–162; 119 Stat. 3108), and the amendments made by such sections, are repealed.

20 USC 1152; 42 USC 3796gg–1, 3796gg–3, 10420, 13975, 14039.

(c) GRANTS FOR YOUNG WITNESS ASSISTANCE.—Section 1136(a) of the Violence Against Women and Department of Justice Reauthorization Act of 2005 (42 U.S.C. 3743(a)) is amended by striking "The Attorney General, acting through the Bureau of Justice Assistance, may" and inserting "The Director of the Bureau of Justice Assistance of the Office of Justice Programs may".

(d) USE OF FEDERAL TRAINING FACILITIES.—Section 1173 of the Violence Against Women and Department of Justice Reauthorization Act of 2005 (28 U.S.C. 530c note) is amended—

(1) in subsection (a), by inserting "or for meals, lodging, or other expenses related to such internal training or conference meeting" before the period; and

(2) in subsection (b), by striking "that requires specific authorization" and inserting "authorized".

(e) OFFICE OF AUDIT, ASSESSMENT, AND MANAGEMENT.—Part A of title I of the Omnibus Crime Control and Safe Streets Act of 1968 (42 U.S.C. 3711 et seq.) is amended by redesignating the section 105 titled "**OFFICE OF AUDIT, ASSESSMENT, AND MANAGEMENT**" as section 109 and transferring such section to the end of such part A.

42 USC 3712d, 3712h.

(f) COMMUNITY CAPACITY DEVELOPMENT OFFICE.—Section 106 of the Omnibus Crime Control and Safe Streets Act of 1968 (42 U.S.C. 3712e) is amended by striking "section 105(b)" each place such term appears and inserting "section 103(b)".

Appendix E
Key Resources Helpful in Understanding Domestic Violence and Alaska Native Women

Frequently Used Publications

Alaska Native Women's Resource Center, *Increasing Safety for Alaska Native Women, An Indigenous Grassroots Curriculum for Alaska Native Villages*, AKWRC (2016).

Jacqueline Agtuca, *Safety for Native Women: VAWA and American Indian Tribes Foreword*, NIWRC (2013).

Roe Bubar and Pamela Jumper Thurman, *Violence Against Native Women,* Social Justice, Vol. 31, No. 4, 73 (2004).

David S. Case & David A. Voluck, *Alaska Natives and American Laws* (2012).

Sarah Deer, Bonnie Clairmont, Carrie A Martell, and Maureen L. White Eagle (Editors), *Sharing Our Stories of Survival, Native Women Surviving Violence* (2008).

Sarah Deer, *Sovereignty of the Soul: Exploring the Intersection of Rape Law Reform and Federal Indian Law*, Suffolk University Law Review, Vol. 38, p. 455, 2005, https://papers.ssrn.com/sol3/papers.cfm?abstract_id=987702.

Carole Goldberg-Ambrose, *Planting Tail Feathers: Tribal Survival and Public Law 280* (1997).

Ada Pecos Melton, *Indigenous Justice Systems and Tribal Society,* In Wanda D. McCaslin, ed., Justice as Healing: Indigenous Ways (2005), http://www.aidainc.net/Publications/ij_systems.htm.

Restoration of Native Sovereignty and Safety for Native Women Magazine

Michelle Demmert, *Extending VAWA Protections to Alaska Native Women*, Vol. 15, Issue 3, p. 32-34 (Oct. 2018).

Michelle Demmert, *Extension of Special Domestic Violence Jurisdiction to Alaska Indian Tribes Advances*, Vol. 17, Issue 1, p. 54-56 (Feb. 2020).

Paula Julian, *Indigenous Organizing Approaches, Addressing the Safety of Alaska Native Women*, Restoration Magazine, Vol. 14, Issue 3, p. 38-40 (Oct. 2017).

Helpful Legal Resources

U.S. Federal Statutes

Family Violence Prevention and Services Act:

Child Abuse Prevention and Treatment Act of 2010, Pub. L. No. 111-320 (Dec. 20, 2010), https://www.congress.gov/111/plaws/publ320/PLAW-111publ320.pdf.

Family Violence Prevention and Services, 42 U.S.C. Ch. 110 § 10409, https://uscode.house.gov/view.xhtml?path=/prelim@title42/chapter110&edition=prelim.

Violence Against Women Act:

Violence Against Women Act, title IV of the Violent Crime Control and Law Enforcement Act of 1994, Pub. L. No. 103-322 (Sept. 7, 1994), 34 U.S.C. 12291 *et seq.*).

Violence Against Women and Department of Justice Reauthorization Act of 2005, Pub. L. No. 109-162, title IX Safety for Indian Women, §§ 901-909, 119 Stat. 3077 (Jan. 5, 2006). https://www.govinfo.gov/content/pkg/BILLS-109hr3402enr/pdf/BILLS-109hr3402enr.pdf

Violence Against Women Reauthorization Act of 2013, Pub. L. No. 113-4, title IX Safety for Indian Women, §§ 901-910, 127 Stat. 120 (March 7, 2013), 25 U.S.C. § 1304. https://www.govinfo.gov/content/pkg/BILLS-113s47enr/pdf/BILLS-113s47enr.pdf

Violence Against Women Act of 2022, Title VIII, Division W, Safety for Indian Women, 847-862, Tribal jurisdictional provisions of H.R. 2471, codified into 25 U.S.C. 25 U.S.C.§§ 1304.

Full Faith and Credit, 18 U.S.C. § 2265.

Trafficking Victims Protection Act, definition of sex trafficking, 22 U.S.C. Sec. 7102 (8).

Federally Recognized Indian Tribe List Act of 1994, 25 U.S.C. 5130. https://www.federalregister.gov/documents/2015/01/14/2015-00509/indian-entities-recognized-and-eligible-to-receive-services-from-the-united-states-bureau-of-indian

Savanna's Act, S. 227. https://www.congress.gov/116/bills/s227/BILLS-116s227enr.pdf. https://www.congress.gov/116/crpt/srpt206/CRPT-116srpt206.pdf

Not Invisible Act, S. 982. https://www.congress.gov/116/bills/s982/BILLS-116s982enr.pdf. https://www.congress.gov/116/crpt/srpt214/CRPT-116srpt214.pdf

Definition of Indian country, 18 U.S.C. 1151.
Public Law 83-280, 18 U.S.C.A. 1152.
Major Crimes Act, 18 U.S.C.A. 1153.
Metlakatla and State of Alaska amendment to P.L. 280: Act of November 25, 1970, Pub. L. No.91-523, 84 Stat. 1358.18 U.S.C.A. § 1162, as amended.

U.S. Supreme Court Cases

Ex parte Crow Dog, 109 U.S. 556 (1883).
Worcester v. Georgia, 31 U.S. (6 Pet.) 559-560 (1830).
Oliphant v. Suquamish Indian Tribe, 435 U.S. 191 (1978).
Alaska v. Native Village of Venetie Tribal Government, 522 U.S. 520 (1998).

U.S. Congressional Resolutions

Apology to Native Peoples, 2009, P.L. 111-118, https://www.congress.gov/bill/111th-congress/senate-joint-resolution/14/text.
National Day of Awareness, 2019, https://www.congress.gov/116/bills/sres144/BILLS-116sres144ats.pdf.

State of Alaska Supreme Court Cases

John v. Baker, 982 P.2d 738 (Alaska 1999). The court found that a tribe had inherent sovereignty to hear a custody case between tribal members in its courts, recognizing tribal court jurisdiction over civil matters.

Federal Reports

U.S. Commission on Civil Rights, *A Quiet Crisis: Federal Funding and Unmet Needs in Indian* Country (2003). https://www.usccr.gov/pubs/na0703/na0204.pdf
U.S. Commission on Civil Rights, *Broken Promises Report, Continuing Federal Funding Shortfall for Native Americans* (2018). https://www.usccr.gov/pubs/2018/12-20-Broken-Promises.pdf
Indian Law and Order Commission, *A Roadmap for Making Native America Safer: Report to the President and Congress of the United States* (2013). http://www.aisc.ucla.edu/iloc/report

U.S. Gen. Accountability Office, *GAO-17-624, Human Trafficking, Information on Cases in Indian Country or that Involved Native Americans,* 23 (2017). https://www.gao.gov/assets/690/686051.pdf

U.S. Congressional Hearings

Senate Committee on Indian Affairs, *Oversight Hearing on The Indian Law and Order Commission Report: "A Roadmap for Making Native America Safer,"* Feb. 12, 2014. https://www.indian.senate.gov/hearing/oversight-hearing-receive-testimony-indian-law-and-order-commission-report-roadmap-making

Senate Committee on Indian Affairs, *Oversight Hearing on Missing and Murdered, Confronting the Silent Crisis*, Dec. 12, 2018. https://www.indian.senate.gov/hearing/oversight-hearing-missing-and-murdered-confronting-silent-crisis-indian-country

Senate Committee on Indian Affairs, *Oversight Hearing "Restoring Justice: Addressing Violence in Native Communities through VAWA Title IX Special Jurisdiction,"* Dec. 8, 2021. https://www.indian.senate.gov/hearing/oversight-hearing-restoring-justice-addressing-violence-native-communities-through-vawa

State Reports

C. Goldberg-Ambrose and D. Champagne, *A Second Century of Dishonor: Federal Inequities and California Tribes*, Report to the Advisory Council on California Indian Policy, 47–59 (1996).

Alaska Violent Death Reporting System 2003-2008 (August 2011), State of Alaska, Department of Health and Social Services, http://dhss.alaska.gov/dph/Epi/injury/Documents/akvdrs/assets/AKVDRS.pdf.

Research

Patricia Tjaden & Nancy Thoennes, Nat'l Institute of Justice, U.S. Dep't of Justice, NCJ 181867, *Extent, Nature, and Consequences of Intimate Partner Violence,* 23 (2000).

André B. Rosay, Nat'l Inst. of Justice, *Violence Against American Indian and Alaska Native Women and Men: 2010 Findings from the National Intimate Partner and Sexual Violence Survey*, 44 NCJ 249736 (2016). https://www.ncjrs.gov/pdffiles1/nij/249736.pdf

Melissa Farley, Nicole Mathews, Sarah Deer, et al, *Garden of Truth*, Minnesota Sexual Assault Coalition (2011). http://www.prostitutionresearch.com/pdfs/Garden_of_Truth_Final_Project_WEB.pdf

Annita Lucchesi and Abigail Echo-Hawk, *Missing and Murdered Indigenous Women & Girls, A snapshot of data from 71 urban cities in the United States*, Urban Indian Health Institute, Seattle Indian Health Board (Nov. 2018). http://www.uihi.org/wp-content/uploads/2018/11/Missing-and-Murdered-Indigenous-Women-and-Girls-Report.pdf

Steven W. Perry, U.S. Dep't of Justice, Bureau of Justice Statistics, *A BJS Statistical Profile, 1992-2002*: American Indians and Crime 7, NCJ 203097 (2004). https://www.bjs.gov/content/pub/pdf/aic02.pdf

International

United Nations

United Nations Convention on the Prevention and Punishment of the Crime of Genocide, 1948, Article 2. https://treaties.un.org/doc/publication/unts/volume%2078/volume-78-i-1021-english.pdf

United Nations Declaration on the Rights of Indigenous Peoples (2007). http://undesadspd.org/IndigenousPeoples/DeclarationontheRightsofIndigenousPeoples.aspx

Organization of American States

The American Declaration on the Rights of Indigenous Peoples (2016). https://indianlaw.org/sites/default/files/ADRIP%201-17-17.pdf

Front Cover Art

AKNWRC Logo, By E. Colleen Hickman, 2017 Watercolor Painting.
The watercolor painting of the arms and hands of five Alaska Native women was created to signify the unity, shared experience in the struggle for safety, and organic relationship the women of Alaska have with each as Indigenous people. Bracelets made of beads, leather, bone, tusks, and silver are commonly created and worn by Alaska Native women. The painting metaphorically indicates how Native women carry their culture as protective factors in their daily lives. The watercolor painting was adopted as the logo of the Alaska Native Women's Resource Center and reflects the grassroots advocacy movement of women across the 229 Alaska Native Villages.

Back Cover Graphic

2018 Cedar Hat with Beaded Hat Band (red and yellow cedar bark and #11 glass seed beads), Woven By Debra Dzijúksuk O'Gara, Tlingit, Yup'ik, and Irish.

The woven cedar hat is traditional headgear used by the Tlingit, Haida, and Tsimshian's of Southeast Alaska and Canada. Today the hats continue to be worn during significant events, gatherings, and ceremonies. Cedar hats are often adorned with shells, buttons, ermine, and other fur and beads. The hat band here is beaded in geometric patterns using the seven colors of what today depicts the pride rainbow commemorating lesbian, gay, bisexual, transexual, and two-spirit (LGBT2-S) people. Two-spirit is a modern-day term to signify Indigenous individuals who live outside of the Western heterosexual norm. Two-spirit and the other LGBT+ terms, were not used or known in traditional Indigenous societies before colonization, because all were accepted without the discrimination known today. Dzijúksuk, a weaver of Chilkat, Ravenstail, cedar bark, and spruce root, as well as a beader, often incorporates the LGBT2S pride colors into her artwork to remind folks that acceptance of diversity is ingrained in indigenous traditional values and should be protected today, especially in the movement to end domestic and sexual violence.

Chapter Title Page Graphic

2015 Beaded flower (#11 seed beads on cotton felt), By Debra Dzijúksuk O'Gara, Tlingit, Yup'ik, and Irish.

This flower, representing the color of summer, is a part of an Octopus Bag, a traditional Tlingit bag, worn today as regalia during significant events, gatherings, and ceremonies. Dzijúksuk sewed the eight-legged bag and beaded a design symbolizing the four seasons using flowers and colored seed beads. The frog in the middle represents her Teehittaan clan's crest, the frog.

Printed in the USA
CPSIA information can be obtained
at www.ICGtesting.com
LVHW022055121124
796318LV00004BA/381
9798396756472